Modernism and ...

Series Editor: **Roger Griffin**, Professor in Modern History, Oxford Brookes University, UK.

The series *Modernism and ...* invites experts in a wide range of cultural, social, scientific and political phenomena to explore the relationship between a particular topic in modern history and 'modernism'. Apart from their intrinsic value as short but groundbreaking specialist monographs, the books aim through their cumulative impact to expand the application of this highly contested term beyond its conventional remit of art and aesthetics. Our definition of modernism embraces the vast profusion of creative acts, reforming initiatives and utopian projects that, since the late nineteenth century, have sought either to articulate, and so symbolically transcend, the spiritual malaise or decadence of modernity, or to find a radical solution to it through a movement of spiritual, social, political – even racial – regeneration and renewal. The ultimate aim is to foster a spirit of transdisciplinary collaboration in shifting the structural forces that define modern history beyond their conventional conceptual frameworks.

Titles include:

Roy Starrs
MODERNISM AND JAPANESE CULTURE

Marius Turda
MODERNISM AND EUGENICS

Shane Weller
MODERNISM AND NIHILISM

Ben Hutchinson
MODERNISM AND STYLE

Anna Katharina Schaffner
MODERNISM AND PERVERSION

Thomas Linehan
MODERNISM AND BRITISH SOCIALISM

David Ohana
MODERNISM AND ZIONISM

Richard Shorten
MODERNISM AND TOTALITARIANISM
Rethinking the Intellectual Sources of Nazism and Stalinism, 1945 to the Present

Agnes Horvath
MODERNISM AND CHARISMA

Forthcoming titles:

Tamir Bar-On
MODERNISM AND THE EUROPEAN NEW RIGHT

Maria Bucur
MODERNISM AND GENDER

Frances Connelly
MODERNISM AND THE GROTESQUE

Elizabeth Darling
MODERNISM AND DOMESTICITY

Matthew Feldman
MODERNISM AND PROPAGANDA

Claudio Fogu
MODERNISM AND MEDITERRANEANISM

Roger Griffin
MODERNISM AND TERRORISM

Carmen Kuhling
MODERNISM AND NEW RELIGIONS

Patricia Leighten
MODERNISM AND ANARCHISM

Gregory Maertz
MODERNISM AND NAZI PAINTING

Paul March-Russell
MODERNISM AND SCIENCE FICTION

Mihai Spariosu
MODERNISM, EXILE AND UTOPIA

Erik Tonning
MODERNISM AND CHRISTIANITY

Veronica West-Harling
MODERNISM AND THE QUEST

Modernism and ...
Series Standing Order ISBN 978–0–230–20332–7 (Hardback)
978–0–230–20333–4 (Paperback)
(*outside North America only*)

You can receive future titles in this series as they are published by placing a standing order. Please contact your bookseller or, in case of difficulty, write to us at the address below with your name and address, the title of the series and the ISBN quoted above.

Customer Services Department, Macmillan Distribution Ltd, Houndmills, Basingstoke, Hampshire RG21 6XS, England

Modernism and Charisma

Agnes Horvath

First published 2013 by
PALGRAVE MACMILLAN

Palgrave Macmillan in the UK is an imprint of Macmillan Publishers Limited, registered in England, company number 785998, of Houndmills, Basingstoke, Hampshire RG21 6XS.

Palgrave Macmillan in the US is a division of St Martin's Press LLC, 175 Fifth Avenue, New York, NY 10010.

Palgrave Macmillan is the global academic imprint of the above companies and has companies and representatives throughout the world.

Palgrave® and Macmillan® are registered trademarks in the United States, the United Kingdom, Europe and other countries.

ISBN 978–1–137–27785–5

This book is printed on paper suitable for recycling and made from fully managed and sustained forest sources. Logging, pulping and manufacturing processes are expected to conform to the environmental regulations of the country of origin.

A catalogue record for this book is available from the British Library.

A catalog record for this book is available from the Library of Congress.

10   9   8   7   6   5   4   3   2   1
22   21   20   19   18   17   16   15   14   13

Printed and bound in Great Britain by
CPI Antony Rowe, Chippenham and Eastbourne

To the youngest, Stefano

Contents

Editorial Preface to Modernism and Charisma

As the title 'Modernism and ...' implies, this series has been conceived in an open-ended, closure-defying spirit, more akin to the soul of jazz than to the rigour of a classical score. Each volume provides an experimental space allowing both seasoned professionals and aspiring academics to investigate familiar areas of modern social, scientific or political history from the defamiliarising vantage point afforded by a term not routinely associated with it: 'modernism'. Yet this is no contrived makeover of a clichéd concept for the purposes of scholastic bravado. Nor is it a gratuitous theoretical exercise in expanding the remit of an 'ism' already notorious for its polyvalence – not to say its sheer nebulousness – in a transgressional fling of postmodern *jouissance*.

Instead this series is based on the *empirically* oriented hope that a deliberate enlargement of the semantic field of 'modernism' to embrace a whole range of phenomena apparently unrelated to the radical innovation in the arts it normally connotes will do more than contribute to scholarly understanding of those topics. Cumulatively the volumes that appear are meant to provide momentum to a perceptible paradigm shift slowly becoming evident in the way modern history is approached. It is one which, while indebted to 'the cultural turn', is if anything 'post-post-modern', for it attempts to use transdisciplinary perspectives and the conscious clustering of concepts often viewed as unconnected – or even antagonistic to each other – to consolidate and deepen the reality principle on which historiography is based, not flee it, to move closer to the experience of history of its actors, not away from it. Only those with a stunted, myopic (and actually *unhistorical*) view of what constitutes historical 'fact' and 'causation' will be predisposed to dismiss the 'Modernism and ...' project as mere 'culturalism', a term which due to unexamined prejudices and sometimes sheer ignorance has, particularly in the vocabulary of more than one eminent 'archival' historian, acquired a reductionist, pejorative meaning.

Yet even open-minded readers may find the title of this book disconcerting. Like all the volumes in the series, it may seem to conjoin two phenomena that do not 'belong', in this case an aesthetic category with a political concept. However, any 'shock of the new' induced by the widened usage of modernism to embrace non-aesthetic phenomena that makes this juxtaposition possible should be mitigated by realising that, in fact, it is neither new nor shocking. The conceptual ground for a work such as *Modernism and Charisma* has been prepared for by such seminal texts as Marshall Berman's *All that is Solid Melts into Thin Air: The Experience of Modernity* (1982), Modris Eksteins' *Rites of Spring* (1989), Peter Osborne's *The Politics of Time: Modernity and Avant-Garde* (1995), Emilio Gentile's *The Struggle for Modernity* (2003) and Mark Antliff's *Avant-Garde Fascism: The Mobilization of Myth, Art and Culture in France, 1909–1939* (2007). In each case modernism is revealed as the long-lost sibling (twin or maybe even father) of historical phenomena from the social and political sphere rarely mentioned in the same breath.

Yet the real pioneers of such a 'maximalist' interpretation of modernism were none other than some of the major aesthetic modernists themselves. For them the art and thought that subsequently earned them this title was a creative force – passion even – of revelatory power which, in a crisis-ridden West where *anomie* was reaching pandemic proportions, was capable of regenerating not just 'cultural production', but 'socio-political production', and for some even society *tout court*. Figures such as Friedrich Nietzsche, Richard Wagner, Wassily Kandinsky, Walter Gropius, Pablo Picasso and Virginia Woolf never accepted that the art and thought of 'high culture' were to be treated as self-contained spheres of activity peripheral to – and cut off from – the main streams of contemporary social and political events. Instead they assumed them to be laboratories of visionary thought vital to the spiritual salvation of a world being systematically drained of higher meaning and ultimate purpose by the dominant, 'nomocidal' forces of modernity. If we accept Max Weber's thesis of the gradual *Entzauberung*, or 'disenchantment' of the world through rationalism, such creative individuals can be seen as setting themselves the task – each in his or her own idiosyncratic way – of *re-enchanting* and re-sacralising the world. Such modernists consciously sought to restore a sense of higher purpose, transcendence and *Zauber* (magic) to a spiritually starved modern humanity condemned by 'progress' to live in a permanent state of existential exile, of *liminoid transition*, now that the forces of the divine seemed to have withdrawn in what Martin Heidegger's muse, the poet Friedrich Hölderlin, called 'The Flight of the Gods'. If the hero of modern popular nationalism is the Unknown Warrior, perhaps the patron saint of modernism itself is *Deus Absconditus*.

Approached from this oblique angle modernism is thus a revolutionary force, but is so in a sense only distantly related to the one made familiar by standard accounts of the (political or social) revolutions on which modern historians cut their teeth. It is a 'hidden' revolution of the sort referred to by the 'arch-'aesthetic modernist Vincent van Gogh musing to his brother Theo in his letter of 24 September 1888 about the sorry plight of the world. In one passage he waxes ecstatic about the impression made on him by the work of another spiritual seeker disturbed by the impact of 'modern progress', Leo Tolstoy:

> It seems that in the book, *My Religion*, Tolstoy implies that whatever happens in a violent revolution, there will also be an inner and hidden revolution in the people, out of which a new religion will be born, or rather, something completely new which will be nameless, but which will have the same effect of consoling, of making life possible, as the Christian religion used to.[1]

The book must be a very interesting one – it seems to me. In the end, we shall have had enough of cynicism, scepticism and humbug, and will want to live – more musically. How will this come about and what will we discover? It would be nice to be able to prophesy, but it is even better to be forewarned, instead of seeing absolutely nothing in the future other than the disasters that are bound to strike the modern world and civilisation like so many thunderbolts, through revolution, or war, or the bankruptcy of worm-eaten states.

In the series 'Modernism and ...' the key term has been experimentally expanded and 'heuristically modified' to embrace any movement for change which set out to give a name and a public identity to the 'nameless' and 'hidden' revolutionary principle that van Gogh saw as necessary to counteract the rise of nihilism. He was attracted to Tolstoy's vision because it seemed to offer a remedy to the impotence of Christianity and the insidious spread of literally a soul-destroying cynicism, which if unchecked would ultimately lead to the collapse of civilisation. Modernism thus applies in this series to all concerted attempts in any sphere of activity to enable life to be lived more 'musically', to resurrect the sense of transcendent communal and individual purpose being palpably eroded by the chaotic unfolding of events in the modern world even if the end result would be 'just' to make society physically and mentally healthy.

What would have probably appalled van Gogh is that some visionaries no less concerned than him by the growing crisis of the West sought a manna of spiritual nourishment emanating not from heaven, nor even from an earthly beauty still retaining an aura of celestial otherworldliness, but from strictly secular visions of an alternative modernity so radical in its conception that attempts to enact them inevitably led to disasters of their own following the law of unintended consequences. Such solutions were to be realised not by a withdrawal from history into the realm of art (the sphere of 'epiphanic' modernism), but by applying a utopian artistic, mythopoeic, religious or technocratic consciousness to the task of harnessing the dynamic forces of modernity itself in such spheres as politics, nationalism, the natural sciences and social engineering in order to establish a new order and a 'new man'. It is initiatives conceived in this 'programmatic' mode of modernism that the series sets out to explore. Its results are intended to benefit not just a small coterie of like-minded academics, but mainstream teaching and research in modern history, thereby becoming part of the 'common sense' of the discipline even of self-proclaimed 'empiricists'.

Some of the deep-seated psychological, cultural and 'anthropological' mechanisms underlying the futural revolts against modernity here termed 'modernism' are explored at length in my *Modernism and Fascism: The Sense of a Beginning under Mussolini and Hitler* (2007). The premise of this book could be taken to be Phillip Johnson's assertion that 'Modernism is typically defined as the condition that begins when people realize God is truly dead, and we are therefore on our own'. It presents the well-springs of modernism in the primordial human need for a new metaphysical centre in a radically decentred reality, for a new source of transcendental meaning in a godless universe, in the impulse to erect a 'sacred canopy' of culture which not only aesthetically veils the infinity of time and space surrounding human existence to make existence feasible, but provides a totalising world view within which to locate individual life narratives, thus imparting it with the illusion of cosmic significance. By eroding or destroying that canopy, modernity creates a protracted spiritual crisis which provokes the proliferation of countervailing impulses to restore a 'higher meaning' to historical time that are collectively termed by the book (ideal-typically) as 'modernism'.

Johnson's statement seems to make a perceptive point by associating modernism not just with art, but with a general 'human condition' consequent on what Nietzsche, the first great modernist philosopher, called 'the Death of God'. Yet in the context of this series his statement requires significant qualification. Modernism is *not* a general historical condition (any more than 'postmodernism' is), but a generalised revolt against even the *intuition* made possible by a secularising modernisation that we are spiritual orphans in a godless and ultimately meaningless universe. Its hallmark is the bid to find a new home, a new community and a new source of transcendence.

Nor is modernism itself necessarily secular. On the contrary, both the wave of occultism, theosophy, and the Catholic revival of the 1890s, and the emergence of radicalised, Manichaean forms of Christianity, Hinduism, Islam and even Buddhism in the 1990s demonstrate that modernist impulses need not take the form of secular utopianism, but may readily assume religious (some would say 'post-secular') forms. In any case, within the cultural force field of modernism even the most secular entities are sacralised to acquire an aura of numinous significance. Ironically, Johnson himself offers a fascinating case study in this fundamental aspect: the modernist rebellion against the empty skies of a disenchanted, anomic world. A retired Berkeley law professor, some of the books he published such as *The Wedge of Truth* made him one of the major protagonists of 'Intelligent Design', a Christian(ised) version of creationism that offers a prophylactic against the allegedly nihilistic implications of Darwinist science.

Naturally, no attempt has been made to impose 'reflexive metanarrative' developed in *Modernism and Fascism* on the various authors of this series. Each has been encouraged to tailor the term 'modernism' to fit their own epistemological cloth, as long as they broadly agree in seeing it as the expression of a reaction against modernity not restricted to art and aesthetics, and driven by the aspiration to create a spiritually or physically 'healthier' modernity through a new cultural, political and ultimately biological order. Needless to say, the blueprint for the ideal society varies significantly according to each diagnosis of what makes actually existing modernity untenable, 'decadent' or doomed to self-destruction.

The ultimate aim of the series is to help bring about a paradigm shift in the way 'modernism' is generally used, and hence stimulate fertile new areas of research and teaching with an approach which enables methodological empathy and causal analysis to be applied even to events and processes ignored by or resistant to the explanatory powers of conventional historiography. I am delighted that Agnes Horvath, a political anthropologist with a deep interest in social and ideological reactions to the liminality which lies at the experience of modernity, has contributed a volume to this series which presents charisma and totalitarian leadership in a startlingly unfamiliar context.

Roger Griffin
Oxford
August 2012

Acknowledgements

I would like to acknowledge and extend my heartfelt gratitude to the following colleagues and students who shared their personal and professional experience with me: Philippe Schmitter, Elemer Hankiss, Harvie Ferguson, Harald Wydra, Bjorn Thomassen, Gianfranco Poggi, Richard Sakwa, Kieran Keohane, John Dunn, Shane Gay, Andrew Gamble, Michael Urban, and also László Adorjáni, Mario Alinei, Johann Arnason, Nándor Bárdi, Tom Boland, James Cuffe, Ion Copoeru, Gonzalo Fernández de Córdoba, Julian Davis, James Fairhead, Patrizia Fara, Bernhard Giesen, Arvydas Grišinas, Carmen Kuhling, Peter McMylor, Eugene MacNamee, József Lőrincz, John O'Brien, Anders Petersen, Mathias Riedl, Martin Riesebrodt, Simon Schaffer, Wolfgang Schwentker, Iván Szelényi, Vilmos Tánczos and Catherine Verdery.

Thanks are most especially due to my family – Daniel, Peter, Janos, Tamas, Stefano and Arpad. Words alone cannot express what I owe them for their encouragement, whose patient love enabled me to complete this book.

A special thanks to Wendy Cook, Ben Davenport, Lottie Garrett and Louise Kay (University Library Cambridge, CRIC Cambridge University) and to Jonathon Fife for helping me while staying in Cambridge as a visiting scholar.

Introduction

A proper understanding of the dynamics of modernity, in particular the paradoxical links between modernism, fascism and communism, requires new concepts, not taken from the usual self-understanding of modernity. This book argues that this can be done through the notions developed in anthropology, based on a systematic and comparative analysis of the most varied cultures. Not every anthropological study, however, is equally useful for that purpose, as it is necessary to overcome those theoretical approaches that themselves were part of the very same self-understanding of modernity and its ideologies. The most important such ideas, developed by long-ignored figures, mostly at the margin of the discipline, owing to their dissent from the ideas of Durkheim, Boas, Marx or Freud, and their disciples, include liminality (Arnold van Gennep and Victor Turner), schismogenesis (Gregory Bateson), the trickster (Paul Radin), imitation (Gabriel Tarde, René Girard) or sacrifice (Marcel Mauss).[1] Interestingly enough, these concepts can be paired with ideas from classical philosophical anthropology, especially those of Plato. Liminal is close to the *apeiron*, the famous 'first word' of Greek philosophy, introduced by Anaximander; the trickster to the sophist; Bateson's entire work had a Platonic inspiration; whereas the best proof for the tight connection is shown by the term 'imitation', central for the anthropology of René Girard, the anthropological sociology of Gabriel Tarde and for the entire philosophy of Plato. The aim of this book is to understand the masquerading capacity of the irrational in the totalitarian experience through the rise of the liminal authorities of modernity, focusing on the case of communism,[2] but with a crucial comparative eye on fascism as well,[3] using a combination of the clues about the irrational mentioned above.

However, to make proper use of these notions, it is necessary not only to combine them, but also to clarify their meaning, as developed by their inventors. This is most substantial in the single most important theoretical tool for this book, the term 'liminality'. The work of Victor Turner has vital significance in turning attention to this concept, introduced by Arnold van Gennep, a main intellectual opponent of Durkheim, who was subsequently diverted out of anthropological and sociological thinking. However, Turner's approach to liminality has two major shortcomings. First, partly because of criticism, Turner was keen to limit the meaning of the concept to the concrete settings of small-scale tribal societies, preferring his own neologism 'liminoid', to analyse certain features of the modern world, like theatre (Turner 1982). However, this book will argue that the term can be applied to concrete historical events, and *should* be applied, as offering a vital means for historical and sociological understanding.[4] Second, again staying too close to his own experiences, Turner attributed a rather univocally positive connotation to liminal situations, as ways of renewal. However, it will be argued that liminal situations can be, and in fact in the modern era are, rather quite different: periods of uncertainly, anguish, even existential fear; a facing of the abyss or the void.[5]

Being pushed to the limit, or on the threshold, is an extremely difficult moment in the life of individuals, or any community. If this happens, it is never certain that there is a way back to life as before; even to any kind of rational existence. A proper way out of such an irrational situation depends on many factors, and it can easily happen that a limited situation can be exploited by some: for example trickster-like figures, as pioneered by Radin, and used by several anthropologists, mythologists or literary scholars. Such figures, as ample anthropological and mythological evidence indicates, might emerge from temporary situations of distress, using and abusing the anxieties and uncertainties of people whose world has suddenly collapsed, capitalising on weakness. Radin's ideas about the trickster illuminate the Weberian perspective of charismatic leader from a new light.

This book is about how this weakness can be transfigured into political capital, owing to the dissolution of certainties that transforms societies simply because the new situations are beyond the reach of cognitive power, and hence effectively fracture cognition. Modern politics, it is generally assumed, is concerned with strength, based on rationality and interests, or on the will of the people as expressed and codified by the law. This is also where the essence of democracy is usually situated, connected to power relations. Tocqueville[6] or Max Weber[7] were searching for emotions and sentiments that were mobilised to influence political systems powerfully. It was to capture this type of mobilisation that Weber developed the concept charisma,[8] taken over from theology, but also using material from anthropology, mythology and ancient history, defining it as a type of authority. The problem, however, is that the term attempts to incorporate emotions and other non-rational elements influencing and motivating political behaviour into an otherwise rationalistic classificatory scheme. How to construct types out of emotions, whose extraordinary moves and possibilities can never be exactly calculated, whose ability for fascination and capacity to mesmerise are never ending and whose strength is so separable from the reality created? Emotions, like so many devices of our mind, are beyond individual abilities and have nothing to do with powerful social possibilities; they belong to the liminal, which engineers their reproduction. This book suggests that the term 'charisma', just as other emotional mobilisations characteristic of modern politics, should be linked with liminal conditions: situations in which the previously taken-for-granted order of things is dissolved, everybody is paralysed with the opposite of power with weakness concerning what to do and is faced with anxiety about what is going to happen.

Liminality, where events happen that are never ending and actions take place that cannot be exactly calculated, is a forbidden territory of knowledge. Classical philosophy was built up on the opposite ethos: on the principle of concreteness; that objects and beings powerfully inhabit reality, whether animate or inanimate, and whatever fills the space between these entities is irrelevant, being empty. In the language of classical philosophy, it belongs to non-being, a forbidden territory of knowledge. Since the Presocratics – but it must have been formulated even before – beings have been considered as given in their unity, with each thing having a character that is always the same. This took no account of any breakage or fraction (Deleuze 2004a: 238):[9] staying close to the real world is primary evidence of every living being, refusing a radical difference between the appearance and the essence, even maintaining an unbroken continuity between the human and divine worlds. However, both these primary and primordial standards are questioned by liminality, where unity becomes weak, relations hazy, order suspended, thus finding themselves in a relative go-between, with the decomposed entities standing in incommensurable relations to each other. The true radicalism of incommensurability, pioneered by liminality, lies in the reversal of the self-evidence of reality. In Being, there is a balanced and harmonious relationship between every part. This is the meaning of rational, derived from Latin *ratio*, which does not mean reasoning, rather proportionality, still present in English with the same meaning; or present in the idea of 'rational' numbers, which means that a number can be written as a ratio of two natural numbers. In liminality, as in non-being, the self-evident reality becomes the void; objects only take up an uncertain position within this empty space, which dissolves meaning, but they are still experienced, however devoid of units. But why is this apprehensibility such a particularly suitable though forbidden vehicle for knowledge?

The forbidden knowledge

The Tocquevillean analysis of emotions and sentiments diverts the problem towards already known or accepted statements. This is quite understandable, as analysis is at a loss in coming to terms with counter-solutions, thinking rather in terms of causalities, like tracing the origins of the French Revolution to the rise of the absolutist state. In this perspective, emotions arise because there was a cause for them. However, this book argues that a genuine proliferation of the incommensurable liminal took place with the rise of modern politics, marked by its revolutions and wars, culminating in the World Wars and totalitarian regimes of the twentieth century that have no causal origins or realistic aims. What is more, exactly a detachment from reality, the liminal void nursed their appearance as alienation, penchant of a kind of resentment. This was first recognised towards the end of the nineteenth century by Friedrich Nietzsche and Gustave Le Bon, contemporaries who also shared the fate of not being taken seriously during their lifetime but having an enormous following and effect soon after. Nietzsche had a great impact on Weber's analysis of charismatic leadership, whereas Le Bon pioneered the study of crowd psychology, influencing Tarde and Durkheim, similar to Simmel and Pareto. Le Bon was interested in the problem of how certain figures can rise to a leadership position under the type of unstable condition that is characteristic of crowds and masses. Le Bon reflected on the feeling of distress that he found around himself; but a series of interpreters and political leaders would soon emerge who explicitly made use of his ideas in unsettled times, not covered by the scientific view of contemporary political philosophy dominated by neo-Kantian categories, to gain power in liminal situations. They are the 'liminal authorities' of the twentieth century, whose appearance justifies and requires an analysis based on the broadest possible historical and anthropological material. This book attempts to draw the picture, and present the exploits, of liminal figures, a disturbance or an irritation in the order of things that use the forbidden knowledge of liminality, much ignored over the past centuries owing to the legacy of the Enlightenment.

Incommensurable liminality so far has hardly been perceived, let alone studied, by social and political scientists, even though it has played a fundamental, decisive role since pre-history, and some of its manifestations, under various labels, have gained a certain degree of notoriety in most cultures and civilisations. There are several reasons why liminality, in spite of the crucial importance I claim it has played in all times and places, have so far not been recognised. First, liminality is incommensurable with unity, order, causes and facts, and so is practically invisible.[10] Liminality hides and disguises itself, stalking either underground or outside the boundaries, at the margins or limits of society;[11] thus, it falls out of perception, and is even often confused with its opposite. This is not even a simple matter of choice, as every community tries to do its best to get rid of liminality, pushing perceptions of weakness to the margins and keeping it there, once its presence has been revealed. Thus, liminality repeatedly disappears, and – under the false assumption that this means the end – vigilance and knowledge about such conditions also vanish, so it can strike again, provoking decomposition.

Apart from its invisible, underground or outcast character, the full identification of liminality and the recognition of the unity underlying its various individual manifestations have also been hindered so far because of the profoundly contradictory and ambivalent nature of liminal persons themselves and their personification into leaders. Political leaders must manage a combination of opposites: an intellectual and a moral dualism. Intellectually they need a practical sense for success and an understanding about differences, where each social act is judged by its own terms, while morally they also must manifest idealism, having knowledge about ideas that make life a value in any community, thus being capable of living a life animated by decency and self-sufficiency. However, these two major character-signs of leadership are completely undermined by the liminal, which is further magnified if it begets a political figure who is ambitiously imitative, miming or hijacking and conceiving. By taking conscious use of such sensitive conditions, liminal leaders might destroy the very conditions of possibility of reality, inciting sensations, using them as vehicles for further liquidating normality. Liminal authorities make use of the classical topos of leadership, while marrying it to their own tenets of disturbance. An example of such figures includes on one side the communist nomenclature with their intellectual cheerleaders, the various avant-garde, covering their brooding mediocrity with super ideology, whereas on the other there is the fascist leaders' nightmarish suspense of order advocated by queer political craftsmanship. Although politics in the classical and even early modern sense can only be carried by figures who exist in the meaningful sense of the word, demanding worthy thoughts and defending postulates that guarantee the existence of a unique normality, in the topsy-turvy world of liminality the distinguishing principles, where counterparts meet in harmony, disappear into the incommensurable.

Liminal figures are those who – owing to their exterior position to normal social conditions – gain an in-depth understanding of the out-of-ordinary, liminal stages of reality. They therefore manage to come up with unusual and seemingly congenial solutions when liminal conditions occur within society, while the central issue in charisma is not the reception of a gift, but rather being a gifted, intact personality. Those figures of the liminal who are themselves divided could easily become omnipresent and indestructible, their dual nature accommodating well to the contradictory space of the incommensurable, while the charismatic is not a crisis person, their appearance being restricted to certain positions and spaces in history. Liminal figures, however, appear at every possible location in space and time, known not only in anthropology and in mythology, but also in literature, in philosophy, in religion, in theatre, in every borderline situation, whether called in-between, go-between, transitoriness, haziness, emptiness, or the void, while they are the trickster or the stalker, the smith of fairy tales or the leprechaun, the dwarf or the spider-god (Horvath 2008). The ancients were familiar with this figure just as the moderns. Plato famously described them in the form of the wandering philosophers, the *Sophists*, under *poiesis* or – as Heidegger expressed it – the *bringing-forth*. The chief traits are the appearance of a break, an ability to launch emptiness in the likeness of the real, just as in an alchemical opus the unit is broken into parts and is reunited again into a new existence. The book will present the exploits of this peculiar disturbance or irritation in the order of things, when it grows into a leading position, for which the name liminal authority is suggested; figures who are particularly able to mimic normal forms and rules of behaviour, even though – or rather exactly because – they themselves lost their integrity. In contrast, a charismatic person is at one with themselves, having coherence and a never-changing attitude towards things in harmonious co-existence.

The idea of catching the dynamism of liminal authorities is derived from the perception that politics in the modern world is not simply based on the rational pursuit of objective interests. Rather – just as in any other human societies – it is deeply penetrated by emotional and sensational concerns, in particular force derived from weakness, visible in the growth of political revolutions, totalitarian systems and media power (the role of political marketing and propaganda), phenomena that are themselves much connected with each other and much improvised with increasingly newer patterns of emotional domination. The study of these incommensurable aspects of modern democratic politics requires the incorporation of broader, anthropologically based terms and perspectives, moving beyond the narrow foundations of modern politics, which can be traced back to Hobbes and Kant (Lefort 2007; Wydra 2007: 16–17).

An excessive focus on causal mechanism led to the systematic ignoring of the detaching aspects of incommensurable moments, when events and actions seem to arise as existent, small groups may suddenly gain the upper hand, give a new cognitive direction to entire societies or cultures and then suddenly perish. The matter is further complicated by the fact that liminality is connected to sensations, and thus the reproduction of similar senses, which gives an unexpected spread to the movements. The consequence is that, owing to the mimetic nature of liminal situations, and the easy reversibility and transference of imitative processes (e.g. a model can become an object, and vice versa), an extremely delicate and manifold relationship develops between sensation, subordination and procreation: just as genuine love cancels individuality in the happy union with the beloved one, sensation can be used to subjugate and enslave; and even subjugation can be desired and loved, if one happens to be in such a desperately unsettled and terrifying situation that otherwise the anxiety of existence seems to be irresolvable. This is key for the growing, procreative and multiplying, and then sudden perishing, character of liminality: it vanishes once nothing remains to be emptied out or desired.

Liminal reconditioning becoming the vehicle for subjugation is the fundamental corollary for the political history of the twentieth century: under unsettled, liminal conditions, societies can be trapped or tricked into 'loving' political figures and movements whose imitative character otherwise they would easily recognise; individuals and movements that, by generating further divisions and antagonisms in social life, can proliferate their power (Clastres, 2010).[12]

However, given the nature of liminality, this reconditioning is divided into parts that are smaller than the original. Once increased in critical numbers, many things take the place of the original condition, endlessly dividing into themselves and into their opposites, making comprehension and reasoning impossible in this general confusion of principles, aims and targets: a typical crisis situation, we should say, that corresponds to the appearance of the trickster. Forbidden knowledge concerns the dual nature of liminality, which is an inconsistent state, representing both creativity and destruction. It excludes the possibility of the unit being identical with itself, but at the same time and exactly by the breaking of units it suddenly opens up the possibility of enormous, indeed infinite, growth. This will be called the 'denominator' effect of liminality, making use of the dual meaning in mathematics of fractions. Liminality provides for unlimited reproductivity from weakness, as it requires neither power (*dynamis*) nor skill, but only one thing: robotic obedience. This adjusted vacuity makes an automatic union with the void, a union that resembles a disturbed marriage or an ill-fated birth, capable of producing only unusual variations, or mutants, altering the original form. Although it bears chemical or psychological aspects of the original image, it does so only in a disturbed, senseless way. These mutants make false demands for unity; their false suppositions cause further divisions,[13] bring things into permanent schismogenesis (Bateson 1958),[14] or pathogenesis (Koselleck 1988),[15] copying infinitely the original image which thus becomes paler and paler, or infinitely split into new fake images. The union with liminality is a tricky device. The liminal is associated with the indestructible void: how could it be otherwise, as the void does not own anything, not even its own matter, remaining always the same, it is impossible to add to or take away from it, and it neither grows nor diminishes. Consequently, it annihilates every form. The void nurses reproductivity, but any motion generates destruction in it, so deceit is needed to hide this ever-same destruction: this is why deceit has an ontological affinity with the void, as the figure of the Trickster shows.

Managing crisis: Trickster mimicking charisma

The problem of how societies managed to solve situations of crisis was a central concern of classical sociology from its beginnings. Max Weber posed this problem in the language of 'out-of-ordinary' situations, whether caused by natural catastrophes, warfare, invasions or economic reasons, and placed the emphasis on the need for charismatic leaders who could solve such difficulties. Emile Durkheim used the contrast between the profane (ordinary, everyday) and the sacred. Ever since the works of Durkheim and Mauss, and of those anthropologists on whom they relied, the link and priority between rituals, myths and actual events has been a central question.

The term 'liminal', and its extension to social and political events, can provide a way out not simply in solving the theoretical problem, but also for extending these concepts to the analysis of contemporary politics and society, as the term builds on but also moves beyond Weber and Durkheim's explanation. The crucial significance of the term 'liminal', as hinted at by Plato in his analysis of the 'in between' (*metaxy*),[16] is that it has an extremely wide range of applicability in its precise and technical capturing of the imprecise and unsettled situation of transitoriness. Any situation where borderlines and boundaries that previously were stable and taken for granted are dissolved generates a 'liminal' situation which needs some solution, as the elimination of such boundaries generates uncertainties in which a decent and meaningful normality becomes impossible, returning the world into chaos, a central preoccupation for the Greeks. On the other hand, however, dissolution of borderlines has its own attractiveness, exactly by being connected to an 'oceanic' feeling of freedom from previous structures, and the possibility of giving a free rein to one's own wishes and desires. Liminality and transitoriness have their own elusive and easily deluding attractiveness, enough to mention all we know about art, theatre or poetry, all the vehicles of enactment, whether by dupe or deceit, or by being cathartic.

At the intersection point of social and cultural anthropology, comparative politics and classical political philosophy, we can situate the particularly important aspect of political modernism, the inspiration behind and effect mechanism of those revolutionary movements that – after major situations of crisis – suddenly gained a mass following by pretending to solve the shortcomings of the present through an escape into a bright future. One must be very precise here: escapism through dissolving boundaries between public and private, or political and personal, of course must not be respected. Personal extraordinary experiences should not be used by themselves as intellectual tools to explain a situation of crisis. However, it is increasingly clear that crisis is exactly concerned with a thorough, long-standing play with borderlines: the escapism has become political, though in a very problematic way. A simple stricture of keeping personal life experiences out of the scientific arena would amount to ignoring the need to be concerned with reality.

Interpretations of the modern condition motivated by personal experiences, animating the works of Hölderlin, Nietzsche, Weber or Heidegger, are central for understanding the contemporary world. However, sensation also establishes a relationship of subordination, which can subjugate and entrap the sensor into one's own feelings, and thus can be used for political purposes. In particular, in modern politics such sensual entrapment was promoted through the identification of political party leaders with party members and even the population at large under totalitarian systems, as sharing the same position of the sufferers. The acceptance of such instrumentalisation of sensation was rendered possible first by a sense of guilt of being asocial owing to the system of 'passionate interests' (Tarde and Latour), connected to the rise of capitalism as a solution for the period of civil wars, and then by the liminal conditions that emerged, especially in Eastern Europe, after the World Wars; conditions that were purposefully perpetuated through staging a sacrificial system. Although totalitarianism has disappeared as a force, contemporary political life is increasingly reduced to a politics of victimhood and suffering, where the search for the good life is replaced by the double negation of eliminating all suffering from the world. Such effort only produces the opposite result, while public reality becomes torn apart by sensual scandals, confirming Foucault's insight about the investment of desire and enslavement to sexuality (Foucault 1980a), bringing out the typical liminal figure of the lustful trickster.

It is, however, difficult to find an approach that would not just further the inciting of sensations. An approach is required that is relevant, yet distant enough to prevent proliferation through emotional involvement. This is why this book combines an in-depth reading of Plato's works with a particular angle from anthropology. It argues that through the all-but-forgotten political experiment of totalitarianism one can understand the contemporary fascination with *sensation* in politics, when figures who lack a proper perception of ratio, reality and good judgement, but rather are skilful in manipulating desires, come to rule the scenery. Although totalitarianism as a political system emerged at a definite time and place, the mechanism it used was rooted in earlier experiences in European history: the artificial maintaining of liminality, thus the indoctrination into a senseless apprehension of liminal sensuality, for which Tarde formulated the term 'passionate interests'.

Tarde's 'passionate interests'

Just before his famous, and much misunderstood, public debate with Durkheim (in 1903), which was shortly followed by his death (in 1904), in 1902–3 Tarde published a voluminous work on modern economics and the modern economy, entitled *La psychologie économique*, of which a resume recently appeared (Latour and Lépinay 2009).[17] As Latour and Lépinay argue, Tarde offers us a language that is completely different from that used by economists during his time and ever since, but one that has striking insights which, especially in its arguments against machine worship and big structure admiration, might be worthwhile taking seriously. The most important of these is the expression 'passionate interests', selected as the title of the resume. The concept can help us understand why and how not only the Eastern part of Europe was no longer 'normal' before the World Wars, but the Western part as well.

Economists – and social and political scientists who follow their lead, well beyond the narrow confines of rational choice theory – argue that human beings are fundamentally driven by the rational pursuit of the satisfaction of their objective interests. The objectivity of interests is just as fundamental a concept for Marxist and revolutionary discourses, except that they root such objectivity in social classes, instead of individuals. There is something striking, but often unnoticed, about such claims, as 'interest' simply means 'inter esse', or 'being in between' (see also Wydra 2009). It is thus a term particularly suited for an analysis that takes its departure from Plato's analysis of in-between-ness in the *Symposium*, a dialogue on 'love' (*Eros*), which is not easily associated with rationality and objectivity.

Latour and Lépinay's book on Tarde offers fundamental insights in this direction. For Tarde, the interests that are the subject matter of modern economics, and on which the modern economy is based, are by no means 'objective', but passionate. They involve a state of passion, a tension and intention, not to be searched somewhere in basic needs or desires. However, they can indeed be fixated, with a degree of skill and trick, if they are purposefully directed to certain objects, and if the satisfaction of such desires becomes tied to the heart of personal identity. When this is done on a mass scale, at the collective level, the result will be a social entity where human life is increasingly reduced to the mechanical and predictable satisfaction of a certain amount of prefabricated interests and desires, which furthermore involves the complicity of individual human beings. Such a situation is not hypothetical, but is considered by Albert Hirschman as an explicit political project that was at the heart of the 'political arguments of capitalism before its triumph' (Hirschman 1977). The conditions for such a project were given by the period of incessant religious and civil wars, dominating the sixteenth and seventeenth centuries, central for the 'pathogenesis' of modernity, according to Reinhart Koselleck (1988). The objectivation of 'passionate interests' into a rational and calculable, manageable and predictable form was considered as a solution to the religious and political crisis that otherwise proved intractable. It also rhymed perfectly with the philosophies of Descartes and Newton, and the mechanical world image they propagated.

However, as over the course of decades and centuries it became increasingly evident, such a solution came at a price on its own. The fixation of such 'objective interests' entrapped concrete human beings in the 'iron cage' of their own calculative self, instrumentalising and destroying both the 'care of the self' (the foundation of ancient philosophy) and the delicate tissue of social life; the very fabric of normality. Communities have never and nowhere been the sum of their members, driven by their own inexorable and objective interests. They were the concrete and historically unique outcome of lives and experiences, events and encounters, where everyone had a certain valorised reputation, based on innumerable acts of mutual recognition (Pizzorno 1991). Events, of course, included crises and challenges, and for them bad or unsatisfactory responses were also given. This could entail the dispersal of the entire community, or alternatively its survival at a low level of existence, where violence and hostility became endemic within a community that became internally split. It is in such a situation that 'individualism' becomes pronounced, as the struggle to survive amid conflict grips the mind. To understand such a situation Gregory Bateson (1958, 1972) developed his Plato-inspired concept 'schismogenesis'. Europe in the sixteenth century, with its religious and civil wars, became a model case of a broken civilisation (Koselleck 1988). The solution, in the form of passionate interests, as governed first through the absolutist state and then the free market, managed to stabilise order, but only at the price of identification with big structures, like the state itself. Order was restored at the price of subjugating, in principle, every single individual being to his or her 'passionate' interests.

In the words of Eric Voegelin, it was an 'order without meaning' (Voegelin 1999a: 153–5).

This was the context in which the forces that opposed the mechanised world governed by passionate interests came to side with and generate energy from an abstract and overarching view of the 'social' or the 'public'. The problem was posed in the following terms. While the state and the market functioned, in the sense that the devastating period of civil wars ended, the price was increasing inequalities and the marginalisation of a substantial part of the population within the new, all-encompassing entity of the national state, as a kind of 'sacrifice' in the name of the common interest. This resulted in the following, double-edged critique of the system of 'passionate interests'. On the one hand, all those who were marginalised in this game had to be taken care of. This led to the idea that some kind of 'standards' should be defined in terms of basic needs which should be satisfied for everybody, associated with maintaining human rights. On the other hand, in a closely connected manner, the perceived anomie and loss of sociability led to the support of an abstract idea of society as the greatest good.

The best minds and spirits felt that something was not right in this contrast between the absolute value attributed to the individual on the one side, and the social void on the other; however, it was difficult to determine exactly what it was. As is always the case with schismogenic developments, one excess justified another. Everyone was forced to take sides in an impossible debate; not doing so meant to be resigned to the position of a weightless outsider. The outcome was an extremely tricky and particular circle, on which the indeed tight affinities between sociology and socialism were based: the sacralisation of individual rights, but only in so far as these were basic and merited through suffering; and the sacralisation of an abstract ideal of society, where concrete human relations and sociability were replaced by the community of sufferers, imposed through moral terror. The acceptance of such an outcome was due to a vague but dominating sense of guilt, based on a looming background feeling that something was wrong with the proliferation of egoism and greed as the very substance of social life, and yet not being able to step outside one's own 'passionate interests'.

As Durkheim (1995 [1912]) argued with particular zeal, God is nothing but society writ large, so in a secular world society is nothing else than God. From here, it is only a short step to say that this abstracted society and the common good, or at least its representatives, should be 'loved'. Following this line, totalitarian movements trapped and redirected *Eros*,[18] urging their adherents to give up themselves in an eroticised environment with loving cult figures. This happened first through the ideology of marginality, which advocated self-effacing by entrusting everything in the hands of the 'party'; and second, by the parallel call for taking up the side of the oppressed and the sufferers, promising to eradicate suffering from the world. Such a relinquishing of personal integrity resulted in split personality, emptying the inside and trusting in the 'outside', which transformed life itself into a gloomy emptiness, in attendance for atonement.

The structure of the book

This book is organised around a series of successive episodes from history, even prehistory, that illustrate the formative and transformative significance of liminality. These capture some of the most important liminal crises in the history and pre-history of Europe and the broader Mediterranean world, positioning contemporary 'permanent liminality' in context.[19] It does not offer an exhaustive, continuous narrative: this would be impossible. Rather, it focuses on some major juncture points in human culture and civilisation when, in a liminal situation, something unusual happened, when the usual sequence of events that accompany an entry at the threshold took a turn different from the standard sequence/procedure that was going on endlessly, and left a clear trace – *had* to leave a clear trace – as reality was transformed, and a new kind of reality emerged: an altered one, characterised by terms like 'irreality' or new irreality, resulting in the experience of a schismatic world (Dunn 2000; Hanks and Linduff 2009).[20] This happened because the usual authorities under whose guidance the anguishing liminal situations were previously lived and passed through – the 'liminal authorities' contained in the title of this book, of which the Weberian expression 'charisma' provides a first, though seriously defective illustration – somehow failed to function. A new kind of liminal 'authority' emerged, which hijacked the scenery, deviating it towards its own character and purposes. As a result the previous order could be captured, in its original Latin sense by the term *ratio*, or, again in its original Greek sense by the term *metron*, meaning a whole in which every element is in harmonious relationship with the others, forming a whole (Clastres 2010: 276).[21] This loss of measure is captured in the expression 'liminal incommeasurability', another central term of the book, which implies a break, a fraction and fragmentation.

The first chapter goes back as far as the Palaeolithic era, identifying the first, and in many ways most decisive, moment of liminal crisis, standing on the borderline between pre-history and history. This can be captured through an 'alternative Lascaux': the unique case of a narrative scenery in the entire 25,000 years of Palaeolithic cave painting, the famous 'shaft scene' in a hidden recess of the most famous and most beautifully painted cave in the entire period, a singular exception through which the unmaking of documented wholeness can be understood. This is not simply a pictorial illustration of a particular event, but the image as *the* event itself, as it represents the first mask in human culture: the transformation of an image into a mask, and thus of a serious, exacting, sacred ritual into a new logic of machination; the emergence of technology. This can be understood through a reconstruction of the historical background: the way the caves were functioning, as a kind of 'rite of passage'.

Chapter 2 focuses on another episode in the history of technological transformation: the emergence of metallurgy, or the technique by which the solidity of rocks – proverbially the most solid objects in human experience – were dissolved, resulting in fluid metal, which then could be moulded and stamped, following the will of the smiths, masters of ceremony of this new, technological ritual, into preconceived, fixed, mechanical and identical forms. It is argued that this technological process gave rise to an entire philosophical system, still preserved in the form of 'alchemy', which contained a secret knowledge about how not only rocks, but also human beings, could be transformed and moulded into a more docile shape, according to the will of the possessors of alchemic knowledge, through a genuine procession, resulting in a sudden, though fleeting and self-destructive, prosperity. This technique is sacrifice, explaining why there is a close historical correspondence, reinforced by recent archaeological findings – for example in Çayönü or Arslantepe – between the invention of metallurgy, culminating in the Bronze Age, and practices of human sacrifice. In its last sections, the chapter will argue that the origins of philosophy, with the pre-Socratics and Plato, can be searched in the attempt to harmonise such technological skill with a knowledge about nature, and the nature of Being; this is a problem rendered particularly pertinent with the appearance of the sophists, carriers of an alchemical kind of knowledge, promising quick fame, wealth and happiness, but stealing the unity of life.

Chapter 3 moves closer to our present, by showing how this kind of technological knowledge, which is based on the denigration of human existence to a lived death, can provide the basis from which the idea of a radical new re-birth, central for the 'palingenetic' ideologies of modernity (Griffin 2007), can exert their influence. It starts by shortly presenting the ideas of Pope Innocent III about the supposed 'misery of the human condition', then Leon Battista Alberti's *Momus*, in which Alberti, one of the most famous Renaissance polihistors, identified the reappearance of the trickster in the midst of the Renaissance. It then discusses the reappearance of theatre and the mask, towards the end of the Renaissance, analysing the figure of Pulcinella, embodiment of nothingness, the zero, or not-Being, thus again capable of a sudden and alchemic transformation of social entities. It concludes by presenting the works of the French etcher Jacques Callot, the first to make an image of Pulcinella, a masked mime, in a not realistic but highly stylised, and thus even more interesting, manner.

The last two chapters are devoted to the modern reappearance of liminal incommeasurability, which would become a dominant feature of the modern condition. Chapter 4 will start by comparing the alchemical–cosmological aspects of the work of Callot, this crucial in-between figure, with the ideas of Isaac Newton, inaugurator of the new world view characteristic of the Enlightenment, in particular through the significance attributed to the liminal void as a 'prime mover' of events. It will then show how the modern revolutionary tradition capitalised on the significance of Newton's discovery of the void, through the 'S's central to the revolutionary mentality, already pioneered in the etchings of Callot, which – just as the philosophy of Newton – merely and literally reflected the liminal void, giving up the attempt to restore measure and harmony: seduction, or yielding to the empting power of *Eros*, or eroticised sensations; senselessness, or resignation to a world without meaning; and sensation, or a futile search for satisfaction at the individual level of gratifying sensory pleasure. The chapter then presents the human equivalent of the Newtonian world of quantities and particles bumping into each other in the void, or the crowds and masses that have increasingly dominated politics since the end of the nineteenth century. This is a human reality that was largely brought into being by the transformation of the social world into the equivalent of the Newtonian vision of the universe, as a kind of 'performative speech act', and the pioneering analysis of the manner in which such crowds select their leaders, through the ideas of Gustave Le Bon, a visionary figure comparable in certain respects to Nietzsche, and continued by Gabriel Tarde, especially in his 'laws of imitation' and the concept 'passionate interests'. Out of the background of this reality came the demagogy of the totalitarian politics of the twentieth century, using and perpetuating the crisis situation of a liminal void into the desired precondition of re-birth. Thus the idea of a new, perfect social order, was born. The chapter closes by contrasting ideas on crowd psychology with Max Weber's pioneering introduction of charisma into political sociology.

The last and concluding chapter returns to the contemporary world. It combines Weber's understanding of charisma with Plato's analysis of *Eros* as an irresistible and potentially destructive force. Weber failed to incorporate fully the emotional aspects of a liminal situation, giving an excessively rationalistic account of the way charismatic heroes emerge, to solve liminal crises. This was symptomatic of a broader ignorance of such processes, characteristic of our era, which rendered modern politics vulnerable to the appearance of a series of strange figures: 'liminal authorities', created by the two World Wars, who increasingly managed to overtake the political scene, at first culminating in the various totalitarian regimes, but currently threatening, in a mutated form, contemporary democracies as well. The success of these movements is based on a joint play with *Eros* (as a result or release of sacrifice) and techniques of sacrifice. *Eros* is a particularly strong liminal force, emerging in the in-between, or the 'metaxy', as analysed by Plato in the *Symposium*, erasing the boundaries of the self; it is thus comparable to self-sacrifice, as if echoing Bataille's 'Eroticism opens the way to death' at more than 2000 years distance (Bataille 1998: 24).[22] It is this same self-sacrifice that totalitarian movements require from their adherents, promising a bright new world, a perfect social order where all individual needs and desires will be fully satisfied, thus luring the incautious to give up personal integrity and leap into the unknown. The promises will not be met; but at this moment, instead of a blissful state of happiness, a sacrificial mechanism will be set in motion, capturing those hooked and misled by their own sense of guilt, because of their unlimited desires for erotic gratification or their readiness to accept the logic of 'passionate interests'. At this stage, the logic of illusionism shifts gear. Instead of the positive image of a perfect society, emphasis is displaced on a double negation: the search for eliminating all suffering and unhappiness in the world. This aim is similarly unattainable, but paradoxically positively never ending, as the failure – in contrast to the failure of positive utopias – will only reinforce an ever more dogged and obsessive belief in the need to persist, because the continuous presence of suffering, increasingly produced by the very effort, will be physically present, in contrast to the elusive utopias. It is this, at once self-fulfilling and self-destructive spiral, which is captured by the expression 'transforming weakness into political capital'. The chapter focuses on the case of communist leadership, but will incorporate, as a reference point, and to prepare the ground for further comparative studies, the works of Roger Griffin[23] about fascism, which introduce the similar term 'liminoidality'.

The Bolsheviks, those obsessive sensationalists, are difficult to deal with as they learned access towards a technicalised knowledge of how to break and divide social links, which caused a sudden malign effect, later called 'totalitarianism'.[24] This is because sensation needs to be controlled; otherwise it is invasive, targeting the soft and the defenceless with its dissolving, annihilating power. This power, at a fundamental anthropological level, in the past as much as in modernity, is rooted in memories, images and dreams, where the basic difference between the original and the copy can easily evaporate, leading to the conflation of genuine and fake impulses. Sensitivity, which searches for genuine properties that are inside a soft tissue, can thus be attacked, ready for possession or take-over through infiltration; it is a very delicate poison. What is more, it lets in, even at a privileged position, those who gave up themselves, taking a leap into the void, thus losing their *ratio*. Its training therefore cannot be restricted to rational comprehension or the law: rather, it poses more fundamental questions of confidence in reality.

However, this confidence is invisible, it belongs to the imperceptible; this is why we need to trace our search concerning the links between charisma and liminality back to the furthest reaches of memory. In our search for retrieving this confidence in reality, we will show how certain prehistoric images were not at all disconnected from the forbidden knowledge of incommensurability, where orders, forms and principles came to be suspended, and with a definite sequence of actions reproduction could be provoked in liminality, which was different from the general veneration exemplified by most cave paintings. In this way it is possible to see how techniques provoking sensations, or 'desiring machines' (Deleuze 2004b: 232–4), leading to an empty consciousness (Baudrillard 2009: 27), could be deliberately used to break and divide the unity of being.

1
Squaring the Liminal or Reproducing it: Charisma and Trickster

The liminal is an endpoint, where things hang over nothingness, being kept apart from life, yet feeling it intensively. It is thus something that has no unity, suffering from this deprivation, having a weakness for forms, which cannot be expressed; yet it is possible to sense it, approach it and exploit it. Liminality can only be expressed through the zero, as only nothingness can express nothingness: it is positional, and can only become visible when something infiltrates it. In the following, I give an account of the liminal incommensurability when it first appeared, as an apprehensible object of knowledge in a peculiar underground setting.

When one enters a place not one's own, not only does one become part of it, but the place infiltrates the person as well, through a strange and uncanny feeling. This experience is even more pronounced when the place itself is somehow unusual, like an underground cave, where one literally enters the void, as if going through nothingness, becoming part of it, although not identical with it. Through those who enter it, this void can gain existence and thus visibility. The experience is identical for any cave, but it gains an additional and striking significance through those caves where very ancient wall paintings have been discovered over the past century or so. These cave paintings express this nothingness with the floating figures and the hazy lines, the beauty and joy in the lightness of forms, the cave being triggered into motion by the presence of people. Letting loose the void, by liberating it from the boundaries that contain it, liberates sensations of sweet delight. The problem is that some can access and approach the liminal properly, whereas others should not have, as eventually a visitor arrived who came up with false demands, based on false suppositions, which resulted in the decomposition of the entire realm of delight. This dramatic revolution is indicated by Lascaux's famous 'Shaft scene', which demonstrates the presence of this intruder, who aimed to possess special knowledge in the prehistoric world.

Though the expression seems hazy, the term 'prehistory' can be given a precise meaning, which corresponds to a substantial co-operation of humans with the order of reality.[1] It does not refer indiscriminately to everything that happened before written history, but can be connected to a particular period: the appearance of harmonious images, which first took place on a mass scale and in a particularly impressive manner through cave paintings.[2] At this moment, with the Aurignacian (the period lasting from about 40,000 to 28,000 BC), we no longer have only to consider sparse objects here and there, like worked pebbles or hand axes, but there appears an astonishing quantity and quality of expression of a sense of commensuration with the world. This is the period when the Upper Palaeolithic started, around 35,000 BC. Palaeolithic cave art survives in Western Europe in about 300 sites, containing many thousands of images. These range from the earliest examples in the Chauvet cave,[3] up to the Magdalenian, with Lascaux and Altamira, the most famous ones, dating from around 17,000 to 12,000 BC.[4] Yet, at about 10,000 BC, the entire development became somehow blocked, the caves ceased to be visited and even their memory disappeared. Around this time people evidently lost awareness about a tradition when bows and other weapons or even hunting scenes were not depicted, when animals were not considered as merely sources for food and when the world was represented as operational without violence in line with one golden mean.

Cave painting generated an enormous amount of admiration among modern scholars and artists, and even the public. Archaeologists and art historians analysed the manner in which they rendered shades, captured perspectives, outlined objects and reproduced movements, underlining the graphic skill for measure and harmony, the figurative realism and expressive strength produced by the delicate use of paint, characteristic of the Western European sites. The discoveries shocked the scientific public and urged it to redefine previously existing notions about prehistory, as no population could maintain these kinds of skills without stable foundations in mind. The paintings expressed principles by people who possessed exquisite taste and native talent, paired with overall excellence.[5] They reveal temperance, which is required for observing and depicting the powerful, running animals; and a similar moderation in painting that is relaxed (Johnson 2004). Cave paintings are unique documents about a unity with nature. They are animated by human passion and power, a delight in an existence without victims, whether hunters or the hunted, with no evidence for killing or anything else that would violate the order of things (the only exception being in the Lascaux cave that we are analysing). Most intriguingly, humans are not present in the paintings; they are implied as taking part in the whole, without any particular sign of their separate presence.[6] These people, who came down there, were their own factorial, their own self, identity, sufficiency and creation in parthenogenesis, raising a unit to a second power by itself. This is probably what charisma means when it is able to square itself by multiplying itself by itself.

Parthenogenesis, charisma

In prehistoric cave paintings, man has no role to play. He does not act, does not exist at all as a separate agent, as if his existence were only part of a bigger picture, which is the whole being-in-the-world. This term, taken from Heidegger, can be understood as a lack of self-consciousness, or lack of self-expression. This can further be illustrated in a particularly lucid manner through Plato's metaphor of wrestling, which captures the heart of the worldview of prehistoric man. Plato, who was himself a wrestler, used this sport, probably the first sport of mankind, preserved through the special esteem in which it was held by the Greeks in their Olympic Games, and in particular the wrestlers' 'method' as a model for the philosophical manner of debating.[7] Further, in his longest and conclusive dialogue, the *Laws*, Plato formulated this assimilation with one canon under established codes, which causes delight and beautiful strength, in the following manner:

> But the exercises of stand-up wrestling, with the twisting free of neck, hands and sides, when practiced with ardour and with a firm and graceful pose, and directed towards strength and health, – these must not be omitted, since they are useful

for all purposes; but we must charge both pupils and their teachers – when we reach this point in our legislation – that the latter should impart these lessons gently, and the former receive them gracefully [*charisin*].

> Plato, Laws 796A–B (translation slightly changed)

With the wrestling metaphor, Plato illustrates two fundamental characteristics of being-in-the-world: gentleness and gracefulness. These are the two outcomes of the delight that is derived from a sense of freedom that is released by working out from hardness of the fight, in contrast to the sinking feeling of a hopeless struggle; out of the tightness of discipline instead of the weakening feeling of pity; out of a tuning towards rightness and tightness instead of being exposed to humiliating shame. *Dynamis* is derived from delight, the strength of freedom, from being in harmony with oneself, in a well-adjusted world. Here the divine is evident reality; but so are humans, who correspond to each other through *ratio*, or harmonious measure, as if they would know that they and the divine are corresponding sides in fair and square relation, that they have common measure in grace and strength. Grace is not a given, but is present in human beings, where everything has a meaningful role in reflecting and proliferating decency. Courage and determination produce a hearty soul, similar to the divine, implying being kind, considerate, virtuous, sincere and genuine. The meaning of unity or wholeness is where things belong properly to each other. In the cave, where the void was evoked, one could reach up to the highest, testing oneself by setting the void over and against oneself, feeling and experiencing how things belong to each other. This combat is complete and absolute, thorough, abundant and satisfying, involving the sensuality of man and God as well. Hence we arrived at a *reductio ad absurdum*, where the proposition of a principle is proved true as it is impossible that it be false. If the human is graceful, then the divine must also be graceful; whereas if it is felt that the human is true, then the divine cannot be false either, and therefore God is true and has a golden mean. A melted heart that is full of sweet adoration is the measure of parthenogenesis, which is bringing forth grace and so charisma, a divinity for those who are themselves equal with themselves; for them it is impossible to be other than graceful, which is at the same time an empty result, as if God becomes united with Himself, which produces the same end as meeting with none at all. Parthenogenesis is a kind of empty result, as the same one is born again who existed already, without any change or break. If you square 1 or 0, you get unity in each case, or one (the unit), the ethos of the cave paintings.

This prehistoric worldview, transpiring from the images, is at one with the whole; the corresponding life conduct does not know change, fraction, division, independence (Fagan 2010: 144), nor identification: one is differentiated within identification, entities come to be in accordance with a principle, while preserving their oneness. Measure and harmony were born from this unity, which was named by the Eleatic Greek philosophers as *logos*. *Logos* does not exist in plurality or in any contradiction. It must be in accord with every quantity that corresponds to the same parthenogenetic rational amount. Picasso famously acknowledged, when looking at the Altamira images, that 'none of us could paint like that' (as in Lewis-Williams 2002: 31). This, on the one hand, implies that we have still the same taste and eyes for *logos* as the ancients tens of thousands of years ago, as we can still appreciate their work. On the other, however, it also contains the astonishing acknowledgement, from a most authoritative source, that their capacities were superior to ours. The viewing of the world of prehistoric man, concerning perfection, harmony or formal beauty, falls within the same general patterns as those of modern man, the difference being that they could still partake in it with their *ratio*. Prehistoric men were not different from us: they saw and judged the world with our senses, though not with our mind, which has become irrational over the course of time. They meant the same thing by beauty and harmony, they did know what order is and what the principles of life are, though with a difference: they did not know about one thing of which we have ample knowledge, which is the *opposite* principle, irrationality; at least, until the Shaft scene, which admitted incommensurability.

The Shaft scene introduced incommensurable irrationality in the simplest technical manner, by breaking up unity, the common measure of the divine and the human. In this way technology was born, which denies a relationship between two sides. Thus something that could not be expressed, the *arrheton* (forbidden knowledge for the Greeks), was born, which was not in line with unity anymore. About 20,000 years passed between the emergence of cave art in the Chauvet Cave and the appearance of this secret knowledge in Lascaux's Shaft scene, where a unique statement occurred on the rocks that attempted to 'rationalise' divisibility, claiming that every unity could be broken, that even the most sacred entities could be forced to give up their dignity, and that this knowledge yields infinite power to its holders.

The caves of Altamira, Chauvet, Cosquer, Lascaux, Le Madeleine and others were all hermetically sealed tubes, often miles long, containing the concentrated essence of a life in delight and strength, with hundreds of paintings expressing – close to saturation point – the representation of the fairest and the best of life: striving and power, and the belief that reciprocity is our greatest blessing (Barry 1997: 76–7). Here every animal had a will and character of its own as they always move together, as if their minds were synchronised with each other. In this sense there is no difference in substance between men and animals, society and nature, gods and after-world: all was represented in vigour and rejoicing with its own particular shape, being deeply thoughtful in its serious and quiet way, reflecting each other.[8] We can in fact even recognise the power that kept all this calm reciprocity together, in the form of a net on the head of the 25,000-year-old and one-inch-high statue of the Brassempouy goddess: 'It seems to have been love that encouraged the first sculptor to carve ivory to depict the woman he loved', said its discoverer, Edouard Piette, in 1894 (White 2006: 269). It represented the power of the void when set against themselves once they entered the cave, and they 'enjoyed the tender joys in the closed cups' with her (Hölderlin), honouring her down there accordingly.

Aiming at transformation: Bringing forth schism

The basic thing about the Shaft scene is that it breaks with the standard distinction between painting animals and engravings of humans by enacting a painted image for the human being as well, and that it depicts a phallic man who is urging for copulation. The novelty of this image, a class in its own, is well defined by the phallus of the masked figure in the Shaft scene, which has again no equals in the cave paintings. It is true that in the caves there were other phallic signs present, but they were only symbols, not a definite member united to a human body. This small figure in the Shaft scene, with its elementary, vulgar pose, entraps and annihilates the whole tiresome effort of dozen millennia of work and art, reducing the magnificent art into one base – rather than basic – gesture. The Shaft scene changes involution, or the entanglement with the divine, into detachment. It thus alternates the process of turning upon oneself by a function of equal strength to its inverse, which is revolution, or the process of turning round and round. In opposition to the paintings, where everything is moving together in harmony, being caught firmly by an operational will that, invisibly, embroiled together the magnificent figures, this scenery visibly separates them into three different entities: the phallic figure, the divine animal and the bird spirit. In between them a new form of communication is enacted: that of the erotically possessive one.

This release from an elementary and comprehensible communication between the human and the divine, or a change from involution into revolution, entails other consequences as well. All three participants are alienated from their own shape and form: the figure from his human form by the mask, the divine from its divinity by lust, whereas the dislocated spirit has received a separate entity in the form of the bird on the mask and on the staff. Furthermore, the pose of the human is in itself contradictory, schismatic, defending and attacking at the same time: the body lying on the ground with wide open arms shows that he is being subjected to external forces to which he gives himself up, while his erect phallus demonstrates his objecting to the perceived violator.

The 'Shaft' is actually a misnomer, as the scene can be found at the end of a small recess, on the right from the passageway that connects the nave to the main hall in the prehistoric cave of Lascaux (Aujoulat 2005: 26, 40–2, 158–61). Its access from the passageway is difficult, as one must negotiate a six-metre drop to reach the bottom level, the ceiling levels being identical; however, it is practically impossible to return from there to the main cave area, which contains the rest of the paintings (Ruspoli 1987: 138). Furthermore, it is now widely accepted that there was originally a second entrance to the cave, from which one could get access to the 'Shaft', though not beyond. It was therefore an authentic alternative sanctuary, outside the main paintings and ritual sceneries, yet closely connected to them, to which some people might have been genuinely attracted, with the promise of initiation into some hidden secrets to which the guards of the ruling cult were unwilling or unable to gain access. The mask is worn by a phallic creature with bird-like claws. He faces on the right side a bison, widely interpreted as a divine appearance, which, however, also alludes to a broken unity through an arrow-like sign. The bowel-like drawing under the bison expresses a maze symbol that has suddenly become visible, as if it fell out of the body of the bison. Finally, on the left, as if alluding to a narrative – which is again quite unique for Palaeolithic cave art, as these images do not have a narrative aspect – there is a rhinoceros and a spectre with a bird on it. They clearly belong to the same scene, shown by the manner in which they are facing each other: the bird's beak faces the rhinoceros's anus, which is opened up in a manner opposite to the way the tail of the bison is lifted up. There are also six dots painted next to the anal area, arranged in three pairs, as if they were just now being born out of the back part of the rhinoceros (for further information about the unique coordinated animation, see Leroi-Gourhan 1982: 42). The rhinoceros is giving birth to something multiplicative, in definite connection with the bird's beak, as if this referred to a difference between the digestive system of humans and birds: although in the case of the latter only one orifice serves both for secreting waste and for reproduction, human beings have three, each well-defined and distinct. All three of these anatomical functions are brought into one line, as indicated by the bird's beak, representing with its phallic, copulative form the cloacae as well, that it is itself the one that is fertilising, excreting waste and laying an egg. A communication chain is depicted here: from the bison's bird-like soul to the man's mask and bird fingers, and from the man's bird essence to the rhinoceros's behind, and then back to the bison, as the rhinoceros and the bison are mirror images of each other. It is not only the circular movement that is astonishing here but also the presence of a third being. The reciprocal links between the bison and the rhinoceros could function perfectly well without an outsider. Now the circle contains two equal beings, which are mirror images of each other, the bison and the rhino. The phallic figure of the Shaft scene is unnecessary in the circle; this is why the interloper is using a mask, mimicking the divine, disguising strength and so leaving a hole in the picture like a knife in the wound.

The bird and the rhinoceros as well as the man are not to be found anywhere else in the cave. The three pairs of dots, however, are reproduced at the very end of the Southern shaft, just after the Chamber of the Felines and a very enigmatic 'house on the tree', though the colours there are different (Eshleman 2003: 188). Given that the Chamber of the Felines is in the area of the main cave of Lascaux that is most difficult to access, and that the images there depict more frightening animals, it might be argued that they represent an alteration to the existing arrangements of the main halls. This lends further credit to the idea that the designers of the 'Shaft scene' intended it to represent something like a difficult and secret trial. Even if they did not want to undermine completely the master idea of the cave itself, they certainly introduced something alternative and grave, in contrast to the authenticity of the animal images in the cave sanctuary.

A new gravity

The interpretation of the Shaft scene as the decomposition of the cooperation between the divine, animal and human realms can be supported by several further points. According to various scholars, there are only some dozen human or anthropomorphic figures among all the cave images found so far in Spain and France, a small number compared with the thousands of animal images. They are also mostly engravings, with the single Lascaux exception of the Shaft scene, and these few representations are usually in hidden parts of the caves, far away from the main paintings (Kleiner 2010: 9). These cave engravings deliberately chose to represent humans through vague images, which contain few details, or show even outright deformed features (Conkey, in Lock & Peters 1999: 328). A contemplation of these engravings about human figures produces the feeling as if one just happened to be in the midst of a puppet show, being surrounded with a bizarre burlesque of mechanical entities, without any strength. They are as if we could not think at all, just allowing ourselves to be overcome with fantasies, living with the ever-opening and closing images of terror: always opening up, always in disintegration, never arriving at a fulfilment. It is true that in prehistoric caves we have a distorting realism, through the twisting of space and the intensification of fantasy forms; but the engraved human images are strikingly modern and outrightly grotesque. They express emptiness, their vacuity producing a dry, monotonous, metal-cold, constant pain; an emptiness that provokes schisms, as it can never lead to satiety. There is no remedy whatsoever for this frightening, tormenting state of terror; these eternal wanderers in the bowels of the Earth are neither really alive, nor completely dead, lurking there to catch something. These flattened, disordered figures that only appear in engravings represent the illusionist space of the cave, which is a hallucinatory, outsider automatism, endlessly looping and circling into bizarre images which, entrapped by the darkness of the mind, are unfinished. The phantom engravings represent something different from the wholeness of the paintings, showing obscure and ambiguous features that do not tell much about order and delight, and reveal little strength or intensity. They are only present in the darkest recesses of the caves, places that represent the real underground inside the underground, where they can exist in secrecy.

The perfect, high aesthetic standard of the cave paintings, their admirable precision, the intensity of movements and the beauty of animal figures, their astonishing reality, their detail; even drawing the hair in the bison's ear, the horse's fur, the different animal characters that were getting shape and form in the paintings; all are in very apparent contrast to the amphibious human engravings. Note that these animals are floating in the air, their legs do not reach down to the earth and their pose does not know gravity; they have no horizon, no landscape, no orientation to earthly living, they are themselves from the world of gods and their appearances require the participative help of an orderly net, which is entirely missing for the engravings of the human figures, who are thrown out into nothingness.[9]

The masked man is reclining, offering his body to violence. The bison is towering over him with his forceful horns. The man in the Shaft scene has a bird mask, representing the spirit-essence of the divine bison that was lured into the mask so that it could be caught and its power taken. Mimicking the divine and feigning to be weak at the same time offers a perfect hiding place for the interloper. In this way he can divert the attention away from his traps, softening up his divine rival, and luring him easily into his own ways. The masked man successfully plays the martyr and the aggressor at the same time: the bison is shown as hurt, disembowelled by a 'love spear', while the mask is also fainting. The mask is lowering and thus humiliating itself by playing the victim and by the same act manages to catch the divine into its grips. For Bataille this scene is a testimony of a crime, or even a sin committed by man against animals, because the separation between animal and human was not totally established at that time (Bataille 2005: IX; Geneste et al. 2004: 102). By showing pain and suffering it empties itself, until it receives a response from the divine powers embodied by the bison. The divine has thus entered into an eroticised contact or communication with the man, as its attention became focused on the man. They are both searching for a sexual unity (Thompson 1996: 111).

The mask identified himself with the bison, mimicking its phallic appearance, and in this way managed to approach the bison and take its power. The mask is ithyphallic; and by introducing submission into the game he became emphatically phallic, as if on the third power: with the sharp beak of the mask, with its erect member and with his two phallic form feet. These feet even have the same shape and size as the horns of the bison, so they are very much each other's equals in terms of fertilising power. This is why his self-humiliation is very much a form of attack: the mask is involved in a violent action. There is a broken arrow sign under the human and the bison, joining them and thus signifying the end of their separate existence and the ensuing mutual subjugation to each other. According to the narrative of the Shaft scene, they both died owing to a love wound, which is indicated by the fact that the arrow cuts across the bison's anus, which is shown open by the raising of its tail. Both the ithyphallic man and the bison with the phallic form horns are indicating that this is an amorous scene, and cannot be reduced to a simple passing away. They are eager for getting more and more from each other, dragging energy from the other, being involved in a cross fertilisation.

It is remarkable that, according the Shaft narrative, it is only the man who receives gifts through his offering of himself to subjugation. Three such gifts are indicated in the image: one is the maze that the bison emanated from his body; the second is the inseminating of the divine, as indicated by the dots next to the rhinoceros; while the third is immortal life, as the shown by the bird on the erected sceptre. This can be understood by analysing the connections between the rhinoceros and the bison (about female–male animals and signs, see Leroi-Gourhan 1982). The bison and the rhinoceros, both emphatically horned animals, are mirror images of each other, though showing some significant asymmetries. The rhinoceros is on the left side of the image, behind the back of the fainting mask, while the bison is on the right. Both have their tail lifted up, and both are pointing in the direction of the mask. As the mask is turned towards the bison, it is ready to receive the human semen in its anus, while the rhinoceros is giving birth. The beak of the bird at the top of the shaft is pointed directly at the anus of the rhinoceros beside the fainting mask, indicating the final goal and target of the action, assisting the multiplicative birth, as expressed by the two rows of triple dots. They consummated their love together, but the benefits produced are one-sided, being only on the side of the man. The god remained in depravity, robbed and in despair, which is quite a significant change from its previous co-operativeness, as manifested by the paintings.

The mask configures an absence of form, as it covers the face. The mask cancels the individual human person, with its character and shapes, and rather mirrors the nothingness of death. Death is an elementary problematic in prehistoric cave art, as the paintings were designed around the question of the absence of shapes: how to give shape to nothingness by strengthening visions on the surface of rocks. It could be better approached through the idea of *dreaming*. People certainly performed some kind of 'rituals' there, but we do not know anymore what they were exactly. But we can bypass this entire issue by realising that coming into the cave and staying there was a ritual *per se*; certainly an act out of the ordinary. Further, sleeping is in itself an involutive act, a moment of turning upon oneself. It is a passive, motionless state from the outside, but an active and participatory state from the inside as the painted pictures show what they have depicted once awoken. As these sleeping, hibernating rituals, and in particular the entry into the cave – in order to dream there – stimulated an encounter with powers, the cave sanctuary was literally a teasing of death, so it is reasonable to assume that people who went there also went through some kind of death experience, went beyond the real, physical world, passed the line between life and death. Not only death entered into their body, but they also participated in nothingness: a creative change, if we consider that they woke up at a certain point.

By creating the cave paintings they managed to keep contact with the void; these images caused the latter to move or function, as if in a natural reflex of remembering. We might say that they were able to 'trigger off' the liminal by their painted images, could work out how they could see beauty, echoing unbearable harmony. The communication with the Beyond, however, had another element as well: the response they received from there was not very different from the type of situation captured by the images pictured on the cave. Just as the cave paintings captured wild animals in magnificent movement and sometimes their struggle, the initial and the later response from Beyond also had the character of a force, constraining them to struggle, to grapple under terror with the powers that got hold of them, and they fought for their integrity with quickness, energy, acuteness. Those upward and virtuous who succeeded literally seized powers, and held the otherworld close to them with a strong grip.[10] People did not come down to the cave to die but to benefit from the powers beyond, to involute growth and power! The cave was the place where opposites agreed, intentions magnified into involution, parthenogenesis.

The Shaft scene was different. It altered the meaning of agreement, because the masked man is giving up himself, a mere pose of prostitution. The mask is hiding instead of sharing, his hands and feet are no longer instruments of his own intentions and he is misusing powers by offering its body to them, alternating their attention, a passive positionality without mental energy. This is visible by the broken image of the arrow, which is the sign of a break, or the mathematical operation of division. In mathematics the result of the division of a unit is called a 'fraction', which is derived from the Latin *fractio*, or breaking.[11] Where corporality (the human being, matter) gets in contact with the divine (spiritual being, nulla) through break or division, the result is infinity; just as any natural number divided by zero mathematically yields infinity.[12] The result is the infinite growth of the set-up captured in the image of the three times two dots under the rhinoceros's anus, the multiplication of the mask's semen. Through the insinuation of weakness and emptiness, the man of the image pulls down the power and repositions it, focusing it on itself, on its own body. The mask is hijacking the idea of giving, transforming it into a knavish sacrifice, offering himself, the unstable and drunken, to the divine.

Of course, this creates a split at the level of the divine power as well, which was tricked into the affair, then caught and abused, its power being stolen. The reciprocity of beauty and gift relations of the cave images, which is based on the squaring of qualities, is becoming corrupted by new techniques that are converting the operation into a new kind of manipulation. This technique is based on a very simple motive of passivity, offering a body to be subjugated and fractioned, but resulting in a complicated mathematical operation. A simple bodily addition to nothing does not bring any result at all $(2 + 0 = 2)$; however, if we break the body with nothing, the result is surprisingly profitable: it is the infinite growth that is turning around, which is exactly the Latin meaning of the word 'revolution'. Accordingly, it is worth arriving at the completion of the operation: whether digging the trap or hanging the bait, one must always show oneself as feeling low – down and out, weak and enslaved, hurt and suffering. Whoever is offering a gift can be sincere; but whoever wants to take something away must always hide behind a mask. The mask is snarly and wilfully playing the role of the prey, feeding an endless and insatiable monster with the sensation of pain, though the success is guaranteed. The divine bison on the one hand safely recognises its inner image in the bird mask, and on the other considers the fainting man as harmless. Consequently it infiltrates its body, while the man also penetrates him $(2/0 = \text{infinity})$, thus releasing the secret of the maze, the symbol of infinite mechanical reproduction or growth (on the labyrinth as representing infinity, see Hyde 1998: 332). The revolution is thus accomplished, with growth being turned over from the bison-god to the technicalised proceduralist.

The growth is caught by the trick of man, but its reward is just as small as its pleasure was. This is the meeting of an inferior god with an inferior man in common consumption, which is aggravating on weakness and on common plundering. In this world man is despotically closed into the mill of a crushing terror under the ever-renewed material abundance by new and newest subjugations, where every fractioning operation brings ever the same results. Its masked victims are never liberated from a troglodyte existence, from the labyrinths that lead nowhere but curling around with every curl into a new schism.

The Shaft scene brings out three new elements compared with the previous, painted pictures of the underground: isolation, as the mask with his abnormal hands is isolated from humanity but linked to the subhuman, being in-between the two; insinuation; and subjugation. None of the three points work in isolation, but taken all together they produce a frenetic result, on the one hand by enacting the technical know-how of mechanical growth, on the other by imprisoning the mind into infinite repetition, stamping it with the evacuation of meaning. Man is reduced to a mere techno-head, indicated by the bird of the staff, which has a reduced (meaning only one) and identical organ for creation, reproduction and elimination, a humiliating reduction for anybody, but quite a fruitful position concerning automatised reproduction. He cannot forget anymore the sour terror of what he happened to learn during the rite, repeating it infinitely, taking the terror on his own back, recalling Zarathustra's dwarf, and is not able to comprehend anything else any more than the dual nature of his own existence, eternal but reduced to the perceptible world of mere sensations (Nietzsche 1976: 268).

Conclusion: Technology, the Trickster's episteme

Images started on rocks ended up on plasma screens. Although some 30,000 years has passed in between, contemporary art has a quite similar comprehension of reality than its predecessor, which brings us back again to the underground, as if to complete a circle whose end and beginnings are now reaching each other. The cave paintings, these rock-solid foundations of grace, can be confronted with their scandalous imitation or forgery. The latter only mimes the authentic, though not in the sense in which each sunrise repeats the first sunrise of creation. Each such repetition coalesces with the original event, with giving, and thus has delight and beauty in repetition. A mimed copy is a rough, idle blockade of sensual movement, alternating the original circle into another one, the mechanism of infinite insatiability, of which the plague is the model, or any other epidemic disease.[13]

The consequence – owing to a permanent alienation from their humanity, which is reductionist materialism – is a metal-cold automatism, which can continue into eternity. There is no remedy whatsoever for this tormenting state of terror. This can be perceived in the much later Deer Cave in Badisco, Puglia, in the Los Dogues cave in Spain, in the rocks of Tassili and many other examples that were made once the Palaeolithic caves ceased to be visited anymore, after about 10,000 BC. The entire mechanism produces a type of depravity that is forever eager, as its components strive after the pleasure of fulfilment, without ever being pleased. The components are schismatic in themselves because they can never be satisfied. This never-ending milling of schisms and re-unifications, which only leads to further schisms and never completes anything, is the reason why any mechanism is always bound to slip out of control (Bateson 1972).

Techne belongs to bringing-forth, to *poiesis*; it is something poetic (Heidegger 1977: 294). Here Heidegger is following Plato: 'Take the following: You know that *poetry* [*poésis*] is more than a single thing. For if anything whatever that passes from not being into being the whole cause is composing or poetry; so that the productions of all arts are kinds of poetry, and their craftsmen are all poets' (Plato, *Symposium* 205B). They are rivals! Both have an episteme of how to create objects, the knowledge of creation, but only the original has the harmonious equity of principle,[14] whereas the technological mode, which switches from a superior to an inferior mode of operation, is wild and intractable with its subjugation and forced passivity. However, it also manages to bring to life the powers of the Beyond, in the form of an idle beast that *techné* is fattening endlessly, whose world is unkindly totalitarian.

According to Heidegger, it is *poiesis* that constitutes the difference. (It is to be noted, however, that the Greek word has a much wider meaning of 'making' than the European sense of poetry). As an attitude, it does not imply respect for the intensive feeling of happiness derived from the experience of the orderly, but the lust of infinitely longing after that. Instead of absorption, it is characterised by 'enframing' (Heidegger), which chases life and throws whatever it caught into the 'melting pot', where every object becomes a deprived automaton, following the same rhythmical repetition of itself. This kind of attitude feeds on a movement that does not require further care, but first presses people into the same container, then spins them further to idle purposes. It represents the vacuity of technology which is not governed by due measure. *Poiesis* is the invention of a novelty that might deviate from the principles of beauty and order, thus the re-creator of reality, the revolutionary in contrast to order, as it deviates from measure. It is repositioning the automatism of order. Hence it does not simply produce disorder; rather, it generates a new centre of gravity, thus 'spinning' or 'forging' away from the original into a direction of automated depravity.

The humble and visionary cave painters of the Palaeolithic era were the first genuine philosophers, who understood that there are no mere facts; that a fact only becomes what it is in light of its framing: true knowledge is invisible and imperceptible, it happens to be true only if one has the proper characteristics for receiving it. The Palaeolithic cave painters tuned themselves for admitting what had just opened up in front of their mind: the delicate, soft contours of emotions, as captured in the Brassempuoy Lady who is dreaming, feeling and resonating together with them. Every mood, disposition, wish, calculation, opinion, consideration, reflection in life, the sensation and the form of the fire, air and water, every movement and motion is present in these under-ground spaces: every forethought, council, joy, grief, confidence, love, and everything else that is akin to it. For them, the gift of grace governs all changes and modifications to their entire world. It reacts and answers to every stimulus or change that occurs there. Our bodies, which are part and parcel of the Earth, Nature or the Divine, are linked with charismas, in their every motion and feeling and act to a dormant existence, which dwells in every object, in all things in the world. The people who went to the caves underwent incubation, but *logos*, harmony and measure did not thrive in them before they developed it in themselves. The cave did not play the role of their breeder; grace is not given but requires attunement. So they had to go through, one by one, the victorious combat for principle, of becoming united with its grace; they had to trust for partaking in harmonious creation.

On the opposite side, a salient characteristic of Trickster *alogos* is that this unity with nature is broken, trust in reality does not work anymore, and man and God became confused; like in the simple geometric sense, the symmetry between the two sides of the square becomes confused if a single line is drawn between them. The two lines, which previously were in measure or *ratio* with each other, suddenly lose their self-support and independ-ence with this action. Their meaning suddenly alternates into another one, they become triangles, and the diagonal line receives an impossible quantity, as it is an irrational number, an *arrheton* (Szabo 1978: 227), a number of the liminal. This counter-factual condition of impossibility gives birth to infinite similar operations, where the result is always the same decomposition. This properly performed practical procedure could continue for-ever, once the recipe is discovered that one unit might be linked into another one by transformation. The treatment for changing this composition always corresponds to the three phases of the *rites of passage*: separation, liminality and re-aggregation, being identical with the technical treatment of a unity, broken through metallurgical processes.

2

The Rise of Liminal Authorities: Trickster's Gaining a Craft, or the Techniques of Incommensurability

Any situation of incommensurable liminality by definition first of all disrupts integrity and unity, breaking the whole down into its composite elements, and thus – in the current sense of the term – produces a crisis that must be dealt with directly. From this perspective the appearance of metallurgy as a technology that divides units into parts can be characterised as an anthropological and historical marker of crises.[1] What is more, this technological process handles crises in a mechanical, procedural manner, thus destroying the original composition of elements. Metallurgy as a technique was developed through an awareness of pain, using suffering to force objects to give up their original physical properties, playing with excess and enacting a new circle by confounding accepted ways of thinking.[2] In situations of crisis, this way of thinking reaches spiritual depth and produces significant effects, as it deprived entities from self-support, reducing life to subservience,[3] as seen in the post- or pre-metallurgical alchemy, whose origins are uncertain, as the knowledge was secret, was forbidden to reveal, was enveloped in mystery (Thompson 1932: 43–4). In this way the crisis was resolved, though only by capitalising on the opportunity and using destruction to generate new and different entities. This is why the god of Bronze Age technology (metallurgy), Hephaestus, and his skill of smithery is a quite problematical story. The Greeks certainly recognised this problem, as according to a related myth he spent nine years at the bottom of the sea in the company of Thetis, learning to become master of skilled metal work (Détienne and Vernant 1978: 300). Several motifs are present here jointly: gaining a craft out of chaos, the sea being a primal element, shapeless yet material essence; the cunning, shape-altering Thetis/Metis; and the character of mimesis. All these gave their characteristic stamp to the changing, bisexual, smithing half-deity figures associated with metalwork, like the dwarfs of the mountains, the Dactyls or the Cabeiri (Kerényi 1980), dwellers of liminal places, and occupied with bizarre activities. Hephaestus was pictured through proto-human features, his ugliness being so alien to *kalokagathia*, the Greek ideal of virtuous beauty. However, this figure synthesised a grotesque and excessive situation, which liquefies meaning, confuses essence and distorts forms, ever oscillating between being and becoming. In Georgius Agricola's sixteenth century book *De Re Metallica*, the smith's limbs are twisted and curved, echoing the form of the crippled smith's god Hephaestus – this decidedly undignified and ridiculous god of the Greeks – who was nevertheless Aphrodite's husband, thus suggesting the erotic connotations of metallurgy, as Aphrodite is the goddess of Love.[4] In contrast to Weber's views of charismatic leadership, crises do not imply presence or representation; rather, they mechanically follow a procedural dramatic plot that always produces the same effects, as visible in the 'ritual process' theorised by Victor Turner. There is a fundamental and so far unperceived affinity between metallurgical techniques and rituals, especially transformative rites of passage. Such technological solution to crises mimes forms and provokes effects, which nevertheless are always exciting, interesting and impressive, though also and necessarily involving victims. Liminal places and situations magnetically attract erotic impulses, which are the most tremendous mechanical and morphological aspect of sensation.

Liminality is where anything is permitted and yet everything is oppressed, where forms become weakness, owing to the rupture of the previously taken for granted order, where emptiness invades both life and death. In liminality one is in between two borderlines, with sex, age, professional qualifications or social status being indefinable. The term has been developed in anthropology to characterise the middle stage in an initiation ceremony, where the generally accepted goal is to help the initiand, and the community, move from one stage in the life-cycle to another: from childhood to adulthood, from being single to being married or to accommodate major events like birth or death. Such transformations are often marked with bodily changes: the initiand's hair is cut down, he is deprived of a proper satisfaction of his bodily needs, his dress is taken away, and in every sense he is impoverished and humiliated, occasionally even beaten: in general submitted to pain and suffering to heighten the intensity of sensations. Any intimate relationship between the initiands and the normal outside world, especially their family, is prohibited and strictly punished, because while preparing for the rite of passage they are under the jurisdiction of an 'alien' power', which is jealous to possess them. Alien power is expressed by the initiators' – and sometimes even the initiands' – masks or hoods, where they hide themselves away from the annihilating nature of this power, and at the same time mime its unutterable essence, its origin in a primal, erotic force, which is shown by the oft-used snake motifs, or by the digging of a circular pit, evoking conception, or by the whole ritual taking place in caves or underground places: 'bottom of the sea', loathing a desolate existence, the womb of the earth.

A central characteristic of liminal situations is that, by eliminating the stable boundary lines, they contribute to the proliferation of imitative processes and thus help the continuous, effective reproduction of the dominant messages about how to be reborn. These messages concerning the form to imitate disappear as quickly as they appear, though not without an impact, just as – using the language of epidemics – viruses infect and mutate, or – in the language of thermodynamics – energy does not dissipate, rather it is only transformed. Their appearance and effects have the aspect of a deadly virus, dissipating into the social body and multiplying their effects in a nick of time; and possessing a particularly strong virulence due to their both destructive and constructive energy. An example is Bazarov in Turgenev's *Fathers and Sons*, who with his fellow anarchists wanted to 'clear the ground'. Everyone considered them as cold-blooded, manipulative and ruthless, and their nihilistic attitudes were nothing more than private vices, until their followers managed to turn, at the opportune moment, despair and self-destructiveness into an attractive, powerful, epidemic social disease.

A sudden flowering of prosperity, attractiveness and mutual sympathy, and a similarly quick and thorough jump into the abyss of self-destruction, far from being neatly separable and radically different, are rather quite close to each other, and can be easily confused by the incautious or the bewildered. Thus, we have to take seriously deceptive image production as a problem, and analyse the conditions of possibility of effective, mass-scale mimetic influencing in artificial liminality. But *how to be reborn* is a tricky question, because liminality can be put into motion unconditionally as it is guided neither by causes nor by ends, but blindly goes after effects. The liminal is a place of purposeless, random roaming, the lowest common denominator, the servant of brutal appetites; but it also nurses generation, therefore its dual nature does not give a blueprint for clear adaptation. A result is only produced if the initiands accept that the meaning put forward was theirs, which means that the unity can be reborn in the process. The classical attributes of the smith, like hoods of invisibility (called the cap of Hades), the magic sickle sword that recalls the form of the uterus but also the female body and their mask, all serve the secret transformative practices to bring forth a new entity. Considering metallurgy as a religious secret should not be so surprising, given that smiths are equally at home in the world of reality and the world of imagination, as the receptacles in which the fluid metal is placed to 'create' the new objects must be designed, and with skill, while their unreality is indicated by the *mask*, the *hood*, the *hammer* and the *sickle*, their phallic and uterus forms having concentric circles, the favourite signs of the alchemical Philosopher's Egg and the Serpent Apophis. The curved legs of Hephaestus are repeated by the classic smith figure, with the magic circles of eroticised emotions. What is more, in the traditional fool's uniform the smith's cap, the mask and a hood gain a second life, together with their common dexterity: they all possess a sureness of eyes: they all have a knack for perceiving weakness, through a senseless and purposeless yet calculating mind, winning every antagonistic affair through their flexible dogmatism. The emblem figures of the liminal, the irrational fools, the mad smith, the rough wild man, the unformed Trickster, all these empty and ugly beings capture beings and transform them into a new shape.

A liminal situation only emerges once the previously stable structures of order are dissolved. Once the integrity of the form is dissolved, the scattered elements continually undergo the experience of self-negation. The matter is blocked off; it is under attack and panic, as the bridges collapse between cognition, understanding, memory, or any other type of self-identification. What remains is pure sensory perception, but also observation, driven by the working of the brain that – owing to the loss of memory and identity – is spinning on unbounded, just like an engine when the gas pedal is pushed forward with the gear in neutral. So there is extreme eagerness for new messages suggesting a new stability and identity, with each disjointed element becoming a 'relay' that receives and transmits the message.

At first everyone finds it astonishing that something exists which cannot be measured, because its measure, its unity, is destroyed; but as far as its measuring relays are functioning, it is considered as existing. In liminality the incommensurable is multiplied, as the unit was broken. Every broken unit obtains a new self and existence, as we are now in the domain of the irrational. In a rational world a unit could not be halved, because rationality excludes the possibility that a unit could be something other than itself. This is why Bateson asserted that a schismogenic system is liable to sudden and multiplicative increase. But in what direction would this process go? This depends on those present in liminality; whether they are able to erect a barrier against *invasion*. But where is the power to create such a barrier if participants are in a state of subordination, without self, identity, quality, property? Two answers can be given to this question, related to the elements that participate in this peculiar void, or creation-situation. The first is that besides the disintegrated, shapeless and colourless matter, there stands a new figure of the Neolithic, the blacksmith (Détienne and Vernant 1978), who is learned and experienced, who has the preparation to provide guidance for the invaded, who can generate a new form out of the formless liminality. The smith does not crave simply for possession, but to command power over shapeless matter, instructing and ordering it to reach a desirable form. But there is a second element present as well, contained in the fact that Hephaestus was Athena's brother, and that they together founded the mighty city, Athens. Athena stands for the opposite craft, necessary for founding a city, guiding towards unity, where real participation is given by dynamism and involution, with a strength similar to mere imitativity, in the *charismata*,[5] or the graceful (*charisin*) being.

Gaining a new craft where strength is in weakness is not just an attribute of a mythological creature, but rather evokes an ancient practice that can be traced back to the origins of metallurgy and its philosophical version, alchemy.[6] The shaping of stones first by hammering, cutting and grinding, and then by using a heat treatment to obtain metals which, when molten, could be cast – or knowledge about the secret manipulation of nature – was the craft of the metallurgists. They thus gained a concrete experience that everything in the world constitutes a reflection of and an analogy with others in the various domains of nature, each clothing itself in a body, unifying its property with matter. There is no other way of existing. The self-support of the metals could be changed artificially, recombining or altering the proportion of the composing elements by literally making them suffer, by violating their previous proportions, thus calling out a new existence through sensations.

These processes are considered by alchemists an imitation of nature, where matter is disintegrated as well as created during the middle, liminal phase of the metallurgical process. As the previously stable qualities of the elements are dissolved by various machinations, like heating, burning, sublimation, descent, distillation and calcinations, they reach the level when they lose their character, becoming mortified, any distinction between them ceasing to exist, so any new form can be printed on them; they are ready for mimesis.

Pre-Socratic thought arguably represents, among others, the philosophical elaboration of the knowledge of metallurgical techniques, the transmutation of metals. Such a convertibility between the elements is contained, for example, in a famous fragment by Anaxagoras, according to which, 'All things have a portion of everything' (Kirk and Raven 1957: 375), but do not contain the demand for man-made image-making craft. The idea that substances can transform into each other was shared by pre-Socratics: fire could become air and vice versa, if dryness came to be replaced by wetness; and each four elements could be changed into water if their essential dryness was replaced by wetness, without taking account of things being transmutated by human practices. Everything new is the offspring of flux and motion, says Plato in the *Theaetetus*, where the stage of flux[7] gives way to creation of the world. Still, artificial mortification and artificial reproduction horrified the Greeks.[8]

Artificial reproduction, or stealing knowledge from void

Working with metal, smelting stones, is a new craft; it was not practised during the time when the only known metal was gold.

Gold was the first metal that was recognised and used. However, as it was obtained in a pure state, without violent operations, and as it could be easily shaped into form, its manufacture cannot be considered a technical practice. The violent industry for obtaining metal only appears with the Bronze Age. The smelting of copper and mixing it with tin emerged around 4000 BC, when their substance was changed into a third property, bronze: the alloy of yellow, flexible copper and soft, pale tin into red, ever-during, hard bronze. This transformation, which is smelting, leaves intact the underlying matter that still remains a metal, but the character of the copper and the tin are both transformed during smelting to a third metal, bronze. Copper, like gold, is found in pure form, but because by smelting and mixing it with 8–30% tin it was converted into bronze, this is considered the first metallurgical product. It is certainly not accidental that the great bronze centre Troy is associated with a significant example of liminality: the Trojan War, the first documented liminal crisis on a world scale, the origin of 'world history'; and the travels of Ulysses, the origins of 'world literature', consisting of an entire series of trials and testing, including separation, shipwreck, meeting with monsters and titans, nymphs and witches (which are not always easy to distinguish from each other), until the eventual return of the enlightened hero. Using a more recent example, 'Bring me my bow of burning gold', says Blake in his Milton, as the 'New Jerusalem' will be built 'Among these dark Satanic mills', implying the absolute acceptance of whatever happens to you on the voyage towards becoming gold, expressing a total subordination to the events that are higher than you, for the sake of reaching the stage of enlightenment. This example also, and not unimportantly, directly links the old and new 'Industrial Revolutions', the price that must be paid for the stolen knowledge. The process of refining or purifying gold has a long history, with important metaphoric uses. The most important point according to this was that gold exists, so does not tolerate any interference or manipulation, because it does not need it, its divine nature refusing to be intruded upon and losing the right on being treated gently. The second part of the story is the story of alchemy: how to multiply, how to be forced to be reborn in a new, happier, multiplied existence. What came out from this manipulation of stealing the knowledge of void is well known, as the gold was never made. Instead numerous kinds of acid were discovered and invested into life, like arsenic, lead acetate, ammonium, chloride, nitric acid, silver nitrate, hydrargyrum, white lead, metallic antimony, sodium sulphate, etc.; all sorts of mineral acids that were used for purpose, with its own theory, which accompanied the corresponding experiments for changing the world (von Franz 1980).[9]

This new craft of metallurgy, invented in the late Neolithic, resulted in ambitious religious principles, the replacements of living units with properly performed practical procedures. The smith's art required mysterious skills and cunning detachments; its task was in some mode to evoke and intensify divine interference, and then to command and master it. The smith swears to the gods, sings songs to their honour, makes prostrations, observes chastity out of respect to his receptacle, fasts and macerates the flesh in their honour, sacrifices beasts and his own blood to get their favour, so that in the next stage his turn would arrive, gaining power over them (Kieckhefer 1998: 71). Smiths underwent self-divinisation in the sense that they made themselves identical with powers different then their own, gaining specific benefits from this interaction, but often receiving abhorrence from the society to which they belonged. They were despised, but always feared; it was considered unwise to curse or insult them because they belonged to an unutterable, desolate existence, their devotion to an unknown power being beyond understanding. Their ambivalent status reflected the perilous nature of their work: situated in an interval (*khóra*) or in between, their practitioners were adepts of the liminal, partakers of a dangerously forbidden knowledge of how to decompose and rebuild units. Their work does violence upon the elements; they are able to change substances with various, suspicious propitiation of the gods. The stones that represented the divine in Neolithic monuments and sculptures are now beaten, buried, heated and crushed in liminal, technological phases, which were linked to the incommeasurable irrational.

'The mysteries practiced among men are unholy mysteries', noted Heraclitus (Fragment 14). The provocation or stimulation of division carried no favour with the Greeks. They rejected scientifically the statement that the unit is divisible. Of course, any unit can be divided in practice, and merchants used fractions from time eternal, but Greek science took no account of fractions until the time of Archimedes (Szabo 1978: 259); it excluded the possibility that the unit could be anything than itself. However, the concept of unit presupposes that one already knows how to destroy the unit by breaking, fractioning or by dividing it, constructing another unit artificially. But these operations were banned as *arrheton*, forbidden practices that gained knowledge of eternal reality at the price of destroying the *dynamis* or ability of the units. The imitation of creation only produces hybrids and a sense of otherness, which is schismatic in nature. At first everyone finds it astonishing that there is something beyond, that break and division produced something that could not be expressed by numbers. Greeks, Romans or Egyptians had no symbol for the void. The smith, however, did make it work, as he on the one hand breaks the unit of the stone, commands and exploits nature, but on the other dedicates himself to an eternal force that is bound up with the perceptible world through the senses alone. Working apart from the community, he is despised and outcast, sacred and untouched, always remaining a dangerous figure for his people as he is linked not to them but to an alien power. He observes strict sexual taboos during his labours to achieve a property through no desires of his own, but a generalised subjugation, like a married union. The helpers of the smith are dwarfs, considered as divine, but also fearful and disturbing creatures, whereas gods often visit him. So he is under divine patronage, as his power is derived from strange sources with which he is in constant contact. The smith has the power of a medicine man, and a sinister one: he is trying to convince the gods to grant him help by promising obedience and dedicating himself to them, though only for further abuse of the divine.

Gods are conjured in various ways. First, during a metallurgical operation, the smith interferes with the harmonious growth of the elements. Second, he steals their properties during an imitative operation, which symbolises submission: the properties are placed in a position of subordination to each other to imitate each other. Third, the *prima materia* are afflicted with a violent passion until they yield to the smith's will, whose disintegrative energy is comparable to a storm or a disease: burning, destructing. All in all, the smith makes his material worse than it was at the start. But he is able to create an obscure situation, rendering his intervention necessary, either because the elements become too weak, unable to survive on their own, or because the overall confusion is accelerating, the smith having the ability to call down curses, so he nurses all those who became his victims, losing their self-support. Also, he is able to reinforce his situation, because the smith before or during the rite offers a sacrifice to compensate for the souls that are diverted, for the gods that are conjured, for nature that is disintegrated, for the state of flux that is generated, and, finally, for tricking the gods into unlimited multiplication (Forbes 1950). Changing the composition of elements through technological treatment often required means by which the transformation could be effected, which materialised in sacrifices.

Sacrifice

The secret manipulation of magical powers, the stealing of properties, the conducting of souls, the phallic fertility characteristics, the wicked, harmful nature of tortuous procedures are all Trickster attributes: he is the demi-god of material abundance, but also of disintegration into death. The smith and the Trickster are keeping each other in check, just as the folk tale goes about the devil who would like to bring the smith to Hell, but the smith manages to outwit the devil every time, and finally remains in his smithy so that he can unleash further wickedness on mankind.[10] Metallic preparations were used by the process of 'killing' the metals, and the smith often brings embryos into the furnace (Forbes 1950: 84–5) to compensate for the killing with the soul of an incomplete, undisturbed being. His special longing to be undisturbed is particularly important considering his aim to gain the state of perfection by manipulations including sacrifice: sacrificing wholeness and sacrificing incompleteness, which bears the signs of being undisturbed or innocence, and is in fact equivalent in Hungarian (*ártatlan*).

On one side, sacrifice is a propitiation for the gods, as if they might have some malign effect over the substance about to be used by the smith; but on the other, sacrifice is properly devouring the gods themselves. It is a popular alchemical symbol, to exploit the vanity of the divine serpent, trapping it in the circle. Accordingly, now the alchemist is the stratagem, killing the god and taking the power of its divine wholeness. The alchemist exploits, he is outwitting the god, capitalising on its lustful weakness, overturning the hierarchy of the world. In a well-prepared poaching on god, the alchemist not merely kills the deity, but reduces the god into servility, steals the god's properties and makes use of the god's force. The smith, who knows the doctrine, becomes an adept, being above the common man, taking the god's place in visible readiness for ruling and transforming the world. Self-divinisation and artificial creation were acted and practised in alchemy as a religion, as it accepted the transmutation of the elements of the material world by forced transformation and obedience, and – even more importantly – with positing the void as the basic principle of the world, where nothing mattered, nothing had any purpose, just disinvolvement and suspension into void. While keeping a cool mind in the midst of turbulence, techno-minds (in a cool distance) compounded chemical preparations, entrapped bodies in closed places and made them suffer until they decomposed and liberated their soul; hence they were collected, undergoing extreme agonies during the process.

In the anthropological literature there are few indications for the pervasive bestiality of liminality, apart from the sexual snare of the initiation ceremonies.[11] Mythology offers some more details, in particular in the story of the Trojan War. Troy was a major city where the ships of Cretan traders carried the hard and shameless bronze throughout the Mediterranean. The same Troy turned out to be a death trap for Helen and her Achaean heroes, who destroyed themselves there: she was dropped cold-bloodedly as a trophy by the vain goddess Aphrodite to Paris. In Italian the word *troia* still exists, with the peculiar connotations of the stultifying love of the prostitute, for a greedy, dirty and oppressive passion or (in Sardinian dialect) *troju sporco*, *troia* the female pig.[12] The occupation of Troy itself indicates that with Troy we are faced with chronic dumbness, showing that the Trojans, with the characteristic obtuseness of people rendered dull and sleepy through technology, did not take any pains to avoid the simple device of the enemy; rather, they waited for divine signs with joined hands so that their destiny would be proclaimed for them. Concerning a case similar to Troy, still in the mythological sense of the lustful and gluttonous pig, we could mention the significance of caves for smelting metal. They embody the same lower dimension of life akin to this stifling, tyrannical animal. The cave in the Neolithic, in contrast to the Palaeolithic, represents stoned heavy stasis, the non-action. It is the heavy incubus, the oppressive love

due to which Calypso for seven years, and Circe for a year, cir-
cled Ulysses;[13] the fear of darkness, the madness of fantasies, the
labyrinthine cave with the underground attack of the Minotaur,
complete helplessness, suffocation, the terror as it weighs down
upon its victims. The cave represents the dwelling place of force;
the circle alludes to erotic experience; the focus of power is to gain
control over cosmic forces (Kieckhefer 1998). In this circle even
the numerical value of human ability to walk on two feet could
change into twice two feet, into four-legged animals like pigs, as
Circe proved when transforming Ulysses' sailors into them.

But the main sign of sacrifice is in fact the sacred clown, often
shown as the wild man, the ape man or the cave man. Here
the participants of the rite of passage are overlapping into each
other: the dismembered, deceived god has thus become a beast;
it expresses aggression and causes terror, or it transforms itself
into satiric wild man. Bestiality and bloodshed occupy the stage,
where man is transformed into a phallic and violent schismatic
being: 'Anyone crossing this border is recruited to clownship', says
Handelman, as void transforms into madness (Handelman 1990:
298). Liminality is the rule of Saturn, the cold night, the dry slow
essence of emptiness, which causes self-indulgence, despair and
self-destructiveness. Images of evil demons appear on the walls
of antique initiation caves: see, for an example, Puglia, *Grotta dei
Cervi* ('Cave of the Stags'), or Nero's underground palace, from
which the term *grotesque* was coined in the Renaissance, once
rediscovered in Rome in the 1430s, to express their horrific qualities, their mocking and tortured essence, as if by their imitation
it were possible to exorcise them. The clown, in sacrificing itself
together with the world, would like to reach the state of complete
immunity from any decay in a continuous attempt to transmute
all imperfections, accordingly even its own body.

During mime plays in ancient Greece and Rome, actors wore
bestial masks, used obscene body language, and expressed disgust
and disbelief to appease the fearful, destructive forces of demonic
spirits. Similarly, the Trickster tales gathered by anthropologists
and mythologists (Guenther 1999; Kerényi 1976, 1986; Radin
1972), or the grotesque medieval *danse macabre* (Huizinga 1990),
which danced off the souls of the living, documented quite plas-
tically the powers of soul snatchers.[14] In fact, this is exactly the
aim of the alchemical *opus*, implying that only destruction could

assure birth and renewal; the release of the soul from the body brings rejuvenated completeness. The beginning of a spiritual quest is always accompanied by sacrifice or death: dying to the old state of things, to make way for new insight and creation.[15] Torture of the body and calcinations here, sacrifice and self-destruction there, this is the manner by which the soul is able to become conscious of its true nature and of the difference between natural and altered existence.[16] In the light of this knowledge the soul desires to unite with the spirit and become illuminated by it. The subsequent reunion of this spiritual awareness with the new, purified body means that knowledge gained about a form or model in an 'altered state' can now be put into action, made manifest in the world. The male and the female energies of the universe are united and balanced within the matter, bringing into being a new, more perfect state:

> [B]y their powerful art they bind
> Volatile Hermes, and call up unbound
> In various shapes old Proteus from the sea,
> Drained through a limbeck to his native form.
> Milton, *Paradise Lost*, 3.602–5

Liminality is not fixed. It is itself the Place (*khóra* in Greek) that assures multiplication and – transmuting itself endlessly if not bordered, by being confined within a concrete ritual process – is present throughout the *opus*, from the very beginning up to the end, always changing its forms, the goal being his own transformation. *Mercurius* is at the same time the matter, the process, and the agent of the work, the *opus*, by which all this is effected. It devours itself and spits itself out, kills itself and generates itself again; makes itself white and red, female and male; brings things forth and guides them to the perfect ending: the reiterated cycle of dissolution and coagulation. Hermes/*Mercurius* is a dual-natured, ambivalent force, both destructive and creative. It is the transformative substance without which the opus cannot be performed: the Mother, the substance out of which everything was created; the divine spirit hidden in everything – the *anima mundi* – which must be released to create the golden aura of beauty. It is also described as water, a water that does not wet the hand: *aqua vitae*, *aqua ardens*, as much water as fire (*noster ignis*), the *prima materia*, volatile and elusive, that takes up many guises during the ritual process. Multiplying 'the circle' is the final stage in the alchemical *opus*, transmuting the base matter into that different being which is able to reproduce itself unendingly (Jung 1989).

The crucial motif is sacrifice; but it can only be comprehended in the context of a compensation for taking something away. The Trickster steals a property and gives a victim in exchange. Pleasing god with confusing pleasures, from music and dance to offering sacrificial victims: all things that nourish the spirit, all that serves to build up sufficient strength are used by the blacksmith to compel and channel the energies of his receptacle according to his will. He is calling upon divine aid for creation, with the sure result of material growth and multiplication (Walker 1958), a state of automated perfection, saved from any decay.

Forced liminality: The alchemical opus

As gold was considered the paradisiacal metal, its successful production, or the creation of a like image, necessarily brought out its entire connotation with the promised land flowing with honey and milk, the land of youthfulness, the blossoming green garden full of virtuous men and virgins. As Hesiod said, the golden race 'lived like gods, with carefree heart/ remote from toil and misery' (1978: 109–13). To achieve this real or metaphoric golden state the alchemic operation consists of forcing the participating elements to undergo a repeated cycle of dissolutions and coagulations. The older form of this matter (the stone) is dissolved into the *prima materia*, or the original chaos, and this material then is coagulated into a new, purer form. At each cycle of dissolving and coagulating the substance becomes more and more purified. In this way, through a cycle of separation and conjunction, the opposites are reconciled, or their differences are united.[17] The adding of alchemy to the discoveries of metallurgy gave a theoretical underpinning to this technical enterprise. Through this the imperfect not only becomes perfect, but the inanimate elements gain the qualities of growth as well; a multiplication that occurs by marrying the male and female ores, wherein new metals are born. The characteristic pair of opposites, the negative and the positive counterparts, the desire to take pain to develop nature goes back as far as the Chinese Lao Tze, in the sixth century BC (Chikashige 1936), who founded Daoism.

Alchemists frequently refer to Plato's work, in spite of the fact that Plato authored no dialogue that dealt with alchemy. The other frequently cited author was Hermes Trismegistos, considered as very ancient in the Renaissance, although in the sixteenth century the Corpus Hermeticum was identified as an eclectic mix of Egyptian, Greek, Roman and Gnostic thought, dated to the first few centuries of our era. The various philosophical schools in the hermetic writings included neo-Platonism, Gnosticism and Stoicism, each influenced by the problem-setting of Plato's *Timaeus* (which is itself a beautiful conglomerate of pre-Socratic ideas) about the pattern of all living creatures having body and soul, the four element theory, about the circle of converting into each other under the influence of heat, about world soul or *anima mundi*, or the relationship between form and matter. Aristotle, especially in the *Meteorology*, with his idea on the natural subterranean formation of metals and minerals, was used by alchemists, who believed that their art imitated creation. So this treatise became an established text on the artificial production of metals and other related matters.

This is why the most widely accepted theoretical account about the multiplication of metals and minerals is deeply rooted in the Taoist–Vedic–Hellenic ideas for the interacting elements (like in the smelted vapours and exhalation), a notion that was taken up with the womb of earth as a furnace for creation, leading to the Alexandrian development of the sulphur–mercury–salt theory, according to which every living thing consists of these three elements. Every ore receives its particular character from a planet, linked to heat, cold, moisture or dryness: the Sun was linked to gold, the Moon to silver, Jupiter to tin, Venus to copper, Mars to iron, Saturn to lead, Mercury to quicksilver. But the common materials of all metals are sulphur (male, the planet Saturn: damp, cold, slimy) and mercury (female, the planet Mercury), whose union produces a child, the metallic stone. Apart from Albertus Magnus,[18] one can evoke Geber (721–800), Avicenna (980–1037), Roger Bacon (1219–92), Ficino (1433–99), Paracelsus (1492–1541) and Newton (1642–1727), just to mention the most well known, all of whom worked secretly on alchemy during their most productive years. They were speculating on and tested empirically Pre-Socratic notions, like 'if the existing is lost thus the non-existing is created' (Melissus, Fr. 7); 'for it is not possible for anything to exist for ever unless it all exists' (Melissus, Fr. 2, Kirk and Raven 1957: 299); 'They would not change if they were real'; 'the solid things come into being out of their own form', 'warm becomes cold and what is cold, warm; that what is hard turns soft and what is soft, hard'; 'A thing that is as cold or as warm as we are does not either warm us or cool us by its approach, nor can we recognise sweetness or bitterness by their like; rather we know cold by warm, fresh by salt and sweet by bitter in proportion to our deficiency in each' (Anaxagoras, according to Theophrastus, as in Kirk and Raven 1957: 394); and 'If they were real they would not change'; 'Immortal mortals, mortal immortals, living their death and dying their life' (Heraclitus, Fr. 62, as in Kirk and Raven 1957: 210); or, as Zeno of Elea stated, 'there will always be other things between the things that are, and yet others between those others' (Fr. 3, Kirk and Raven 1957: 288); up to the reflections of Leibniz, inventor of infinitesimal calculus (Yates 1976), about why it is that things exist, rather than not existing.

Just as there is no surprise in an initiation ceremony (Augé 1992), which always goes through the same levels, steps and stages, the alchemical *opus* of the chemical wedding (Yates 1972) also goes through the same mechanical steps. These are the following: separation, or sublimation, descent, distillation; liminality, or calcinations, solution, coagulation, fixation; and re-aggregation, or creation. The process of purifying or refining a precious metal has affinities with the creation of the philosopher's stone (*basanos*; see Foucault 2001), the effective gold or the divine love essence, which could transform mere mortals into divine beings. In Alexandria it was called *anastasis* (resurrection), turning human savages into full humans; just as Seth, the Egyptian sun-god brought water, light and life to the world, saving it from suffering.

The alchemists were ultimately concerned with the unification of different substances, which was often called the marriage between feminine and masculine qualities, or the reconciliation of opposites.[19] Through the 'marriage' of opposites the goal of the *opus*, the production of gold and its metaphysical equivalent, was finally obtained. However, such marriage does not always take the form of a direct union, but might occur through a third, mediating principle. This is mercury, the *prima materia* or *seminal* matter (black, *melas* in Greek, *melancholos* melancholy, the viscous fluid of the Earth), again composed of both female and male (androgynous, hermaphrodite). In alchemical union *Hermes/Mercurius* is a revelation (as *Hermaphrodite*). The elements correspond to the cosmic order; every element has its own planet; as planet, *Mercury* is the closest to the *Sun*, hence to gold; but as quicksilver, he dissolves gold and extinguishes its sun-like brilliance. But *Mercurius* is also the servant of the *opus* (*servus, cervus fugitivus*), the fugitive slave or stag. *Mercurius* is the lowest as *prima materia* (chaos), but also the highest as *lapis philosophicum*. He is *psychopompos* (*spiritus mercurius*) (Kerényi 1986), the guide for good luck, but also for ruin, being dual natured (see Goethe's *Faust*; Goethe studied Paracelsus (Gebelein 2002).[20] He is *aqua permanens, argentus vivum* = the water. He is the *serpent mercurialis*; *Mercurius* who unites two natures (male and female, Sol and Luna, with the help of the *caduceus*) in the alchemical vessel. From this alchemical vessel is produced the *filius hermaphroditus*, flanked by the six gods representing the planets.

Mercury is known as the glue that ties together the female and male. For the union, reconciliation or re-aggregation of such basic substances – male and female, fire and water – into divine love, alchemists and neo-Platonists used a particular word: 'conversion' (a new interpretation of qualities), when the forces within the properties that were previously divided are reconciled in a new state that can heal, through an epiphany, all the diseases of the world (Agricola). Hermes in the Egg is a favourite alchemical image, indicating the inability of souls to escape. Matter is heated and cooked in abnormal, timeless liminality, and the dying souls so released try to escape from their bodies. As there is nowhere to go, they turn back to their bodies, with a new image-form imprinted on them.

As Arnold van Gennep and Victor Turner already realised, it is the middle stage of the liminal process that is the most important. Creation always involves sacrifice and death, so in the middle stage of the *opus* the female and male consume each other; this is the extinction of the earlier state, before union. Dissolution and coagulation assume each other in liminality. Without this stage, the so-called Nigredo, *Putrefactio* or Regression, the goal of the opus over the graves (the endless course, impenetrability, no exit to be found, dullness) cannot be reached, the expanse cannot be crossed: the end of the journey, where every desire is to be realised, being independent from its former self. The forms are in dissolution, and the conscious mind runs parallel to the schism that the breaking caused in it.

The end result is limitless growth in the sense of unprecedented multiplication, just as in mathematics if you divide any number by zero you get infinity. Altering your interior composition by removing attributes from yourself, drinking and eating up your form, your own integrity, consuming yourself, you devour yourself, but now gain the outstanding abilities of any interval or in-between situation, which gives space to new forms.[21] Now nothing is definitely posited in you, your identity is flexible, becoming the womb of anything to be born, where everything passes, but in which nothing is retained. You become a matrix of images and emotions, the one who gives birth to new sensations.[22] The liminal submits the divine to torture, until its spirit ascends like a white dove, with the liminal circle enclosing it. The *opus* is capable of chaining down the divine for as long as the master of ceremony wishes. The gods remain prisoner to complete the *opus* and so the *tekmor* (aim) is reached. You enclose the divine inside your own body, which becomes your hidden metaphysical substance, now enriched with new divine power. You become a being of in-betweenness, neither being nor non-being, but an interval between them, yourself the liminal being (Couliano 1981).

This new being as the alienated, divine Sophist appeared in the works of Plato, 200 years later than the more or less contemporary Chinese and Hindu developments, as Lao Tze, the Chinese philosopher lived in the sixth century BC, just like Buddha, who developed further ideas from the Hindu Vedas.[23] All these 'axial age' philosophies focused on nothingness and alienated being.[24]

The estranged Sophist in Plato

> For now, you see, we have barely passed through
> the non-existence of being, which was [the Sophist's]
> first prepared line of defence, when we
> find another line ready; and so we must prove that
> falsehood exists in relation to opinion and to
> speech; and after this, perhaps, there will be
> another line, and still another after that; and it
> seems no end will ever appear.
>
> Plato, *Sophist*, 261A–B

Plato's discussion of 'place' (*khóra*), its dual nature as destroyer and as nurse of generation and growth, contained in the Timaeus (358–356 BC) has such a striking relevance for modernity. It is about the appearance of phantom images in a liminal space, which has an infinite desire for the possession of forms. The 'place' has neither quality, nor reality, nor even meaning; it is neutral, a peculiar kind of 'clotting factor', which is capriciously fixing, setting, blocking or releasing features or images from reality. It represents a challenge even for contemporary thinking, which transforms every living being into a construction. For sophistic dogmatism, things exist only in so far as we can see, touch, sense and possess them; a pervasive and categorical thinking that denies reality. It is 'bastard reasoning' that gives meaning to senselessness and proclaims reality to place, which is only an incidence of variability that 'provides room for all things that have birth' (Timaeus 52B). For Plato, 'place' (*khóra*) existed before the world was created; in fact, creation represents an intercourse or mingling between forms and their imperceptible coding in ideas (*noeton*). Place is the source of the new;[25] it is the randomness in images, the emergence of division and separation (*khorismos*), the discontinuity of the form, as place has neither mass nor extension in itself, but is the deceiver of both, playing a fluid game with images: 'for when we regard this we dimly dream and affirm that it is somehow necessary that all that exists should exist *in* some spot and occupy some *place*, and that that which is neither on earth nor anywhere in the Heaven is nothing' (ibid.). All the unusual variations, all the diversity from the forms and their DNA are in the chemical, psychological component of reproduction in this dual natured space, outside the real.

Place is a forbidden dual-natured incidence that takes part in life, but only to degenerate it, to divide it, to bring it into permanent division, 'where the same thing becomes simultaneously both one and two' (52C–D), copying infinitely the superficial images of the forms, but never the proper forms: imitating the image, but also producing renewal and rebirth. Place goes after the form, has an insatiable appetite for possession; it is associated with indestructibility: how could it be anything else as it does not own anything, not even its own matter. Place is the phantom of forms, which has no essence, it is just empty being associated with the invasion of the images, set to conquer the outer world of substantiality. The personalities who fill this *khóra* are discussed in a dialogue composed shortly before *Timaeus*, the *Sophist*.

Beyond the usual, amiable teasing typical of the start of Platonic dialogues, when the topic of Being/not-Being is posed in the *Sophist*, where Plato gives his account of the nothingness, he repeatedly calls attention to the difficulty involved in such an investigation. This is not the first time in the history of philosophy, and not the last, that the problem of the *void* is posed; it preoccupied Asian philosophy much before Plato. Plato's dialogue, the *Sophist* always puzzled scholars. It is too long for defining a concrete problem, as the usual Socratic dialogues proceed, but too short for a full treatise, like the *Republic*. It starts and restarts the argument, until it seems to reach a complete confusion about who the sophist is: is it a concrete or an abstract notion, is it hidden or visible, etc. What makes reading really difficult is its circular argumentation, which never really reaches its peak and does not say what it wants to say. Even further, Plato here goes beyond the horizon of the pre-Socratics, and is doing so quite consciously. He cites more than once Parmenides' stricture about the impossibility of this search after non-being, even stating that he might be mistaken for 'a sort of parricide' (241D). Plato gives the illusion that his dialogue critically tests the theory of his 'master' Parmenides that falsehood could not come into existence.[26] However, he does the opposite, affirming the perspective of his master, by demonstrating, through the nil that he called the Sophist, that nothing cannot be in existence, though it is able to pull and drown others into non-existence (into the divine sphere), by copying the divine.

God which is One and 'just some gods' refer to two different types: 'some god', and especially the god of strangers – and here certainly the *occasionist* (Burke 2005; Horvath 2009),[27] Hermes is in question – is a kind of god of refutation, a higher power that takes peculiar and dangerous interest in human affairs. The divine is also a power, though it can be possessed by humans (or rather it takes possession of them), and is shared by poets, actors and philosophers, all that kind: 'though I do not think [the Stranger] is a god at all, I certainly do think he is divine, for I give the epithet to all philosophers' (216C). This peculiar way of thinking characteristic of the ancient mind means that earthly reality and the divine sphere are separate; this is why Parmenides warns men: 'Never let this thought prevail, saith he, that non-being is;/ But keep your mind from this way of investigation' (237B). This means that non-being (some gods) can never become real; the non-local cannot become local. It can only imitate it – and here comes Plato's central idea – and thus the local itself could become estranged, being led into, pushed, caught or hunted into the position of the non-local, becoming *ek-static* (the Greek word means to stand outside of itself, to transcend oneself), if one transforms oneself into the vehicle or vessel of the divine, or even into nothingness, into the *nulla*. The *nulla* (the Sophist) never assimilates, but makes others to be assimilated to itself; it annihilates Being by a foolish mime.

The foolish self in the *Sophist*

Non-being has no presence, but it longs for units, linking it to the forms with sensations. Its desire for every kind of possession is well shown by its attraction to grotesque, absurd or obscene representations. Plato put the following statement in the mouth of the Stranger: 'the term "not-being" cannot be applied to any being' (237C). The question even ventures into the beginnings of the creation of matter, as – and here we must very carefully adapt our knowledge about of the *void* to what Plato is saying – this non-being has the quality of adding or attributing itself to other things. This is the moment when Plato arrives at the problem of *Place*, or the third component of Creation, which will be so emphatically developed in *Timaeus*. In fact, the *Timaeus* is generally considered as continuing the theme of the *Sophist*. Non-being does not evoke any feeling, except the feeling of a hiatus,[28] which violently drags down everything, laying its hands on any existing thing. As Plato formulated, non-being is what 'lacks something of being' (245C); whatever is deprived of being, deprived of having feeling, understanding, experiencing. Of course, Plato always remained a student of Parmenides, following the traditional philosophical idea that being is held together by enmity and friendship (von Heyking 2008). Therefore anything that lacks this passionate anger or love has no existence whatsoever, as it is not able to experience feelings and understand them properly; it only mimes them. But the mime is in itself a disturbance in the proper order of feelings, as it cannot help trying to be acquisitive, hunting down and selling feelings: 'they are all engaged in coercing, by deeds or words, things which already exist and have been produced, or in preventing others from coercing them; therefore all these divisions together might very properly be called acquisitive art' (219C). Non-being, or the 'fantastic class of the image making craft', as Plato called it at the end of the *Sophist* (268C), is an aggressive art that captures and encloses secretly, appearing disguised in all sort of Protean shapes, a topsy-turvy juggler of the human soul. The unreal is 'the part of appropriative, coercive, hunting art which hunts animals, land animals, tame animals, man, privately, for pay, is paid in cash, claims to give education, and is a hunt after rich and promising youths, must – so our present argument concludes – be called sophistry' (223B). But what do they offer, should be the next, reasonable question. They even present themselves unveiled as non-being, the being without bonds and restrains, the being of ecstasy. Plato examines Place from the point of view of non-being in the *Sophist*, and takes into account the three components of creation, bringing Place in the middle – in between being and becoming – as the likeness of the true (real) things (see 240B: the true one is the real one), the one who is dissolving boundaries, thus the liminal (the zero as a liminal number). 'Do you see, then, that it is impossible rightly to utter or to say or to think of not being without any attribute, but it is a thing inconceivable, inexpressible, unspeakable, irrational?' (238C). This is a state of trance, when something existing becomes deprived of its own existence, becomes dismembered, thus turns into non-being: 'when being is deprived of being, it will be not-being' (245C), which, however, is even a generative, reproductive state.

Beyond the conventional understanding of Plato's critique of the acquisitive Sophist, who is hunting down wealth and youth, there exists another level, the divine Sophist, the ecstatic being, who is estranged in its existence. Here Plato expressed the philosophical notion of nothingness in the figure of the Sophist, a liminal being that has no existence, which is an incommensurability, for whom no common measure exists. The Sophist is a mask without face (236E; 237C; 239C; 245C) with a desire to generate division into further and further schism, a technique that identifies the basic operational rule of every technological device, even in philosophy and knowledge.

3
Liminal Mimes, Masks and Schismogenic Technology: The Trickster Motives in the Renaissance

Technology is more than a simple device: its products look, and are perceived, as unnatural and false, as indeed they are artificial and forged. For anything that moves from non-being into being passes through technology, which fashions it into a new shape and form and identity. Technology composes new entities in space and time, thus defrauding reality by giving a new centre of gravity to life, pushing units out of self-support, and repositioning them into relativity – without doubt into a submissive and schismatic state of deprivation. This happens in the same way in politics, in the life of the state, very visible in the dual-faceted character of the modern state: on one side it tries to elevate its subjects out of their supposed crude humanity, leading them to brotherly, heavenly lights, into universal happiness, but combines this with an iron fist for subordination. Trickster motives are traditionally connected to Machiavelli's famous work, *The Prince* (1513), which gives advice to the political ruler about how to gain control over his subjects by changing their mode of thinking. Machiavelli's Prince is the hero of political games, accumulating political power, the Janus-faced politician who is guided exclusively by ice-cold calculations based on actually believed truths. This voice, however, appears much before Machiavelli, in a prominent text of Pope Innocent the Third (1161–1216), *De contemptu mundi*, which belongs to a series constituted by the works of Petrarch, Poggio Bracciolini (1455) or Giovanni Garzoni (1460), reflecting on a type of emptiness characteristic of their times, driven by distrust in a meaningless world.

From Petrarch to Machiavelli there was an increasing awareness about the gulf separating their own outlook from that of antiquity. It was based on the recognition that happiness cannot be acquired by repressing the desire for anything that one cannot obtain and keep: quite on the contrary, repression actually breeds excessive desires; just as salvation is not assured by the monastic individualism of self-sufficiency, and serenity does not emerge out of mere detachment and isolation. The humanists searched for the confidence and gaiety, serenity and fortitude that they found in the Ancients' attitude concerning the good and the true, looking for the mild power of the truly devoted that should be the energy and wealth reflecting the trust and goodwill emanating from God.

For the humanists God seemed withdrawn from an antagonised world, falling prey to the opposed yet closely connected idols of warfare and justice, represented by the sword and apple of medieval sovereignty, and sustained by the symbol of the Cross. The Christian bliss that was the hoped-for union with the divine turned out to be a grim world in which man was subjected without appeal, where politics became moralised, while the value of life undermined by serfdom. However, this tone of crude and violent sensualism, characteristic of Gothic Christianity, from the Duecento onwards started to alter into a softened, sweet enthusiasm. Still, among the great early humanists, there was not a single author who could orchestrate a change, a breakthrough.

The humanists showed little originality, rather a meek servility towards Christian dogmas, and their work and thought could hardly pioneer the profound change of mental substance that the Renaissance meant. Even before them, there was a peculiar hatred against life, based on a moralising accusation about any pleasure; inhibited thinking was characteristic of the religious writings of Lotario di Segni, future Pope Innocent III, from the end of the twelfth century.

The pope of human misery

Segni used the argumentation, style and mode of thinking, even the exact words and expressions, that would re-appear in the later humanists, from Dante to Boccaccio and beyond. This is especially visible in the set-up of a kind of dialectical trap between the self and the world: once these factors are placed in opposition as guiding principles of life, one is unable to relate one's senses to what is happening around, and a liminal incommensurability grows. Lotario di Segni wrote *La miseria della condizione umana (De contemptu mundi)* around 1190, before he became the 'Vicar of Christ' as Innocent III in 1198, the reformer pope who recognised in this miserable little man, Francis of Assisi, the source of the renovation of the Catholic Church, in spite of a strong opposition by the prelates.[1] Innocent set himself between god and man – below god, but above man – having been given not only the universal church, but the whole world to govern.

Accordingly, Segni's book *De contemptu mundi* is a compilation of Christian feelings, morals and ethos, driven by an astonishing self-satisfaction for being able to see, record and handle all these miseries. In three books he elaborates on this squalid reality, giving an overview, starting from the filthiness of human conception: 'Man is constructed from semen, in uncleanliness; to the lasciviousness of a similarly nasty image of death: Why not to die in the vagina' (Segni 2003). The book characterises the entire human existence in similar terms, as if humans never even lived, because their whole existence is just a displacement from the womb to the tomb. Segni assigns himself the task of examining from what the human race is made (the excrement of the earth); what is the occupation of humans (wicked, illicit, indecent actions); what are humans (food for worms); in sum, nothing but 'a mass of shit' (ibid.).

From this horrific dirt of being, as Segni describes him, this ignoble beast of nature, who is fed in the womb by the menstruation blood of the mother which dries the plants, which makes the green fields die, which makes the trees lose their leaves, from this corruption nothing comes out, only leprosy. Children are moaning, weak and ignorant, they are less than animals; women conceive in foul, deliver in sadness, nurture with fatigue, alleviate with anxiety and trembling. The only fruits that mankind produces are lice, worms, spittle, urine, excrement, vomit. The heart of the elderly becomes faint easily, their head is trembling, their breath is smelly, their form's vigour dissipates, their face is wrinkled, their back is curved, their eyes are obscured, their arteries are vacillating, they lose their hair, their hands are trembling, and they are greedy, mean, gloomy and always complaining.

All in all, concludes Segni in Chapter XIV of his book, everybody, the rich and the poor, the servants and the patrons, the married and the single, the good and the wicked, are all preoccupied by anxiety; all of them are subject to the torments of the world, and are also tormented by their afflictions: 'Death is better than indigence' (ibid.: 39). This is because our enemies are always ready to capture, to cause harm, to chase, to massacre. They are the demons, full of vice; humans, full of bestiality; the whole world, with its four elements; the flesh with its senses. Our opponent, the Evil One, is like a roaring lion, looking for its victims. Death can arrive through the window, the eyes mislead the soul, and the whole world is always in war. Pestilence, earthquakes, the fall of kingdoms, all earthly terrors are coming close. 'Better thus dying for life', he writes 'than living for death, [as] nobody can escape' (ibid.: 47).

This is the basic message of each of the three parts of this late twelfth century book. It helps us better understand the burial customs of the long period from the fifth to the eleventh centuries, with common graves that were filled up by cadavers, or the wealthy buried in the dirt under the flagstone of the church, as the dead person was given to the church without any special ceremony so that it could take care of the body until the day of the Resurrection (see Assmann 2002; Ariès 1985). In such a co-existence of the living and the dead, these are characters and attributes that can easily transmute into each other, and thus life becomes nonsensical and disgusting.

Innocent's text presents an interesting mental combination: the despising of man on the one hand, considering humans ripe for destruction, but on the other keeping for himself the role of the solace. It is a generalised moral accusation of man being corruptive, both through the instincts and through reasoning, as the latter brings about the debilitation of will, the desire for comfort, the loss of vitality, the longing for submission. There is no longer any question of victory, strength and glory, kingdom or authority: a new element appears, the assumption of sheer passivity, and consequently the search for pleasure as the centre of life, in contrast to the pain that is to be avoided. Past and present are split into two, and one is not able to control the latter anymore. His book assumes – and certainly rightly, as it will also transpire from the account that follows – that this self-humiliation was insinuated, generated and then spread solely by itself, gobbling up life; but paradoxically this subjugation is also attributed to the necessities of the times.

Following Nietzsche, we could say that whoever is searching for pain in life tries to escape life. We can assume that this motif *wants* to hear about torment, *wants* to see anger, *wants* to experience the neglect of the self, thus accumulating all the gloomy aspects of life; but on the other side, and as a sheer consequence of this polarisation, it also longs for whatever remained intact after the calamities, looking for pleasure, gold, richness and pomp. The same intoxication from the ugliness of being that proliferates worries and discontent also has a schismatic twin that nurtures the longing for luxuries, which is to say gold-like shining power. This is well developed in the double bind theory of Gregory Bateson, which captures the situation in which small initial differences step by step turn into escalating disorder and conflict. In Batesonian language the question concerns the nature of *difference*, the new piece of information that caused the lethal consequences as it appeared in Innocent's text. This shifting information must have been strong enough to gain access to the centre, then to find a way to exert an impact, and then again influential enough to be able to radiate corruption from the centre, and finally – it is now only a small step – to make rivalry assuming malevolence into the guiding principle of life. Although all these are necessary elements for schismogenesis, a central aspect is still missing, exactly the naming of the element that was missing then, thus rendering schismogenesis possible: an improper response, the failed identification of the spreading evil or demonic force, and the missed opportunity to gather strength to resist it, the lack of a decisive answer to the provocative impulses of evil. It is the lack of such a response that provides unprecedented opportunities for the mimetic and repetitive spreading of the error, and thus the rise of the schism.

The alienated trickster misinforms one's own self, deliberately choosing from every kind of information the piece that corresponds with its already estranged being. This type of self-referentiality dismisses the totality of information, preferring those that comfortably fit one's own despair.

The Renaissance twist: Momus, or the travesty of truth

The recognition of the presence of an idiosyncrasy, the intemperate, miserable misfit, lying beyond and opposed to the cult of *eudaimonism*, is a great and still mostly unrecognised discovery of the Renaissance. Leon Battista Alberti wrote his *Momus*[2] around the same time as Cusanus (1401–61) wrote his book *The Idiot or Learned Ignorance*. The *Idiot* of Cusanus follows the teachings of Plato, that the images reproducing reality are constructed by our own mind and therefore do not represent a grasp of reality, but only produce a series of associations that catch pieces of the truth, but never the whole or real one. *Momus*, a book about the trickster demigod, shows unique qualities of extreme far sight (Wind 1958). Momus is a peculiar, erratic, trickster creature who manifests hostility towards the world. Thus he deliberately creates a world religion out of the bitterness of his own heart. He is an empty, vain being, neither good nor bad, living in idleness and consuming by his activities and very being all the ordered relationships around him; so he is permanently endangering the very foundations of reality.

Alberti's *Momus*, which he started to write probably just after he left Florence for Rome in 1443 and finished before 1450, is something new in the general tone of the humanists. It is not only that *Momus* is biting, as Boccaccio is often like that; or that he is sarcastic, as so is Dante; but Alberti, with a unique eye beyond the ideological debates of his times, perceives liminality even before the height of Renaissance, giving a detailed description of the process of its slipping into the social.

There are three fundamental aspects of Alberti's moral enterprise, three diagnoses of deception: first, the weakening of piety; second, the loss of the idea that man is *imago dei*; and finally, the direct outcome from the previous two, a search for guilt and the subsequent self-victimisation.

Alberti's anti-hero, the Trickster god Momus, violates all laws, successfully corrupting the human world, while also confusing the divine Olympus by letting loose all aberrations, claiming that he is absolutely free to perpetuate any tricky act he feels like doing, as previously he suffered enough to deserve exemption from all conventions and absolution from all crimes. Among human beings and among the gods the trickster, this down-to-earth god, is working without mercy or generosity, but committing crimes and promoting victimisation, as if he explicitly pursue the goal of annihilating stable structures and moral strength, refusing any compromise. In the analogy of Nietzsche's over-man, a being presumably standing a step above mankind, the trickster is the under-god, the reverse and underside of the divinity, who leads to the road towards liberation as carelessness, to a state of exile from all sorts of order, to the transformation of the world into a spiritual desert through the imitative repetition of his own degraded position.[3] Alberti's account of this road towards degradation can be formulated in four theses:

1. There is no piety, value or moral structure that is saved from deceit. Both men and the gods are defenceless against the corrosive influence of the trickster, once a proper key or 'access code' for perpetuating deceit is found.

2. This code usually functions on the basis of a principle that can be called 'homeopathic': only the similar can coexist successfully with the similar. As if turning upside down this principle of 'like cures the like', Momus uses the principle of 'like ruins the like'. Hence, to corrupt the pious, what is called for is disingenuous piety and idealism; something that looks like pious, but is a travesty of piety through excess. The logic of corruption is based on the principle that the frequent, routine repetition of lies and insinuation – as totalitarian regimes and closed institutions abundantly confirmed in past decades – will eventually be taken for granted and accepted, just as it happens with normal everyday truths.

3. The human ability to discriminate between truth and lie is very limited. Ordinary human beings are in a fragile situation when they are confronted with such a choice, because true statements and lies are composed of quite similar elements; only their combination is different. Lies, especially really effective and dangerous lies, are not unrelated to the truth. They only take up some of its elements, a series of half-truths, and bring them together in a coherent system that looks convincing, but which leads to consequences that are exactly opposed to those of the truth: they do not solve problems through lifting up and ennobling; rather, they increase the confusion by throwing dirt and pulling down to the mud. When faced with a skilful hypocrite like Momus, even the gods are beguiled. Men who convert to Momus cease to think of themselves as *imago Dei*, as being capable of benevolence, elevation and nobleness of spirit. This implies two consequences. On the one hand, they

will increasingly become victims of the continuous tortures of Momus, which is rendered possible by their accepting the position of victim, and thus feel justified to commit acts of malevolence that degrade; on the other hand, at the same time and with the same movement, they become enchanted and fascinated both with codes and laws, feeling the need to limit somehow their own excess (assumed, owing to their own self-degradation, as the necessary part of the human condition), but also with the obligation of breaking the very same codes. The trickster spins the movement by inciting to excess; this excess calls for the need of strict and detailed laws and regulations; but this suffocating and increasingly ritualistic legalism, covering more and more areas of existence, stimulates on its own, by a kind of natural perversion, its own transgression. This process can be easily explained by the schematic 'slave-as-trickster' and the 'trickster-as-slave' motifs, which reinforce each other. The more men violate the codes the more Momus punishes them, thus reinforcing the slavery; and the more Momus terrorises his slaves the more eagerly they try to escape from his constraints, which at the end does not bring anything else than ever-new violations of the taboos and ever-harsher punishments on the part of Momus.

4. Finally, concerning the interpretation of Momus as a trickster, Alberti added to our understanding of this figure an aspect that is still novel, after decades of abundant anthropological research: the idea that the trickster is somebody who is simply unable to give gifts. The book starts with the assembly of gods, where everyone salutes Jupiter for the creation of the world, giving him abundant gifts of gratitude: except for Momus, who refuses to do so, and is thus thrown out of the heavens, becoming an outcast. Thus he falls down to the created world, into the humans, and starts to create trouble, corrupting the inhabitants.

At this moment we should rather step back from the argument to perform some stock-taking; as, strictly following the logic of Alberti, we have imperceptibly moved from such (allegedly) trivial issues as gifts to the heart of politics, the question of power.

The return to the idea that gift-giving potency is power was a crucial development in the Renaissance, in the literal sense of resurrecting an ancient Greek tradition (MacLachlan 1993). The gift given was initiated by the donor, and therefore had to be returned or reciprocated.[4] Reciprocity establishes a smooth circulation of the movement starting with the first gift. The role of gifts is to give pleasure to their beneficiary.[5] Those things that gave happiness, hence are designed 'naturally', in a matter of fact way as good, formed an integral part both of the Roman legal tradition and the Christian theological ideas, and particularly so in Medieval Europe. For Thomas Aquinas, it is a virtue to give the right amount to the right person, and for classical Roman law the defining feature of giving was the *animus donandi*, meaning a benevolent predisposition of giving. This implied the intention of giving gratuitously; that is, without contracting for return, according to the principle *gratia gratis data, gratia gratum faciens*. Honouring and adoring is a release of power, a liberation of excess energies, which always leads to action.[6] The purpose of gift-giving as a social action is not to conclude the entire relationship with the equivalent return of the original gift, reducing social life to a series of strictly regulated symmetrical acts, boring automatism where one slips into passivity, a sort of sickness or impotency. This frustrated state brings with itself that unrelieved violence, inexpressible anger and the all-too-well-known hatred that characterise the Trickster god. The trickster could not act from grace, could not perform generous acts of gift-giving; rather, owing to his suspicious, doubtful, untrusting character, his uncertainty and impotency required an immediate equivalent return, he evoked the power of fallacies. This is exactly the way in which the trickster established his realm in Alberti's book.

Momus should have given a gift to the gods, but he refused, which – in light of Marcel Mauss's classic book on gift,[7] according to which giving and accepting gifts is foundational for social life – is quite a significant act. As a punishment he was expelled from Heaven and thus proceeded to Earth. Momus is incapable of giving gifts, he is sterile impotency personified.[8] His literal disgracefulness (as he is not returning gratitude for Jupiter's benefits) is one of the main reasons why the gods are expelling him from Olympus, so he falls through a hole on the land of the Etruscans, the most pious nation on Earth, rich in receiving divine blessings and graceful in gift-giving (I.26). This is how Alberti's first book on Momus starts.

'Hey, catch the criminal', shout the gods after Momus, 'the naturally perverse' (I.2), the bloody-minded, hostile and annoying exile, who is provoking friends, is irritating both in word and deed, and is 'being hated by anyone' (I.2), as he 'filled the world with all those nasty little creatures, similar to himself' (I.5). They thus denounce Momus as a public enemy guilty of the highest treason: boasting of 'giving nothing to no one' (I.3). Once arriving on Earth, he encountered the Etruscans, 'a race wholly devoted to religion' (I.26). Momus, a political allegory of dirt has met with cleanness, a set of ordered relations, a world based on dignity and honour. Dirt is matter out of place; likewise the trickster is a figure of marginality, a contrary and thus the counterpart of order, which includes everything rejected by a well-ordered life, like hatred, revenge, criminality, lie, guile, cunning or deceit. Thus the Trickster, an embodiment of the spirit of negation, is hostile to every existing society. He is standing on the borderline and draws everybody who is getting in touch with him into his liminal unease, alienness or un-accommodation. The 'danger' aspect of the polluter, which figures in the title of Douglas's classic book, alludes to the finality of the Trickster's deeds, as they lead to the threshold, to the danger of liminality, to the peril of nothingness or death (Douglas 1966).

Corruption is polluting the clean, contaminating or destroying integrity, which was exactly the task set up by Momus upon his arrival: to lead the Etruscans away from worshipping the gods and imitate him instead. To realise his aim, Momus first posed as a poet singing the shameful deeds of the gods, then as a philosopher who denied the influence of divine providence on human affairs (I.26). Finally, when his demagoguery had already successfully paved his way towards the heart of the people, 'arguing that the power of gods was nothing other than vain, useless and trifling fabrications of superstitious minds' (I.27), he even found the way of putting himself into the centre of worshipping. He did so by claiming that instincts and not spiritual factors were the real moving forces of all living beings, and that nature was the only deity that is common to all. Thus, the only rational system, which at the same time is the road of liberation from the perverse order of the gods (I.27), is what Momus was setting up for them. Instincts keep us together, and only in instinctual essences is it possible to discover the secret of life, because 'whatever nature fashioned had a proper and preordered function' (ibid.). Thus, the knowledge of instincts gives access to the origin of all things and to the destiny of the world. According to Momus every other belief is just a cheat, every other order is a sham, a trap, a perpetuation of an age-old deception; every other faith is a pitfall to nothingness. Under the mask of the philosopher, Momus is teaching human beings that the gods favour the wicked and oppress the just, whereas nature is fair, as it is shaped in a proper and preordained fashion, which is common to every living being. Instincts are the sole sources of truth and promote equality, because they are the most democratic of all existing things. Common instincts are driving us together to live, to move, to perceive, to care for, to protect ourselves, says Momus, and the acquiescent Etruscans began to abandon their gods (I.28). 'Truth became mixed with falsehood, and the number and infamy of these crimes grew daily in the telling, so that the person of every god and goddess was considered unclean and lost in debauchery' (I.26).

In the meantime Momus changed his outlook. Although he started with a long-bearded, sidelong look and shaggy eyebrows as a sensitive, poetic soul, he finished as a keen and hard warrior of the truth. As a result of his success he regained his old spirit and intentions, and became ready again for doing more harm (I.55). However, as usual, he prepared for his acts very cautiously, 'so that while he was embracing everything in wickedness, he would appear to be acting piously and righteously' (ibid.).

These skilful changes of masks, from the homeless fanatic who presented himself as a public menace, whom everyone had a good reason to despise, to the distinguished friend who trained himself to applaud and flatter everyone around himself, empowered him to receive favours and rewards from the very persons he had injured (II.11). Momus maintained his position among the learned, while ordinary people regarded him as honest, though he only waited for the opportunity to avenge himself and to punish his enemies. In the meantime he concealed his anger in his mind and considered everyone's word as equally untruthful, as he trusted no one, but pretended to have confidence in everyone (II.103). Down to the last details he imitated the life of the good and meek, as though following a written scenario, and hid carefully his own plans, covering them with all signs of trustworthiness and innocence: 'Oh, what an excellent thing it is to know how to cover and cloak one's true feelings with a painted facade of artificiality and studied pretence!' (II.14).

Momus became increasingly popular because he preached easiness and liberation. The people happily gave up the fear of the gods, claiming that they themselves were totally at liberty to perpetuate any act they felt like. Hence higher gods did not exist at all, or if they did, they were surely benevolent by their very nature and would quickly pardon the wanderers (I.31). However, this liberation had two unpleasant consequences. First, the Etruscans lost their trust in themselves, because they stopped thinking of themselves as divine, and started to lament the state of their affairs, begging one another for help as people do when all seems lost (ibid.). They behaved as helpless victims of their fate. Second, they also started to abandon themselves to all kinds of aberrations and excesses, and Momus consequently was quick to express his deep disgust towards them. Their dependence and helplessness increased, just as the intensity of their search for pleasures (II.47). On one occasion Momus himself gave a faithful account of their behaviour, overlooking of course the fact that it was he who incited their aberrations.

This occasion came with his reinstallation by Jupiter in the second book, where Momus gradually regains a leading position among the gods. Jupiter is holding a dinner, and Momus starts complaining about the humans, how they suddenly were overcome with animal lust, caring only for their own pleasures and utility, satisfying their desires by violence and wickedness. Momus laments the impurity of mankind, the fact that men are living without religion and devastated by conflicts and cruelty (II.40). This general state of mankind makes Momus sad and worrying, because owing to the carnage and 'infernal events' (II.41) the earth is full of the smoke and ashes of the ruined temples. Momus severely disapproves the crimes of the people and their flight from their native land, the unbound, uncertain vitality and that elusive, confused and confusing mode of existence that was previously his unique trademark.

At the same time he continues to play the double cards of the vagabond and the meek (II.47). On the one hand, he boasts the freedom of carelessness, turning his own outcast status into a bonus, a justification of his egocentrism: 'You might do many things for other people, but the beggar does nothing either for

you or for others. Whatever he does, he does for himself' (II.51).
On the other, he could pretend himself to be the worthy fellow
(II.65). In doing so he even manages to influence the gods themselves (II.66). He extols the life of the beggars, just as the ancient
cynics did, claiming that it is the only perfect way of life, as it
does not require care or the performance of duty. The only skills it
deploys are carelessness itself, negligence and the attitude of 'who
cares'. Beggars have that pleasure and freedom, which is incom-
patible with the duties of a genuine statesman. However, after all,
Momus, who could not care whatever turn things took, hoping
for nothing and fearing nothing (II.56), became paradoxically a
politician, somebody who cared for everybody:

> Thus the man who until that day had purposely laid himself
> out to be the prankster of all the orders, now took it as an
> insult that he had been invited for his humour rather than
> as an honor. In addition, he now laid aside his previous mask
> and put on a novel one. When he realized that the mob of
> gods valued him because of the prince's favour, carried away
> (as usual) by success, his greed and sense of entitlement made
> him start to seek greater things for himself. He abandoned his
> humorous approach to social intercourse, and through mature
> behavior and seriousness he worked gradually to make himself
> seem worthy of Jupiter's favour and deserving authority among
> the gods.
>
> (II.71)

He managed to secure for himself the favours of Jupiter, gaining authority among the gods, feigning seriousness and mature
behaviour. He never spoke without a meek and quivering voice,
showing a sad face, and with his sly and demagogic tricks he managed to insinuate a fatal disturbance in the affairs between gods
and men. At the instigation of Momus, Jupiter finally started to
give serious thought to the idea of annihilating mankind.

The end of the second book is rich in details about such
destruction. But perhaps the most interesting idea is Momus's
suggestion of doubling the number of 'silly little women' among
mankind, as it would certainly irrevocably damage human affairs.
Women are the most effective 'executioners of souls', a 'bonfire of
cares' (II.112). Their 'essence' works like 'plague'; they are 'plain

destruction'; and the gods do not need any more help besides women to ruin man, once this 'disaster of all peace and relaxation', the gender of females, is at hand (ibid.). Momus, however, failed to convince the gods to destroy humans, as the gods could not agree on the mode of their destruction. This ironic paradox resumes the essence of the Trickster god: its impotency demonstrates itself even in its success. The greatest and most reassuring paradox of the trickster is that the very moment of his victory becomes his demise, as the instance he acquires power he demonstrates that he is unable to do anything positive with it. He is only capable of repeating his own essence. He is the par excellence parasite, who lives only by drawing out the life energies of his host, but is doomed the very moment he kills his victim. Although at the end of the third book Momus is disgraced again, punished for another series of crimes committed against his fellow deities, now condemned to be tied to a rock under the sea, the fourth closes with Jupiter's appreciation of the notebooks of the Trickster on the maxims of good government, where simple common wisdom is written in the form of paradoxes, and where Fortune is assigned as the last arbiter of human affairs (IV.101).

Since it was written and first read, Alberti's ideas contained in *Momus* have baffled audiences and scholars. The work gave rise to the most diverse interpretations (Borsi 1999; Grayson 1998; Grafton 2003). Is this piece a pure entertainment, as Alberti instructed his readers, or an agony of nihilism? Is it a disillusioned satire of his age, with biographical reminiscences, or a positive criticism of the policy of the 'architect' pope, Nicholas V? Although its autobiographical allusions are evident, it is also clear that it is simply not possible to consider Momus as Alberti's alter ego. As similar masterpieces that advanced their age by centuries, like Shakespeare's *Troilus and Cressida*,[9] it can be said to have become intelligible only through the optic of the re-emergence of political trickster figures in modernity.

Late Renaissance masks

The power and visibility of the masked mime during the entire medieval period was very limited. At the centres of power, it was either pacified as a court jester or diabolised as the devil. As far as popular festivities were concerned, mimetic acting played a very circumscribed role in the medieval world, seen with rather apprehensive eyes both by the secular and especially the religious authorities. Although popular festivities survived and kept their importance in the forms of carnivals and other seasonal rituals, they were met on their own terrain by similarly popular religious festivities, and certainly did not interfere with normal everyday existence or the dominant spheres of cultural life.

A radical change happened towards the end of Renaissance and the rise of the Reformation, especially at their point of intersection, whether in Italy or in England. On the one hand such forms of entertainment gained immense popularity, on the other hand they became persecuted with renewed and even vicious energy, a movement comparable to the prohibition of images. The case of Shakespeare is particularly interesting in this regard, as new research has shown both that his work was strongly motivated by his dual, both Catholic and Protestant, allegiances, and that the *Commedia dell'Arte* most probably played a decisive role in the genesis of his art (see Greenblatt 2001, 2004). This helps us to explain the striking insights he gained about the exact mechanism and significance of mimetism (see Girard 1991).

The *Commedia dell'Arte* grew out of the lowest, most vulgar kind of popular entertainment, having deep historical roots in antiquity. In Greece examples include the Dorian mime or the Atellane theatre (Nicoll 1963a); but it had much deeper historical roots in Middle Eastern civilisation, in the form of the Egyptian deity Bes or the Mesopotamian demon Humbaba. It survived in the underworlds of society as a hardly tolerated artistic practice, and only became a major force in Europe after the Turkish occupation of Constantinople in 1453, when Byzantine mimes arrived through Venice in Italy, sparking the rise of *Commedia dell'Arte*.

Mimes performed their acts without a pre-established text, basing the performance on their powers of improvisation. Out of the many characters thus generated, the most important turned out to be Pulcinella. Originating in Acerra near Naples around the turn of the fifteenth and sixteenth centuries, in a zone where already during the Roman period the Atellane theatre had its centre, it soon spread northwards, becoming the single most important figure in the carnivals in Rome, then – as if by contagion – further to Northern Italy, and eventually – in spite of the strongly Mediterranean character of the figure – generating a double in practically every European culture, known in France as Polichinelle, in England as Punch, as Kasper (or a similar name) in Germanic Central Europe, as László Vitéz in Hungary, as Karagöz in Turkey and as Petrushka in Russia, among others (Paërl 2002: 17).

In spite of this variety, the basic behavioural characteristics and closely related bodily features of the figure have become stand-ardised over the centuries. Pulcinella wears a long and broad wide shirt, brought together by a belt and three big white buttons. If we compare these attributes with the libidinous medieval 'Wild Man' figure, with his mask, animal fur (sometimes feathers) and bewitching faculties, the similarity is visible. Both are living off scene, outside civilisation, with a loss or absence of faculties that make us humans, while also being the harbingers of fertility, with Pulcinella's buttons alluding to semen, and his broad shirt that stands for shaggy rugs or animal skin (Bernheimer 1952). The belt, furthermore, alludes to snakes, or the chthonic power beyond, whereas his pointed cap is called the Phrygian beret, best identi-fied with the demons of death, even associated with the most mysterious and powerful figures of the Greek myths and rituals, the Kabirs or the all-powerful dwarf gods, masters of the famous initiation rites at Samothrace (Kerényi 1980; Paërl 2002: 25, 87). These two features immediately identify one of the most impor-tant contrasts at the heart of this figure embodying ambiguity and ambivalence: on the one hand, Pulcinella is the simpleton, possessing no qualities whatsoever, but on the other is associated with the magnetising powers of death and fertility, easily laying outside not simply the common, but outright the human.

Such ambivalent characteristics are illustrated by a series of fur-ther striking bodily features. Pulcinella has an enormous potbelly, representing his insatiable appetite for *pasta* and wine; a series of deformities, including disgusting facial warts and a strange chicken breast, illustrating his frightful character; and especially a huge hump. In Baroque images this sometimes appears as sign of pregnancy, from where the little Pulcinellas are born, and so again marks an outright non-human status, while at the same time ren-dering evident the vulgar character of the popular entertainment of which he is a part. Finally, he has a long and crooked nose that (just as another aspect, the Phrygian beret) can easily be identified as a phallic symbol.[10] Pulcinella is thus the stage character repre-senting, in a particularly exaggerated, even distorted, manner, the most basic bodily functions: eating, drinking and sexuality, and the most superhuman ability, fertility.

Moving from description to narration, we get a better understanding of the character and its exploits. Pulcinella is not only eating and drinking on stage as if he had never done it before, but even defecating and urinating with great nonchalance, even fondness. Furthermore, Pulcinella's performance not simply generates a contrast between 'nature' and 'culture', but clearly aims to undermine the value of both. He even intimately connects these activities to the fifth 'natural functioning' of the body, sexuality, even extending it to childbearing. Even further, as if to crown all these activities by taking them to their utmost limits, Pulcinella also embodies sexual ambivalence, even in his name. Ending with the letter 'a', the name 'Pulcinella' is feminine, even if his bodily attributes are strongly phallic; whereas his offspring are called 'Pulcinelli', which is again in the masculine and thus grammatically incorrect.

As a conclusive description, let me quote here Thelma Niklaus's short but pungent characterisation of Pulcinella from her excellent book on another *Commedia dell'Arte* character, Harlequin, filtered in particular through the English version of Pulcinella, Punch: 'He was the supreme egotist, determined to secure for himself riches, fame, women, and fat living, at whatever cost to others. Beneath an apparent good humour lurked a cynical depravity and the smouldering volcano of his brutal personality. His megalomania was wonderfully exposed in his song: "When I march along the whole earth trembles. I am master of the sun." He delighted in sowing seeds of dissension among his fellows, fomenting discord, provoking violence' (Niklaus 1956: 39).

Ambiguity to normality or the zero

The manner in which Pulcinella represents the close, allegedly even intimate, relations between the basic bodily functions is captured in a scene between Pulcinella, Cicerella (local dialect for chicken) and the cock Chirichichiò, up to recent times often performed in Naples puppet shows (Paërl 2002: 74–5, 87–8). In it Cicerella flirts with Pulcinella, who lets himself be seduced, and mounts her from behind. After a few seconds of movement, however, he gets off, lifts the chicken by her tail and smashes her head on the theatre wall. Then he disappears, only to return a few seconds later with a roasted chicken whose back parts are turned towards the public, and takes a small repose. Sure this is an aberrant narrative, that is ob(off)-scene, and definitely disrupts the feeling of the concrete, human endeavours. There is something subhuman present: we are dislocated out of our everyday experience. But exactly this shift is what makes us laugh.

At this moment the cock Chirichichiò, Cicerella's lover, appears, and – noticing her beloved one prepared for lunch – weeps heavily and calls for revenge, evoking Farfariello, a demonic spirit in Dante and the devil in Naples dialect, who performs a spell. At this moment Pulcinella wakes up and devours the whole chicken – in fact, his beloved one – in a hardly disguised act of cannibalism. But he cannot go back to sweet sleep, with his enormously inflated belly, as he starts to develop cramps. He is crying for a doctor, but instead a midwife appears who delivers from under his shirt an enormous egg. The whole scene is quite funny with its endless re-reformulation of reality, though also absurd and grotesque in a highly disconcerting manner, and the egg motive requires some further lines, as the egg is a characteristic zero form.

Zero is a subnormal number, owing to its characteristic role of altering numerical and operational value, a kind of logical scandal: 'Of the counting figures there is one which is called the nothing (*nulla*) which is the figure for nothing because in itself it counts for nothing. But joined with other figures and figured with figures it makes their value grow'.[11] The representation of the zero always posed a certain problem for writers on mathematics since it appeared in Europe in the eleventh century, not only because of a multiplication in language, as zipher and nulla mean the same thing: nothing; but as the symbolic representation of this 'nothing' was also modified, from the Hindu/Arabic dot and sometimes represented as a hyphen-dot-hyphen sign sequence (-.-), sometimes as a dot in a circle, into a whole empty circle, as we use it today: 0. It is not very clear how this change has taken place; we know that Petrarch still used the Hindu/Arabic form, the dot in the circle; it is quite possible, though, that the change can be connected to the work of Leonardo da Vinci, who connected reflections on the zero to the special characteristics of the 'dot'.[12] At any rate, it was only through the work of Italian mathematicians of the sixteenth century, like Recorde and the Tagliente brothers, and the French philosopher Charles Bovelles, that this usage started to become widespread.[13]

Returning to Pulcinella's egg-child, this scene demonstrates a world completely turned upside down, nevertheless possessing a strange coherence. Pulcinella reveals here his full constitutive ambivalence, his hermaphrodite nature. The cock is the animal most closely associated with Pulcinella, with the donkey, another animal considered both stupid and libidinous. Even Pulcinella's highly pitched, shrieking voice evokes association with sounds emitted by poultry, and has an asexual aspect. Furthermore, the significance and ambivalence of the name again enters the game, as 'Pulcinella' is derived from *pulcino*, Italian for newly hatched chick. The donkey, on the other hand, is his closest friend. Both animals, even in their names, betray further, evident and obscene sexual allusions. The cock in many languages is euphemism for the male genital organ, whereas the donkey, or the ass, evokes the behind. Both these links go back to antiquity. One of the classic mimes in the Athenian scene was the 'cock type', and there are surviving representations of mimes with an ass head (Nicoll 1963a: 74–5). As elements in a chain of transmission from antiquity to the early modern world, we might evoke the cockscomb of the court jesters, or – with a revealing name – Bottom in Shakespeare's *A Midsummer Night's Dream*, who has been turned into an ass; a transformation effectuated by Robin Goodfellow, a folktale trickster character, and emphatically commented in the text.

However, something fundamental is still missing from our description; in fact, exactly what is missing from Pulcinella as well: he has no face; he wears a mask, and of a particular kind, which indicates his indiscriminate standing for anything and everything. Every living being has concreteness, shape, form, locality and given qualities, and so is called by a name. This is not case with figures without name; and 'Pulcinella' is not really a name, as we have indicated. Rather, it is a representation of things without qualities: 'Zero seems to be definable by some general characteristic, without any reference to any special peculiarity of the kind of quantity to which it belongs' (Russell 1903: 184); or, using an earlier quote, 'with the sign 0, which the Arabs call a zephyr, any number whatsoever is written' (Fibonacci, in Sigler 2003: 17). Pulcinella in itself means nothing, the denomination itself is standing as well for the trickster, for the ass, the serpent, the coyote, the fox, the stork, the pig, the rabbit, the monkey/ape, the spider or other masked or not masked non-places (Augé 2008),[14] with entangled properties, while at the same time they cross-refer to other creatures, reordering and rearranging the unique properties of others with mimesis.

The mask worn by Pulcinella, or the mask that *is* Pulcinella,[15] is black, with evident allusion to this nothingness, to the dark night, which effaces all distinctions. This makes it stand apart from the basic principles of drama theatre, which is transformation, interaction, changing to be better, *catharsis*. Here theatre remains connected to its origins as a cult drama, as a transformative and participatory rite to alter ourselves, in the form of a tribute to the gods, asking for participation in their qualities. But in the mime play, actors perform endlessly and simultaneously the same stock characters (see Rusten and Cunningham 2003), like the flattering parasite, the greedy, mistrustful old man, the shameless pimp, or the braggart soldier, without any ethical purpose, as their actions are not discussed, neither are the motives rendered clear behind the characters.[16] The mime negates our concrete experience of the world, where the actions of others are connected to our own behaviour. Thus we can directly exert an impact on the world even with our presence, by simply participating, being here. But the act of the mime refutes our beliefs; the masked Pulcinella violates our reality, contra-poses human virtue with its own insubstantiality and indistinctness. It suggests that our world is empty, as its value depends on the position of the *nulla*, and we are reduced into believing that what he says is true.

Apart from the nose, the facial mask contains other characteristic peculiarities, which over time became rigorously defined. These include three big warts, one on the front, another at the root of the nose and the third on the left cheek; and three deep wrinkles on the front and close to the eyes (Paërl 2002: 24). More than anything else, however, the mask is marked by an absence that, after the missing face, covered by the mask, can be defined as a 'second order hiatus': the mask is only partial; it does not cover the mouth. This is no small difference, as the perhaps most important and certainly shared characteristic of the ancient mime's mask is the grimace into which his mouth is contorted. It was this threatening smile of a frozen hilarity, a distant memory of an unbridled laughter, that suddenly turned into a mortal shriek, which is missing from Pulcinella's mask. The absence, however, is not complete, as remains of the grin are clearly visible in the pulled-up cheek of the mask. This absence became a great asset for Pulcinella, as it increased the versatility of figure, leaving room for improvisation, for frequent but always sudden changes of the facial expression from laughter into sadness, from melancholy into hilarity and back again. This is widely considered his most important aspect, underlining his character as a counterfeit, meaning that he can mime and forge anything, as he is purely fictional void.

Masking nothing

The emergence of the standard form of the figure was the result of a long development. In this, apart from actors, an important role was played by visual artists, especially painters and engravers. This link between mime-actors and image-painters is of crucial theoretical importance, as it puts the emphasis on the close, etymological connection between imitation and image, and thus on the central, magical role played by images in sparkling processes of mass-scale imitation, particularly effective through the mechanical reproduction of images due to the discovery of engraving, a practice as old and just as influential as the printing press, but much less known and studied. An image in itself has no meaning; it must be joined to others to become meaningful, so it epitomises contingence.[17] An image is just a fiction until it is seen and experienced by others, until it encounters a willing public who would perceive and understand it. It is this reception that makes it real, and in this way immediately modifies existence.

The image creates a mood in which the real and the fictive coexist and therefore become interchangeable. This is possible because of the similarities between a fantasy image and the manner in which a perception is preserved in memory.[18] Memories are preserved in our mind as two-dimensional images, or *pictures*; and they can be displaced under the direct influence of similarly two-dimensional fantasy-images, altering our understanding of reality, just as new perceptions alter this understanding. In this way a non-being, an image, becomes really existent, by altering our own past – and therefore future – perception of reality. We 'realise' thus the zero (literally 'real'-ise, or 'render it real') in so far as reality and image become equal from the moment we all, participants or observers in this fiction, accept this image, the zero (*nulla,* *zipher, zephyr*), the pure representative of nothingness, and its value dissolving and sublimating character, giving it a name. As a consequence, we do not see the difference anymore between a real thing and a fictional thing, as both gained a name, and so a value, the original measure and proportion of things breaking down.[19] A single figure of nothing (zero) thus generated an entire system of effective 'second reality' representations,[20] which so attracted Leonardo by its interface zone of stability that he regarded it as a fountain of creativity (see Vendrix 2008: 85), but horrified Plato. It is this realisation of non-being (*nulla*) that explains Plato's horror of mimesis, as it can be seen for example in his early dialogue *Ion*. Socrates refuses to listen to the performance of the actor, interrupting him continuously, as he does not want to become transformed by his witnessing of the actor's presentation.

The first iconographic representation of Pulcinella appeared in the 'Balls of Sfessania', the most popular work of Jacques Callot (1592–1635), the famous etcher. It contains scenes from Italian public festivities, sketched in Florence and published upon his return to Nancy in 1621 (Callot 1971, 1992). The 24 drawings of the 'Balls' were used by Callot as an occasion to introduce, for the French and the wider European public, some of the main figures of the Italian *Commedia dell'Arte*. In this first, inaugural iconographic representation, Pulcinella is not alone, but with Lucrezia, engaged in an activity of *flirting*.

Images of flirting recur frequently in the depictions of Pulcinella and Lucrezia, called also by various other names, of which eventually Colombina became something like a standard over the centuries. The preoccupation is reciprocal: Pulcinella is always flirting, but the same holds true for his female companion. Particularly revealing are those images where Colombina is embracing Pulcinella with her hands, but her eyes are elsewhere – already searching for the next partner in flirting. With this generalisation of flirting as an activity, love is shifted to the same level of abstraction as money: everything can be exchanged with everything else; the realisation of love as a concrete encounter does not imply existential commitment, only the pocketing of a conquest, necessitating an immediate move on to the next stage. Matter – the concrete, the real, the existential – does not matter; or, said by Colombina, 'what does it matter that I have another lover'?

Apart from Pulcinella and Colombina, Callot's series also introduces the ass, his most faithful companion. The first image of the

'Balls', after the frontispiece, depicts two *Commedia dell'Arte*-like figures in a very strange and contorted pose: Captain Babeo (a name no doubt alluding to the baboon), dressed as a Spaniard, is thrusting forward his sword from between his two legs, while Captain Cucuba meets this gesture by turning back and thrusting forward his behind. As if the meaning of this first scene would need decoding, in the background of the image an ass can be seen, mounted by Pulcinella but backwards, while a fourth person, dressed with a Spanish hat and performing dancing steps, is pumping air with a fire-kindler into the behind of the ass. This entire image system requires the reality-producing fictionality of the zero: one by one every element that we used here, the ass, the Spaniard, Pulcinella (Cucuba), Babeo, is a set apart element (ob/off-scenic) in an aberrant narrative order, which is disrupting the order of locality or concreteness, the sequence of experiences.

In the centuries that followed Callot's inaugural depiction, the figure became increasingly standardised, gaining its by now familiar features. In this path leading up to the decisive formulation by Tiepolo, three artists made important contributions (Greco 1990). The first is the Rome caricaturist and collector of antiquities Pier Leone Ghezzi (1674–1755). His elaboration on the Pulcinella theme has two main points of interest. In his series of drawings entitled 'New World', Pulcinella outgrew his *Commedia dell'Arte* character and became a figure of everyday life. Furthermore, the ass motive gained a particularly extensive elaboration. In another oft-discussed image entitled 'Pulcinella at school', a very shrewd-looking donkey is visible behind Pulcinella, with a signpost in the background identifying him as the 'Plato of the Pulcinellas'. In this way a figure of absence, the vacancy of a mask, happens to define the value of the figures around: the school, even an academy (as it uses Plato's name), where Pulcinella, a figure of nothingness, becomes the king of educator-mimes, just as Plato is the king of educator-philosophers.

The second artist is William Hogarth (1697–1764), the English painter. He drew only one image of Pulcinella, but this played a major role in the history of the figure and has a special interest for our purposes. The image depicts electoral corruption where, as a picture within the picture, there appears Punch as the candidate for Guzzledown: a multiple pun by excessive behaviour on the mime who won the heart of his electors by his interest in their vices and not in their virtues (Greco 1990: 156–7).

By far the most important figure connecting Callot and the Tiepolos is Alessandro Magnasco (1667–1749). Magnasco painted a series of six small pictures about the life of Pulcinella (Camesasca and Castellotti 1996). In these images Pulcinella is involved in his usual activities, getting the best from everything, filling his stomach, enjoying the pleasures of life, endlessly reproducing his own image: he is either eating, courting or playing music, often surrounded with an evidently infinite number of small Pulcinelli. The figure of nothingness just as easily stands for one hundred or one million as for a dozen, as it is exactly his absence that mimesis renders valuable and meaningful: just as the sketchbook of a great painter is easier to copy than his masterpieces. He is totally absorbed in what he is doing, oblivious of the total mess and disorder surrounding him. The only disturbances in his circular and closed world are the repeated stomachaches caused by his voracious, unlimited appetite.

With his unusual flair for the singular and the macabre, Magnasco made crucial steps in intensifying the character of the empty space, bringing out the deeper recesses beyond the evident hilarity. But the very extremism of Magnasco's own temper also prevented him from exploring the full potentials unleashed by the figure. The occasion became ripe with the Tiepolos, who recognised in the Pulcinella figure that the empty place, the 'nothing', is also full of potentials, as seen in 'The New World' (1791).

Nothing, or the zero, is ever growing, spinning out of control, evacuating meaning, being the only mathematical element that is capable of melding two others. Its power of blankness signifies a new way of apprehending the world by opening it up to all sorts of possible manipulations: '0 called cipher or "nulla" is the figure of nothing, since by itself it has no value, although when joined with others it increases their value.'[21] The nothing or nulla has a positional value, which was not easy to comprehend in Renaissance mathematics, nor to convey outside mathematics; however, with this picture, Tiepolo can be considered as apprehending this positionality by the three figures linked to each other: Pulcinella showing the 0-shape on the edge of the fork to the showman with the stick, and with his own (doubled) painted image observing Pulcinella's act (as in 'The New World'). Furthermore, the crowd plays a fundamental magnifying role, enlarging what they see into an event bigger than it actually is, according to the contagious logic of imitative processes so well analysed by Tarde or Girard. The zero's fictive and purely quantitative character (it is without qualities: no shape, no name, no value) thus becomes transformed into multiplicity through pure observation by a multitude, visible also in the famous Pulcinella drawings.

In this set of drawings everything is connected to everything else, the borderlines being eliminated; and the series, far from simply documenting the life of Pulcinella, rather depicts a society of Pulcinellas, generated through the force of Pulcinella, his mysterious multiplicative capacity. This fertility, it is easy to guess, has something to do with the mimetic nature of the figure; but this talent for imitation in this context ceases to be the occasion of laughter and jokes. Pulcinella's face is often contorted into a grin, but his grimace is enigmatic, falling in between pain and laughter, and when depicted together, the 'society' of Pulcinellas are often shown around with a particularly grave expression. This 'society of Pulcinellas' is a *par excellence* example of Girardian undifferentiation; it knows no difference between social ranks and classes, as the penetrating regression is not a monopoly of one or other social class, but includes every single one.

The key word of Pulcinella is ambivalence; but we must go through an entire range of ambiguities to understand what the term means here. Pulcinella starts from low-level, vulgar burlesque, and pulls everybody down to this level by provoking hilarious laughter with his acts and gestures. Tiepolo, however, is also accentuating the frightening, absurd aspects of this figure, even in the deformations of his body. Laughter can at any moment turn into the opposite feelings of emptiness (Pulcinella's own) and compassion (of the public); those who at one moment were shrieking with laughter at his stupidity and ugliness the next moment would pity the miserable character with his terrible deformities. With Pulcinella, everything becomes different than it looked in the first instance, though the original impression is eventually also confirmed as basically correct, starting another vertiginous circle. What seems casual is not so accidental at all, exampled in the fact that he always happens to turn his behind towards the spectators.

The series of drawings end with the execution of Pulcinella. Pulcinella is condemned by a judge who is a Pulcinella in front of a crowd of Pulcinellas, and executed by a platoon of Pulcinellas commanded by a Pulcinella. In these figures interpreters recognise both members of the revolutionary tribunals and Napoleon, demonstrating the radical manner in which Tiepolo failed to find a difference between representatives of old and new politics.

The scene of execution represents the height of the ambivalent sentiments provoked by Tiepolo's Pulcinella designs that – with their alternation between farce, brutality and tragedy – provoke at the same time laughter, horror and reflection, and even emotions that are impossible to describe. The central theme of this last work is the problem of death, though the link between the death of Pulcinella and Pulcinella as a symbol of death is not evident; this is a point not fully clarified even by Calasso (2006). The ultimate tragedy of Pulcinella might be that he desperately desires forms, but is not one of them, only a figure stuck in liminality. But even more, he needs training, as the central characteristic of liminality is the loss of a discriminating dynamics of values, owing to the dissolution of being and its replacement by awkward figures of incommensurability, who insist on imitating or copying them. The key word related to training is propaganda, and the Enlightenment was ready to provide both, in art and in science, for all those who lost the balance and accord in being.

4
Attraction and Crowd Passions: Isaac Newton and Jacques Callot

The question of the multiplicative automatism that can be derived out of the liminal again takes us back to the heart of classical philosophical anthropology, or the very foundations of social and political analysis. In particular, we can consider the work of Plato, who argued that imitation had become a threatening moving force of then contemporary forms of social and political life, which he identified in several writings as being simulated and stimulated by the Sophists. 'Every occasion for whatever passes beyond the *non present* and goes forward into presenting is *poiesis*, bringing forth' (Plato, *Symposium* 205B). Rationality or reliance on the *power* of reason, for him – and for Aristotle – is not a simple anthropological constant; rather, it is a capacity to be acquired and developed to see measured relations when confronted with the *alogos*, the irrational fake problematic of artificiality. Ignoring the driving force of imitation, as propagated by a 'new class of image makers' in politics (Plato, *Sophist* 268C–D), implies that the mind will be reduced to the instrumental use and furthering of imitative processes, deployed to promote particular political agendas, which is exactly the central problem with the newly emerged public figures of art and science in the seventeenth–eighteenth centuries, leading the path towards the Enlightenment.

Newton gained fame by the idea of universal gravitation, a property that determines the spatial relations between bodies. Could anything be more solid, serious and real as gravity, where the emphasis is understood as being on massive bodies that move along a straight line until they encounter another body? Bodies themselves, with their different individuality, standard and constitution, however, for Newton do not belong to the essential nature of things. The central word in this Newtonian revaluation is not gravity, mass or body, not even movement, but the *void*, where things have only to appear for the whole to be triggered into motion. Their being, entity, identity, power and dynamism do not bring any condition to comprehend the whole; they are identified with the void, and it entered or slipped into them, the eternal and never changeable. Newton argued about the necessity of granting existence to the void between the constituent particles of solid bodies (Newton, *Principia*, Book III, Proposition 6 and Corollary 4). In this way, Newton elevated the void into a primary principle of natural philosophy:[1] it is the void that keeps things in infinite movement and power. All things consist of indivisibles, thus they can be divided indefinitely, without losing their qualities. With this understanding he shook the world of knowledge, not because the world view that he reformulated was not present before,[2] but because in this way he gave a scientific legitimacy to infinite acquisition by extending finite matter into the infinite liminal (Newton, *Principia*, Book I, Section I, Lemma II).[3] Contemporaries[4] were much surprised by Newton's notions of the 0, struggling to understand the true depth of its meaning: that, for Newton, the 0 was a sort of total cosmic fact contained in everything, thus crucial for describing central terms in his cosmology like fluxion of time, velocity or quantities. But Goethe went further than this: he was an outright critic of Newton's scientific methods, which according to him confused, entangled or pushed aside the opposing facts, thus reducing facts into slavery (see Goethe 1995, XII: 320).

The central idea was to procure knowledge of the world. This implied its conquest, in the sense of an ability to influence, manipulate and transforms things, by splitting identities and eventually reconstructing them into a new entity, just as nature generates quantities by continual flux and increase, without ever exhausting itself.[5] The Newtonian view of the world thus discarded the Platonic notion of the form as an eternal *ethos*, just like the singularity of reality, by liberating void through violating the borders of things. A void liberated from one concrete being will keep dissolving and corrupting, though not by attacking every other object in a general way: rather, by searching out their point of weakness, through which another void can be liberated. Thus another solidity is turned into liminal flux. The eventual end product of such dissolution is stasis, a state of chaos where further improvement is no longer possible; for human beings, this implies a state of terror, living under the tyranny of disempowering due to a lack of forms, standards and constitution. The end product of such accelerated motion into infinity is not only puzzling, but also counter-intuitive, as it gains force by dissolving borders, destroying the entity that feeds its own development.

The true radicality of the Enlightenment vision of the world, which Newton pioneered, lay in the reversal of the evidence of the ability or self-support of things. For them, the primary reality was the void; objects only took up a certain position within this empty space. Once this reversal of perspective was accomplished, it had only to be taken to its logical conclusion. The void had to be absolute; and as in such an absolute void, any innate force was absent, particles would move continuously all the time. So in his second law of motion Newton moved beyond the Aristotelian vision of the world, where things are stable and complete with force. For Aristotle, things needed a substantive force to move them from stasis, whereas Newton saw the world as permanent movement, thus recalling in his *Principles* the Greek vision of *chaos*, in opposition to the world as *cosmos*. What is more, Newton's third law of motion states that the nature of interaction in this world-as-void, or chaos, is a perpetual fight of the moving particles, as they bump into each other, moving continuously, without any inner strength.

Void

For Newton, the void itself became a sort of container of substance, instead of just being in-between bordered things, or beings put into shape by Forms. In this way he changed the bearer of substance from the Form (*eidos*) to the void. However, the problem of giving substance to void did not appear for him. He considered the matter as the mimetised aspect of the void, where extension, solidity and gravitation were to be explained by the force of the vacuum that is alternately attractive and repulsive, depending on the range. The void could easily mask itself as wholesome form and generate a huge release of energy by breaking the bonds that held the unity of the bodies together,[6] alongside a chain reaction, with every break generating fragments that could furthermore be broken into ever-smaller fractions.

'Excited sensation' was Newton's most significant innovative idea in this context. Its significance lay not simply in rooting sensation in attraction towards forms[7] – or, as Gabriel Tarde called them, the 'passionate interests' of the Enlightenment that animated the rise of modernity (Latour and Lépinay 2009), and its scientific and social revolutions. Rather, it implied a turn away from the Socratic principle of knowing oneself, which was the basic task of philosophy, and even of classical culture and life. The introduction of the void, with its desire for impulses, or its eagerness for possession, into the centre of the modern scientific world view involved a basic change in thinking, by posing the question how something that is void can move things. There can only be one answer to this question: the void can only move if it mimes, or if it takes a body as a coat. Newton's approach implied a radical shift from the form and its concrete constitution as authentic to its mimicry, ending up legitimising the existence of void though imitation.[8] Only in so doing could Newton reach into another layer of reality, which from the perspective of the standards of the world of living beings implied an unreality, arriving at the idea of the continuity of matter and the continuity of space. Thus, concrete individual standards became irrelevant, losing their authentic forms, and continually dissolving into the liminal: 'conceiving things to be continuously diminished without limit' (Newton, *Principia*, Book I, Section I, Lemma XI).

Taking the void as real can only happen if after decomposition the fragments of the full body sink into imitation. This creates an alternated reality, no longer keeping the borders of the fragments that bound them originally, but trying to keep the newly acquired fabricated images until a new attraction arrives, given that the loss of the original forms renders the fragments vulnerable. One of the results is undetermined fluxion, which is a spiralling, perpetual motion that keeps things in eternal variation. This regularity formed the basis for Newton's application of dynamics, attraction and vacuum to nature, which is still rolling around,[9] as an unreal copy image of the real. However, this truly ultimate and fundamental feature of the void, its mimicry, which leads to the sudden and unlimited reproduction of non-being, can only be rendered intelligible, even if not fully explained and analysed, by the characteristics of the zero, this truly enigmatic number, first before the first and last beyond the last. Newton called it the *naked point*,[10] not without reason; the zero is nullity and nothingness; it does not count, it is indiscriminate; it does not know the difference, being a slave number. If we add zero to any number, the result is the same; if we subtract zero from any number, the result is again the same. That addition and subtraction yield identical results is not something to be taken lightly if we try to reflect on the possible social and human meaning of such operations. Addition implies an increase, an act of giving, to make something more; and subtraction the opposite, to make something less by taking body away. It is thus not surprising that in several languages the mathematical operation 'addition' is connected to the term for giving, whereas to 'subtract' is a synonym for taking away.[11] This indicates that a number which produces the same result for addition or subtraction is beyond ordinary life, which is based on giving and receiving; it is not a 'natural number'; it is 'beyond good and evil', paraphrasing Nietzsche for things that are without character.

There is a further point about addition: the adding of a zero after any number. Different from adding a zero to any number, this makes a difference; even a huge, magnitude growth. This game is a typical illusionist technique: adding a zero after all numbers would leave the relationship between them unchanging, thus again, seemingly, not making a difference; but deep in our heart we know that something does not fit. This is not a purely mental game, as it goes into the heart of neoclassical economic theory. The Walrasian general equilibrium is indifferent to the price level. We get the same equilibrium if the unit price is 1 dollar, 10 dollars, 100 dollars or any other number; and yet in real life, changes in the general price level evidently matter. It took long decades and a series of enormously painful economic crises before economists, with the help of Keynes, started to understand, and even then only dimly, that something was not working with their models; the real world refuses to accept their theories. At the most basic level, however, this simple paradox indicates how profoundly the modern world, driven by the 'economy', is entangled in the mimic Trickster logic of the *nulla*.

Things start to get even more complicated with multiplication. If we multiply any number by zero, the result will be zero; in other words, the zero turns every other number into itself. This conclusion is most significant, as multiplication is the generative operation by which, with normal, natural numbers, we get multiplicity, growth or development. Not with the zero as, if we perform the same operation with it, we get nothing.

How did Newton develop such a radically counterintuitive idea, replacing inner movement due to substance and force by the idea of the absolute void? By what method and procedure? He was certainly helped by previous developments in science, in this case most significantly by the air pump experiments of Boyle and Hooke. It is most significant in this regard that Boyle published his famous work on the air pump in 1660. It was countered in 1661 by Hobbes's, which resolutely argued not simply against the concrete findings of Boyle, but against the very vision of the world implied by it. The debate between Boyle and Hobbes thus began when Newton, at the age of 19, went up to Cambridge (Westfall 1993: 66). The enormous influence exerted by Boyle on Newton is well known, emphasised by the fact that it was also in 1661 that Boyle published his most famous book, if not his most important, *The Sceptical Chymist*,[12] which sparked Newton's interest in alchemy.

It was this debate between Boyle and Hobbes that became the subject matter of the by now classic book of Shapin and Schaffer, *Leviathan and the Air-Pump* (1985), which was influential in redirecting attention to the social and political correlates of the rise of the modern science. Newton's work fitted into a pattern and a context. One might say that it was purely due to the genius of Newton, the power of his mind and thus his ability to abstract, to tear himself away, more than anybody in his broad age, from the taken-for-granted aspects of reality; this, combined with the luck that he happened to be just entering university when the most important scientific debate of his age was being contested.

In the spirit of Shapin and Schaffer, however, it seems that, taking a step further, it is worthwhile investigating the possibility of taking the void as the starting point for a comprehensive vision of the world. The novelty in the view of Shapin and Schaffer is that the link between science and politics concerns not the answers, but a certain commonality in the thematisation of problems. It is in this direction that we must take a further step to understand just how radical Newton's view was about 'nature'. This step might at first seem a regression, because Newton's thinking indeed 'mirrored' the characteristics of his times: a liminal, unsettled age, marked by an absence of order. This seventeenth century 'mirroring' seems to have a certain affinity with the nineteenth century Marxist school of social history. However, it is radically different from it, as Marxists looked for something 'positive' in the socio-political world which could be, supposedly, 'mirrored' by scientific developments: aspects of social structure, class struggle or the presumed optimism of the rising bourgeoisie. Disorder or chaos is something purely negative; it cannot be 'mirrored'; the mirror of the nothing is still nothing else but the nothing itself. And yet, this was exactly what Newton did: to reflect in a new, radical manner on the nature of this nothingness, arriving ultimately at the absolute void as the principle of the universe; making use of the terminology of Marcel Mauss, the void for Newton represented, in the analogy of a 'total social fact', a 'total cosmic fact'.

But what does such reflection mean? Its novelty lies in its implying a *direction* of thinking that is radically different from that of Hobbes or even Boyle. They were still driven by the fear of chaos, the anxiety of living in a 'time of trouble', searching for a return to order. Newton, with Callot, however, chose to move beyond such anxiety, and actively reflect exactly *on* the nature of disorder, persisting in looking into the abyss of chaos and void, until he found its organising principles, or its truth, regarded as universal; thus he ended up *reflecting* disorder, as the foundational layer of the real world. So the central question of this chapter concerns the significance of their persistence: how can we make sense of this truth of perpetual movement, the force of the 'void' continuously moving *away* from reality, further and further discovering the nature of void? Where does the attractiveness of the void lie? What could have been the path-breaker model in this respect?

Modernity and charisma: The first revolutionaries

Here this book will introduce another revolutionary figure who has hardly been connected to the thinking of Newton, although this figure is fundamental in its very condition of possibility. This figure is the French etcher Jacques Callot, in particular his cosmic series of the *Balls of Sfessania*, containing 24 images. These images, it will be argued, represent the vision of a world turned upside down, or literally 'revolved', through the lens of the void, as if fallen through a hole. In the frontispiece of the series, in the closed, alchemic space of a stage, covered by a curtain, two figures try to force a third to enter an empty box. The other 23 show two gigantic figures endlessly fighting, in contorted obscene movements, on a completely open and free public space, mimicked by minuscule humanoids in the background predicating revolutions that soon followed.

Zero has no value in itself. It only gains meaning through a 'magical marriage' as it is a purely positional number (see the initiating picture of Callot's *Balls of Sfessania*), with numbers having characters; only in this way is the 0 able significantly and magically to alter their value and form. This operation is also the source of fertility and thus the basis of reproduction or multiplication or growth. However, multiplication by zero results in death; or, still in other words, through multiplication the zero turns every number into its own empty self. The *nulla* is impotent, it is the nihil itself, but this does not mean that it has no effect whatsoever; quite the contrary, it does manage to change any other number into itself, into nothingness. In the words of Foucault (1980a), it has no power over life, only over death.

Division as an operation leads to even more tricky results. Normally by this operation, natural numbers become smaller, reflecting the fact that division or the breaking up of unity or any kind of cohesion is indeed a way to make things smaller, for example by halving them. Not so again with the zero as, if we divide any number by zero, the result will be a sudden and enormous, indeed infinite growth. In spite of its impotence, the zero not only manages to turn every other number into itself (by multiplication), but even produces boundless growth as well by division, or the principle opposite to growth.

Yet, this is still not all, as the most powerful operation is involution, or the raising to powers. Involution refers to numbers that are repeatedly multiplied by themselves, or are raised by powers; a growth called exponential. The zero even here behaves in a strange way; perhaps the strangest way of all. Any number on the 0th power becomes one; or the zero, this slave number of nothingness, or pure positionality and subordination, suddenly becomes the architect of unity, as it manages, unfailingly, to turn any number into the unity. The culmination of this logic is reached as a genuine liminal case, both mathematical and philosophical, when we realise that asymptotically even zero on the 0th power yields one, or unity. The zero, not when multiplied by itself (which only yields zero), but when taken to its own power, as if by an act of *auto-fertilisation*, produces unity.

The void is naked: it has no inside, no midst, no centre; but it *is* all of this itself (centre, inside and midst) at the same time. The question is how it might exist inside the matter: how to insert it or to pull it out of the matter, how can it mime the form, as if taking it into its own power, thus to gain the creation or auto-fertilisation. There was only one answer to the ancient rebus of infinite divisibility, which was obtaining the form of the thing by mimicry. Nobody gives up their own character, their dignity and morality easily for the void; the void needs to deceive to gain position. This is the only way the void can get a position in the body.

The central claim of this chapter is that Newton's deceptive proposition about the void, belonging to the heart of the history of modernity, has an exact counterpart in the history of art; a visual representation advancing the same idea, about half a century before Newton. This is found in the *Balls of Sfessania* series of Callot who offered a 'rolling wheels' vision of monstrous creation, which is generated and moved by mimetic attraction derived from the energy stored in bodies and revealed by the impulse of the void. Attraction takes place when the borders of the bodies are disturbed.[13] Normally this should bring bodies into inertia, except when the insulting aggression is masked to evade recognition and pre-emptive destruction by the threatened body. By using masks, Callot's figures not only secure their survival, but even proliferation and survival, as this encourages them to behave in ways out of their original, given forms. Breaking the bonds that bind things to themselves and to each other causes that chain reaction that repositions the normal constraints of the world, the result being growth or reproduction. This can be followed through Callot's figures, as the same type is multiplied and is fighting with itself or struggling for copulation with each other after the initial 'sacred marriage' takes place between void and mimicked forms.

Acquisition

Callot, just as Newton, did not invent things. Rather, he captured the very essence of his liminal times in which the mime play

(and of modern theatre) developed, showing mechanical reproductivity as the outcome of the proliferation of insipid characters
and trickster figures into life.[14] Above all, he was a cold artist
who searched out horror, painting torture, execution and assas-
sination, proving himself a pitiless witness to all the miseries of
mankind: never in inertia, but in continuous search for horrific
images. Examples of his works include *The Miseries and Misfortunes
of the War*, *Massacre of the Innocents*, *The Temptation of St. Anthony*
and *Grotesque Hunchbacks*. These are unending reports of a coming
final age, where space is homogeneous and time is indifferent, as
it 'flows equally in without regard to anything external'.[15]

Callot deliberately sets the masks at each other's throats, with
the backstage mirroring the front, thus showing its multiplicative effects among the crowd.[16] The fighting masks are shown as
giants compared with the size of the back crowds: they are either
naked or dressed in loose grab closed with semen-like buttons, but
always wearing indicative feathers, on the head or as if grown out
of their arms (see No. 14; the numbering follows Posner 1977).[17]
Insemination or multiplication is central for Callot, as all males –
except those in loose fitting garments – wear a phallus enlarged
with a cloth wrapped over it, while a row of pompons, representing
semen, runs down their clothes, from neck to groin, underlining
the generative meaning. His *Balls* scenery is about a begetting:
it is like a cosmic machine that never stops its generative zeal, a
numerical composition of time and eternity, a *perpetuum mobile*
with its gigantic demonic fights and births, which have no winners and no losers, but continue into infinity, swallowing up the
old to the subtle generation of the new.[18]

Callot entertained his audience as nobody else did or could
in his age, pushing excitement to its extreme limit, to the pleasure of ironic macabre, presenting his *Balls of Sfessania* in the
ritualistic–ecstatic form of popular mime-dance.[19] At the same
time, he delivered a fatal judgement on the world as a meaningless place of mechanical vengeance, an eternal spectacle of cruelty, vanity and vengeance, which is moved by a foolish, stupid
and inferior non-sense. This vision became extremely powerful,
as it was formulated and published in 1621–22, thus in the very
first years of the Thirty Years' War (1618–48). He executed all this
with technical perfection, visible in the virtuosity of his mannerist curvatures, forcing the spectators to take the images presented

seriously, by provoking repulsion, attraction and reflection at the same time.

The first picture of Callot's *Balls of Sfessania* is a mocked *hieros gamos*, establishing a union with an inferior but powerful spirit.[20] The consecutive pictures show brilliantly the identical ambiguity of the dancers: their more-than-human ability to change their appearance, their positions and their mental attitude. For them, cruelty and sexual enjoyment is identical (see No. 2);[21] they are equally feared and fearing (see No. 6), easily changing identity, clothes or names, and in every way they have an ambiguous, fluid existence. All parts of the body that are targeted by curse are painfully squeezed: twisted, distorted, cramped or convulsed,[22] in grip of an ecstatic madness caused by the unity established with the spirit, which reveals an erotic character. It is a form of savage spectacle with queer marionettes in a monstrous union with the demonic.

In the *Balls*, Callot's genius successfully caught the transformation from the initial scenes, with the trap motive of secret marriage into a new transfiguration of the fighting masks (see No. 2). The pale, trembling central mask of the initial image is turned by Callot into a fighter, a competitor, an invader or an intruder who is chasing the world into transformation. It is well known that there were never any *Commedia dell'Arte* troupes with this type of dance, or these types of character, with all those names (Posner 1977). Every picture pairs and designs the macrocosm and the microcosm, where the fighters are set up and separated, then lash out at the flesh of the other, fighting for copulation with bulging phalluses and bottoms (see Nos 2, 16, 22), miming their unification and re-aggregation, and then starting the same phase again (see Nos 5, 9, 12, 21). Their foreground acts are multiplied and mirrored in every case by similar acts in the background, ensnaring the acquisition of every possible person from the audience pictured. Nurturing a profound obsession with brutality and terror, Callot was also fascinated by comedy and popular entertainment. He was among the first important artists to depict explicitly some characters from *Commedia dell'Arte*, the early modern Italian form of theatre that resurrected the ancient mime play, with its deliberate and routine presentation of a world turned upside down.[23] The mime discovered that everything that is not embedded in, and covered by, forms is ridiculous; just as bodily parts could be obscene, when getting out of their hide. The term ob-scene (out of the scene) in itself illustrates its point, if we look at the *hieros gamos* scene on the Inandik vase (*ca.* 1700 BC) from Anatolia (Idil 2001: 45; McGovern 2003: 175–7), where gods copulate with men in daffy images; or at Leonardo's grotesque faces, which are dumb in so far as they are stripped of all forms, standards, compositions or constitutions; they are simply unreal.[24] Void does not appear; repositioning does not occur – except in the grotesque, the absurd or the obscene; in eerie environment, with the help of the mask that covers such unreality – or covers the nothing which thus becomes real, through possession (Pizzorno 2010). This is Callot's unrealism, a sign of his being estranged, ek-static (the Greek word means to stand outside of itself or to transcend oneself) and evidently ob-scene, as showing on scene, in a theatrical, mime spectacle the process of estrangement, demonstrating how one becomes ek-static if one transforms oneself into the vehicle of emptiness.

Cosmology

Isaac Newton's cosmology considered that quantities exist in continued motion (*Quadratura Curvarum*, 1704), where motion takes place in the void. This brought him to the idea of *fluxions* or the eternal movement of things, the ultimate *ratio*; the determination of quantities from the velocities of motion, differing from its theoretical predecessors and sources, Aristotle or the Epicureans. There was no reason for Newton to introduce or deal with forms any more: 'I was willing to show that, in the Method of Fluxions, there is no necessity to introducing figures infinitely small into geometry' (*Quadratura Curvarum*, 1704); instead, the 0 was used to substitute small finite quantity (Cajori 1919: 34), thus giving substance and form to 0. Taking the 0 as the starting point, Newton set up a challenge by identifying the finitely small with the absolute zero, which provided him with an entire conceptual arsenal concerning *gravitation, vacuum*, the *constant velocity, attraction and repulsion*, the theory of *light*, the *laws of motion*, the *indivisibles* and the *relative* as the infinite essence that glues matter together, the manner in which bodies act upon each other and thus manage to raise, compress, transfer energy.

Transmutability and the conquest of the other's qualities was a crucial problem for Newton. Already as a young Cambridge theologian it was through pursuing the claim that all matter consists of light that he arrived at the idea of liberating light from its composing form.[25] This soon led him to the idea of an active exchange of qualities taking place between things,[26] to raise them into a new significance, just as Callot did earlier. With Callot he shared the importance attributed to surrealistic impulses that served to move things, to pulverise or annihilate their essence by putting them under pressure, forcing them to move and grow. Significantly, both ideas met with resounding and instant success. Newton demonstrated the existence of impulsive forces that reconnect and divide reality, explaining the nature of attraction between things. He epitomised the new model of the scientific establisher of the existence of a design in the universe; the one who provided proof for artificial providence.[27]

The basic problem of the void is its individuation (how to liberate it, the enslaved, from its original constitution), as, according to Parmenides, the nothing cannot have a position (Parmenides 8B). Although every being has a standard, determined through the ordered relations of the whole, the void is missing this quality; it is merely subjected to the entities. Newton solved this discrepancy between the individual form and the enslaved void through a high level of abstraction, when he turned upside down the constitution of our real world and nominated void as the objective standard. However, the concrete unity of things resists change, defending its identity and intactness, becoming unsociable if its concrete existence is threatened. This is the reason why the main problem of Newton's *Hypothesis*, and his *Queries*, is how to deceive them with mimesis or with mirror images: tricking the water to dissolve copper by melting it with sulphur, or deceiving lead to mix with copper by adding tin or antimony to it.

As it is true for every liberation, the liberation of the void – which moves freely and perfectly in its boundless and bottomless fluxional – needs a beginning, a creative initiation. This is shown by the initial picture of Callot's *Balls*, which is not so much a composition as a decomposition, and a malicious one at that, with a transparent erotic allusion at the resulting new constitution through a marriage with the void: a *hieros gamos*, a sacred marriage image, though a rather scoffed one, between a possessing, acquisitive spirit and the possessed worshipper who would otherwise not mix.[28] So that an interchange between the void and the new entity can take place, another requirement must be met as well: that identity is broken, never to become the same as it was before.

The frontispiece of Callot's *Balls of Sfessania* depicts five actors on stage in a tense movement, enacting a secret performance. Two are hiding behind the curtain, peering out with a voyeuristic look at the three front figures. The audience is a willing onlooker of the game, standing on the peak of a ladder (on the left), or just gazing as if through a high window (on the right), at the three figures in the front of the stage, who are involved in an obscure activity. The figures on the left and right are wearing masks and are mirroring each other in dress and appearance, tightly encircling the central figure in between them, who is called Bernoualla. The left mask with the guitar frames the action, chasing Bernoualla with rushed, exaggerated steps towards the right mask who displays similar step-gestures, who has an open box in his hands and whose 'sword positioned between his legs serves as a phallus; its proximity to the open box suggests a vulgar meaning' (Castagno 1994: 207). The vigorously phallic gesture of the stick under the box,[29] however, simply mirrors the form and the exaggerated length of the guitar-neck in the hands of the left mask; while both together terrorise the central mask, who shyly tries to turn his head away, covering it with his arms, while still shaking the tambourine.

Certainly, the central figure is dancing: his left foot is raised and shows a kind of dancing movement. But the figure does not seem to be enjoying himself much, as his back is curved, which is usually a gesture of fear, and is turning his back to the left mask, often the expression of somebody who is chased (Kahan 1976: 10). So he seems to measure the distance between himself and his pursuer, though this pursuer has a guitar and not a weapon in his hand. The central mask is evidently pushed toward the open mouth of the box.[30] This parodic performance of conquest, and the clearly sexual symbols of the long guitar neck, the sword, the open and empty box, and so on, gains its meaning by Callot's inscription, which gives some instruction about how to interpret the opening scene. This inscription can be read as the names of the three masks, but can also be interpreted as a full sentence: 'Lucia mia, Bernoualla, Che buona mi sa', or 'My Lucie, Bernoualla, I really like it', as if giving two female names to the two masks orientating themselves towards the box would indicate the substance (female goodness) of the box, kept in the hand of the third one.

The words 'Lucia mia', handwritten under the picture, allude to a Neapolitan burlesque song, which belonged to the Tarantella dances,[31] where Lucia personified the cock, the transition between sexes (Bragaglia 1930: 66). The central mask is pursued towards the frightening slapstick and the box.[32] This starting and initiatory image of Callot's *Balls* is by no means a simple call for copulation. It is secretive, pregnant with symbolical and mystical meaning; it is ritualistic, with the peculiar purpose of generating something extraordinary from disintegration, through contrasting opposites. The 23 scenes respond to this initiation in their own identical ways. Nothing is noble in these scenes. They are rather bestial: one cannot help the feeling of witnessing beyond the burlesque style, a mythologised travesty of liminality. The *Balls* ridicule the divine, attributing to it a stupid libido, showing it up as an inordinate and vain god, improvising and unordered: a kind of fool's god or a divine idiot, a sacred clown that is inferior to man.[33] The names of the giant masks are all weird, grossly insulting or vaguely threatening: Franca Trippa (clearly alluding to the French malady), Fritellino (the greasy one), Babeo (the blockhead or baboon), Malagamba (the lame), Cucuba (recalling the seventh dwarf, Dopey, *Cucciolo* in Italian), Scaramucia (the skirmisher), Fricasso (the hubbub) and so on: quite a kind of terminology for images of cosmic giants that are mirrored and imitated in the back stage of every picture.

Callot shared with Newton a new conviction about the presence of the effective force of the void in the composition of every concrete being. The central issue for both was conquest, and they both found in the void that indivisible infinity which is able to dissolve cohesive identities, thus breaking the protective borders, unleashing motion and gravitation.[34] They both agreed that what enabled the void to perform this action is its nothingness, because of which it can imitate any form and magnitude leap or transformation. It was posited that there is no need any more to assume a concrete force that keeps moving the cosmos and the concrete beings inside it. Once the void is liberated from a concrete being or sinks into another one it alters its composition, and so now the fragmented matter that comprises a disruption is able to split infinitely. Therefore it does not fall into inertia; instead it is able to strive and prosper, breaking and acquiring without any limit, driven by its own innate depravity. Bodies incorporating depravity are in continuous schism; see Callot's liminal figures as well as Newton's 'fluxional'. In this way they perform their actions separately and in isolation, which deepens their void; but the deeper it is, the closer it comes to fulfilling their void essence, the nothingness. To maintain this circle, where end and beginning meet, individuals do not need to act further in any way: it is enough to empty themselves, subjugating themselves to the void, which results in a self-begetting circle.

Consequently, according to Newton, it is impossible to assign individual names to infinite domains and there is no criterion for identity: only relativities obtain. Nothing is final or local; space and time are infinite, implying, as a consequence, the infinity of all conquest. Nothing is nameable; the standard constitution of forms is unimportant. Hence void is liberated from it. In Newtonian empiricism the essential and fundamental property of bodies is their void, not even needing force to maintain position. With this, Newtonian science separated itself from Euclidean geometry and established a new basis for philosophical comprehension, the new perception of a fluxional world.

The fluxional

Once Newton stated that space and time are ontologically independent of their occupants, this suggestion started to work and proved its worth. It came to mean the impossibility of distinguishing between places, specifying the conditions in which concrete beings could obtain their identity, and so the relative became for Newton the means for talking about the real. Callot, for his part, showed that things in flux, in the void, behave in an unlimited way. How could anything be measured, when there is nothing to compare with it, if things are indistinguishable and cannot be distinct, their nature keeping them inseparable in a meaningless way, being thrown into the mere *sensorium* of infinite space, into the agitation of vibrating motions which progress, irresistibly and victoriously, towards the annihilation of every form.

Once the world is reduced to fluxions and infinite decomposition, we are at a loss about how to conduct or know ourselves, so instead we keep agitating more and more for attraction. The gigantic, macabre spectacle of the French Revolution, in which the Enlightenment culminated, illustrates this point well, with its secretive art of violence, which captures and encloses, dragging down every form, structure, and authority, imposing its binding boundlessness on any existing value, moral and authority. It proclaimed freedom, but ended up coercing, whether by deeds or words. It even presented itself unveiled – in the form of the 'Supreme Being' – as non-being itself, a being without any bonds and restraints, the being of ecstasy, accompanied by songs and marches into nothingness. The Revolution was a ritual breaking of the system, the loss of measure for an entire community, the (dis-)organisation of terror, chaos, disorder, confusion, bringing about the havoc of war and disruption, which was not incidental and externally imposed, but the logical outcome of its waging a mortal war against society itself. It broke all established ties and identities, thus destroying society in the name of the social; a total, inexorable destruction of all social links, a radical change of all forms, evading the surrounding reality in the name of liberation, a release from the self (which is identical to death), establishing a permanent state of struggle as the essence of the human condition, and finally culminating in ecstatic possession, thus passing beyond death. It thus recreated a unity with the fertile, generative force of the void, at the price of the initial stage of violent, dramatic tremor – slowly or abruptly sliding into the unreal, into ecstasy, into orgiastic mimesis.[35] Newton denies even Descartes and introduces space and time as fundamental categories, which are furthermore 'affections': 'Space is an affection of a being just as a being' (as cited by Stein in Cohen and Smith 2002: 267).

Fluxion means that things are divided by the admission of the void (Newton, *Questiones* 2 88'). The void may get entirely inside each of these halves in a critical moment and thus continue their division into eternity; there is infinity in division. The principle of division is the void, which breaks into unlimited number the parts of the matter, objecting to wholeness, size and shape of matter; or the Newtonian supposition that the body is infinite. Although the infinity of division, or the fluxional, reduces authentic things to nothingness, there is always a new stage of life that gives them survival in their new, mutated mode of existence, because it could be infinitely extended. Beyond all this exaltation there is an immobile, unchanged and absolute entity, a vast and hideous demonic being.[36] Newton widened existence over the threshold of life and death and rediscovered the Platonic notion that reality and unreality merge into each other. The material world is not limited to reality; there is a vitalising principle that connects life and death, the existence of the ob-scenic, as it is also present in Callot's wilfully ugly images. Until Newton the infinity of division, which would reduce things to death and non-existence, was a territory banned for man. Newton, however, just like Callot, dared to play with the prohibited, as if anticipating Kant's *sapere aude*, showing a death/birth that revitalises and leads to the generation of new mutations. In his *Optics* Newton called it fermentation: the force that confounds into boundless chaos, but then re-aggregates again.

Infinite series or the axiom of Maria

We immediately encounter difficulties if we try to capture this uniform boundlessness in words. Infinity and void are the terms used by modern science, yet they are not quite right. Void is mute, as is the mime, but is present on the stage in indefinite finiteness. Void – as *nulla* (zero) – only appeared in Arabian mathematics around the eighth century, though not yet with the same sign and name as we know it, rather using a still obscure Indian symbol. The zero only arrived into Europe in the eleventh century, with the Crusades, and for a long time it only had a peripheral usage. Its wider application can be traced to the turn of the sixteenth century. However, only the age of the Enlightenment disseminated it as a mathematical device, much connected both to military architecture and the legacy of Leonardo da Vinci – the first European explorer of and convert to the 'philosophy of the nulla' (Marinoni 1960). But as a numerical extension the void, with the name of nothing, cipher, zephyr, nil, null, nulla, zero – having many names, unknown to the Egyptians or the Sumerians, the Greeks or Romans – only gains power in certain situations when position in mathematical terms comes into importance. We still do not buy zero bread, and we still count from one. Zero is a slave number, but that particular type which is able to enslave others. Our everyday culture still stubbornly clings to things that lack void: numbers are sorted from one and not from the zero, our desperate efforts to express in familiar terms the frightening alien vision of the world discovered by Newton and proposed as the true nature and the real world. Newton's unprecedented success lay in this notion. He combined the discontinuity of matter with the continuity of space, by accepting the brokenness of matter itself by putting indivisibility and continuity inside it, through the void. When we divide, multiply or make involution (raise to powers), the zero alters the normal arithmetical operation, causing growth or unity.

According to this philosophy of emptiness, which moves Callot's masked dancers, entities become generative owing to the void they contain. They are able to divide/multiply infinitely in a nick of time. This is the liminal *flux* that helped Newton to overcome the *vis inertia* problem: that things in resistance lose their motion and fall into inertia, so motion is always in decay. His question was how to recruit matter through an active principle, which generates endless division without losing motion, attraction or power. Void, this obscure structuring aspect of matter became a solution for Newton, implying the inevitable next step of introducing it into reality by breaking it, as otherwise the remaining problem – how the void sinks into the matter – would not become a problem.[37] Consequently the fluxional is connected with acquisitiveness, or the continuous breakage of existing entities, which brings forth the generation of power. In Jung's *The Psychology of Transference* there is a citation from a third century AD Alexandrian alchemist, the so-called *axiom of Mary*: 'One becomes two, two becomes three, and out of the third comes the four', as this progress through the series of numbers is a formula for the alchemical process (Jung 1989). But this infinitely multiplicative nature of schismatic division is even better illustrated by the infinite series in geometry, first discovered by Archimedes (287–212 BC), about how to break up a number, form or figure into an infinite number of infinitely small parts: $1/4 + 1/8 + 1/16 + 1/32 + 1/64$ and so on, through the method of *exhaustion*; a very telling word. Here void makes a difference, because if you divide by zero, you are not distributing anything anymore with the progression of growth.

Nulla means void and emptiness, nihil and non-existence. Callot's masks are first and foremost deprived beings, marginals and outcasts, or those who are subjugated, though at the same time also over-human, tyrannically demonic. The void is the condition for strife; it desperately tries to behave like the others, wants to be 'real', grab the real, 'get a bite of the world', mime it, unite with it and digest it; but at the same time its grabbing ends up annihilating it. This is why these images reproduce, in order to diffuse, only the lowest, most vulgar and obscene aspects of the 'sacred marriage' scene of the opening image. Such traits might be termed animalesque, but this would not be correct. Callot's masks do not behave like animals; at worst, they perform things that animals would never be able to do, demonstrating a genuinely monstrous depravity. We wonder at the masks not because they show up the animal-like vigour of a state of nature, but because they fiddle with the abyss inside us. These radically contrasting aspects of the sub-human and the superhuman are brought together by a third main characteristic, which is something positive, even the most important feature of the *void*: its imitative character, its essence as a mime. The *mask* is a nullity, the embodiment of the zero, but it also has a positive identity: it is miming. It is pure nothingness, a fake, which is unproductive, impotent, unable to complete anything and to be real or true; and yet, at the same time, it is capable of miming to gain position, which is instrumental for marriage and so can cause sudden multiplication. In one moment, it is just an obscure, marginal figure, ignored or enslaved by everybody, not taken seriously, an object of laughter and the butt of bad jokes; but in an instant, without any precedent or warning, with a quick and sudden leap it is up to gain possession, hunting down the others, forcing them to copulate with its void and in this way multiplying itself out of all proportion, becoming the dominant character. Copulation can multiply the unreal that would soon rule the scene, and order everyone else to copy it.

Callot and later Newton both perceived a precious asset for gaining position, exploiting their age in every conceivable manner. The power of the people of their age, their intelligence, energy and wealth became their own: an acquisition they gained as a result of their skills, or their position in art, philosophy and science. But this is not all, as they both have become icons, inexhaustible treasures of imitation and mimesis, thus growing into a generative force[38] as well, as if the 'axiom of Maria', a formula for the alchemical process that describes germination, would have been realised in them. Although the Greeks tried to avoid dividing units,[39] the new era inaugurated by the Enlightenment continued to exercise vigorous power over its subjects, promoting subservience to the big structural machine, which became realised repeatedly as *incubus*, parasitic body or supernatural abstraction. Hobbes and Marx, among others, attempted to build up consciously an artificial construction to subordinate the units to its logic of artificial perfection, failing to realise its perversity and intrinsic irrationality. Indeed, this idea is very similar to the alchemical dream of artificially creating man, so it is not surprising that it produced an identically unexpected result. Alchemy searched for the excellence of gold, and discovered instead hydrochloride acid, nitrate and sulphate,[40] all kinds of acidic metals suitable for aggression and violence against natural objects, perhaps analogous to the modern states that combine bureaucratic rule and colonisation with 'pastoral care'.[41]

Revolutions, however, could not even work their way out of liminality, as they purposefully identified themselves with the void.[42]

Revolutions as the evocations of three 'S's: Seduction, senselessness, sensation

Revolutions are guided by definite types of 'empty' contents, like seduction,[43] senselessness, sensation, or the three 'S's: all unstructured, yet at the same time highly structuring emotional forces. Under their influence the basic norm of personal integrity is questioned, and terror and fear about the meaning and very existence of the world creep into the mind, propelling a sliding back from harmonious Being to the bare level of the taken for granted. This is produced by the contagious spread of a new social content, as channelled through the three 'S's, dissolving accepted norms. Callot was a peculiar but paradigmatic example, the 24 images of the *Balls of Sfessania* providing a 'rolling wheels' vision of human attractions, as generated and moved by seduction, to reposition the world. It helps to understand instances where the relationship between structure and agency cannot be easily resolved or understood through the by-now classical 'structural' or 'structuration' theories, as suggested by Pierre Bourdieu or Anthony Giddens, but the central place is taken over by emptiness, covered by a wafer-thin layer of structure network, as organised by the state. Revolution – a phenomenon studied so extensively in sociology and political science, without yielding a result beyond self-complacency – can be understood as a highly problematic 'carrier' of social change in the original Weberian sense, which reframes the disrupted integrity, as anticipated by Callot or Tiepolo in art and Newton in science.

A central characteristic of liminal situations is that by eliminating the stable boundary lines they contribute to the proliferation of imitative processes and thus to the continuous reproduction of image appearances of reality. Bacon did not take up, rather managed to ignore, this aspect in his famous critique of idols, in opposition to his much more perceptive contemporary Shakespeare; this was an omission that would much limit the relevance of the 'scientific' method in the social sciences and the humanities, as it ignored the power of weakness and formlessness, trying as if to exorcise them by declaring non-effective the non-existent but reality-influencing void. Imitation and images are closely linked, even share a common etymology. In uncertain, fluid, 'liminal' situations they jointly exert a considerable even all-encompassing power, as the contagious impact of liminal authorities, whether for good or bad, is transmitted through an appealing, attractive, evocative imagery.

These phantom images and trickster figures disappear as quickly as they appeared, though not without their impact, just as – using the language of epidemics – viruses infect and mutate, or – in the language of thermodynamics – energy does not dissipate, rather is only transformed. Both languages are particularly appropriate for the phenomenon of liminal authorities, as their appearances and effects have the aspect of a deadly virus, dissipating in the social body and multiplying its effects in a nick of time; and possessing a particularly strong virulence through its both destructive and reproductive energy (Wydra 2011b). A sudden flowering of prosperity and a similarly quick and thorough jump into an abyss of self-destruction, far from being neatly separable and radically different, are rather quite close to each other and can be easily confused. Thus, at the first level, we have to take seriously deception as a problem, and analyse the conditions of possibility of effective, mass-scale delusion; whereas at the second level, we have to extend our analysis to awareness, involving a sense of distinction, discrimination and discernment.

It is at this level that we encounter a series of cases that, although seemingly unconnected to the political revolutions or mass movements and ideologies of the twentieth century, they reveal themselves to be particularly illuminating if we look at the rise and fall of revolutions in the context of liminality. What happens under liminal conditions is a joint stimulation of unconscious imitation and strictly purposeful deliberative calculation. On the one hand, as is well known from crowd behaviour, among an unstructured mass of people, for example during a panic or in outbursts of political violence, imitation takes place extremely quickly, spreading like a forest fire, and the selection of the leaders to imitate can be completely accidental or – even worse – might propel forward the religious or political technologist, for all the wrong reasons. On the other hand, the same conditions also provoke and stimulate calculations, and in two different senses: first, because isolated and atomised individuals have to fall back solely on themselves, and thus they have to find their own 'natural inside' or their so-called interests; and second, because a proper solution to the liminal crisis would indeed require a certain possibility of distancing oneself from the existential anxiety and emotional turbulence that encompass everyone and thus provide a way out. This dilemma was formulated by Norbert Elias in his classic work *Involvement and Detachment*. The exposure of corrupt practices on a broad scale is used by revolutionaries to advocate the classical alchemical themes of *happiness, perfection, liberation* or *immortality*. Alchemy, this thousand-year-old ruse covering the propagation of technology for producing artificial life, aims to acquire power through a *spagyric*[44] art. But the separation and joining together of entities is only possible in liminality; this is why it has a forbidden, *arrheton* character.

A potential charismatic hero, far from being an accommodated figure in the disciplinary order over an organised state, must be a person who can stand in oneself. Consequently charisma is not compatible with modernity, which requires uniformity, as if canalising people into an alchemical opus, as illustrated well by Ostrogorski's classic analysis about the rise of the party whip. Not surprisingly, the best analysts of modernity, from Nietzsche and Weber to Ariès, Elias and Foucault, all emphasised the significant role played in the genesis of modern world by closed institutions, proliferating in periods of transition: asylums, hospitals, prisons, monasteries, courts, barracks, boarding schools; a typical alchemical topos. It is not due to the values and merits of professional education and bureaucratic order, rather to its defects that somebody might become a charismata. But who are these pre-modern entities who do not need legality, state-discipline and formal education, but who are at one with themselves? What eventual positive features do they possess, and what happens with them in the liminal situation?

These are indeed the most difficult questions for the entire theoretical framework presented, indeed for the actual solution of the real crises; and this question cannot be settled before reviewing the actual evidence. Just as the logic of a liminal crisis, as analysed so perceptively by René Girard, is to eliminate all distinctions between the members of a community, leading to a situation where the only remaining distinction – from the view-point of state, order, education and discipline – lies between the large mass of homogenised people and the singular nullity, the eventual 'solution' would also lie in a certain elimination of this last remaining difference, between the 'proto-charismatic' *nulla* and the great mass of people. Either the great mass of people would be drawn into and reduced to a *nulla*; or this nullity itself would participate in the liminal situation and by the force of a collective undertaking will start to share understanding at the level of the lowest common denominator of sensations. It is this incorporation of the nullity into the social that is equivalent to the genuine 'creation' of a charismatic hero.

The case of Napoleon offers a particularly illuminating example. The manner in which Napoleon, a typical nullity figure, became a 'charismatic hero' in the context of the liminality produced by the French Revolution and the ensuing endemic warfare is well captured in the classic study by Dmitri Merezhkovsky, written on the basis of his experiences with the Bolshevik Revolution. Two episodes will be used: a description offered of Napoleon as he arrived in Paris, after Toulon (Merezhkovsky 1929: 58–9); and the events of eighteenth Brumaire (ibid.: 116–21).

Concerning the first, Merezhkovsky captures the way in which Napoleon handled the ups and downs of his fortune: 'In the army he was already Napoleon, but here in Paris a nonentity, or worse still, a "suspect", a disgraced general of the Convention. He was reduced to abject poverty, having lost in unsuccessful speculations all the money saved in the army. With nothing to do he paced the streets. Sometimes he would indulge in fits of utter despair, as evidenced by his later autobiographical reflections: "I am almost ready to give way to the animal instinct which prompts me to suicide [...] I am very little attached to life"' (ibid.: 58). Or, as 'a clever woman' described her impressions, '[h]is gloomy eye made one think he was a man one would not care to meet at night on the outskirts of a wood [... he] did not look a general – but intelligent; at least uncommon' (ibid.: 59).

Merezhkovsky reconstructs the crucial series of events of eighteenth Brumaire with great empathy: 'Bonaparte feels there is no time to lose, delay is fatal. Across the long suite of rooms he makes his way alone [...] In violation of the law, prohibiting an outsider to enter the Assembly Hall uninvited, he enters quickly, almost at a run; halts in the centre, near the Presidential Tribune, and begins to speak. He speaks badly, confusedly as always before an assembly; forgets what he has to say, muddles his speech, loses himself in pompous phrases; the words seem to stick in his throat, now to escape in an incoherent torrent' (ibid.: 116).

He starts by evoking an impeding apocalyptic doom: 'Citizens, you are upon a volcano' (ibid.: 116; the image of 'sitting on a volcano' would be central for the *International*, the hymn of the Communist movement). He presents himself as an innocent, persecuted victim: 'I am a victim of a calumny' The next trick is demagogical mobilisation: 'Let us save liberty, save equality!'

He responds to the objections by playing with the guilty feelings of his opponents: 'You have yourselves violated the Constitution.' He also uses a revealing self-defence: 'I am not an intriguer'; revealing, as otherwise he could not feel the need to utter such a statement (ibid.: 117).

The series of tricks still fail to produce an effect: 'He was conscious that he was not making headway and his confusion increased, like that of a *débutant* on the stage or a schoolboy at an examination'. He starts losing his head; all his efforts to evoke sympathy and find supporters fail; a full-scale pandemonium is about to break out, and he is only saved by his grenadiers, recording his purely military exploits: 'His face is deathly pale, his features distorted and eyes half-closed; his head drooping on his shoulder, lolls like that of a wooden doll. Is this "the god of battle, the god of victory"?' (ibid.: 119).

Everything seems to be lost; yet he stumbles upon the solution, through a doubly negative mobilising call, once all his efforts at a positive mobilisation failed: he manages to galvanise and channel enthusiasm to 'save the President' (ibid.: 122–3).

The successful solution of a liminal crisis thus has two preconditions. The first is the actual presence, within or near the community, of this (still not clearly defined) nulla figure. Without this nullity, which is constitutionally outside the normal condition of modernity, no solution is possible. But the mere presence of the nulla is not sufficient; on the contrary, the nulla might just as well only trap everyone else into its own idiosyncratic status. What is thus furthermore necessary is a selfless self, radiating innocence, because 'even the most sublime nothingness gives birth to nothingness' (Hölderlin, *Hyperion*), so nothing comes out of the nothing if there is no condition of wholeness. So our preliminary thematisation about liminal figures leads to two main results. First, the successful resolution of a major liminal crisis, especially its transformation into a vehicle for spectacular flowering and prosperity, requires the presence of a very special type: a premodern character that is selfless, undisturbed by indoctrinations, the one who feels oneself. This is why everything that happens in liminality depends on us, not on void. The void enters, slips in, but does not determinate actions, characters or outcomes. In fact, at any moment it is as one conceives it, taking up reality only through comprehension. As several historical examples demonstrate, promising, hero-like characters might just as well turn out to be harbingers of doom, instead of guides to a bright future; aimless eternal wanderers that just happen to stumble on a particular community in a moment of crisis. Although weak idiosyncrasy is the outcome of becoming identical with nulla, somebody can only become a unit by becoming oneself.[45]

Here we need to go into the socio- and psycho-genesis of the nulla; pursuing – beyond even his own work – certain insightful hints by Norbert Elias. The real appearance of the nulla, the materialisation of void, requires nothing in particular; rather, it requires the sudden appearance of a desire for nothingness, in the form of doubting.[46] Doubting moves beyond meaningful order, undermining in thought the existing authority structures of an ordered social reality, thus contributing to its eventual dissolution; but, at the same time, it can open the mind to new modes of thinking that are a necessary precondition of solving actual situations of crisis that emerge when real events undermine or destroy the existing order of things. Doubting or hopelessness help to see things 'differently', in the full ambivalence of 'difference'; as 'difference' can be relative and destroy every value, it can also render one sensitive and emphatic towards others, situations and realities that previously were ignored or misunderstood. In fact, this schismatic nature of doubting, and the split personalities it produced, was the main cloaking of ideas of alchemy inside the labyrinth of Christian thinking in the late

Renaissance.[47] In this context nullities can enact understanding and the care for otherness, helped by the fact that doubt is close to despair,[48] a cloak for their frustrated egoism (as they insinuate themselves as the unspecified 'other' who should be cared for and loved), being devoid of the wholeness that loves and honours life.

Liminality does not require a major collective crisis like a war, a revolution, a general economic depression or a particularly devastating natural catastrophe: quite often the exact opposite happens, as the greatest prosperity of Athens brought upon them the Sophists; similarly, the peak of the Renaissance resulted in the proliferation of hermetic Gnostics who escaped from the crumbling Byzantine world.[49] To provoke a liminal crisis, methodological doubting is sufficient in itself, even as a relatively minuscule aspect of the ruling culture and its values. It gradually undermines normal, everyday social order, gathering up momentum in a spiralling manner, like a storm, into the real threat of a catastrophe or revolution. Under such situations the ordinary becomes questioned and the limits set to contagious imitative processes are broken down. So one can expect a multiplication of that type of schismatic behaviour that is particularly imitative.

Strangely enough, sociology is particularly ill equipped at identifying such processes, because of the combined effects of neo-Kantianism, transmitted through the great classics, Durkheim, to some extent even Simmel and Weber, codified by Parsons; and the Cartesian rationalism so characteristic of Marx. Sociology for a long time thought in terms of structures, functions and institutions, transmitting such ideas to anthropology, through Radcliffe-Brown and Malinowski. It failed to recognise the spiralling dynamics of the void; whereas those who did so often ended up simply celebrating chaos, disorder and 'liminality', failing to pay attention not simply to the schismatic consequences of a liminal crisis, but to its generative, enactive character. An anecdote about Karl Mannheim, told by Lewis Mumford, is particularly instructive in this regard: though a refugee from Hungary, still in November 1932 he predicted that within a few months nobody would even know who Hitler was, as he was just a non-entity, a fool, a person not to be taken seriously.

This time Mannheim was not right, as fascism proved that all the assets of liminal conditions can turn into liabilities, promulgating mediocrity, the pursuit of the whimsies of a schismatic self and the destruction of the stabilities, and thus could grow into an empire in a nick of time. The break-up of meaningful order, of stable structures and identities creates the situation of an opening for the fluid state of uncertainty that is easy to master with a single recoding technique. This is why rituals are particularly secretive institutions, and were only supposed to be performed in the presence of 'masters of ceremonies', able to trap spirits and emotions, leading – and occasionally misleading – the initiands, and keeping the whole thing in *arrheton*.

This is especially pertinent when such cases of liminality reduce a large number of people at the same time to an identical and highly deprived condition, thus posing the problem of the crowd.

Crowds and their leaders

Crowds, of course, have always existed in history. But they were temporary phenomena, associated with transitory, temporary liminal events like warfare, pilgrimage or carnival. The novelty of modernity lay first in the political importance crowds played in violent political revolutions, and then in their permanence as a consequence of mass society. This led to the realisation that crowds have their own peculiar features, and, most importantly, that crowds behave and can be influenced in a way that is different from other, more organised and structured kinds of human groups. The Enlightenment, dissolving stabilities with its lethal and indiscriminate weapon of doubting, increasingly brought forward a kind of actor that did not exist previously in such a form or manner: a crowd without leaders.

The emergence of crowd psychology that deals with the tyrannical emotions of the crowd can be connected to a single author and to a single event. The scholar is Gustave Le Bon, who published in 1895 his book *The Psychology of Crowds*. Le Bon is certainly an odd character, an outsider to Enlightenment intellectual circles. He was deprived of the academic recognition he sought so keenly, even considered a charlatan.[50] His works, however, were quite popular. His ideas about the psychology of crowds were almost immediately taken over by some of the most important social theorists of his times. Le Bon was approvingly cited by Durkheim (1995 [1912]), his ideas were a main source of Freud's book on mass psychology (Freud 1949 [1912]), and he was an inspiration for the sociologies of Tarde (1969) and Pareto (1954, 1966, 1986), and of course to the anarchism of Sorel, which oscillated between left- and right-wing extremism.

The single event that can be identified as the main historical source behind the theories of Le Bon was the Paris Commune, especially as interpreted in Hyppolite Taine's classic work. The Commune was certainly not the first event of political violence on a mass scale, even during the nineteenth century. But perceptive observers noticed a new quality, and identified a new problem. Acts of political violence in the past were products of warfare, or the outcome of an accumulation of injuries suffered or provoked by repression. The Commune, however, was produced by a chain of events that was determined by the dynamics of interaction characteristic of crowds.

The central new idea of Le Bon, derived from his study of the Commune and similar observations, was that a crowd has a 'soul', or its own sensation. The specificity of his approach and the source of the admiration and ridicule it received both stemmed from the fact that he did not consider this idea just a metaphor. It seemed to him that when joined by several others in a crowd, human beings were capable of committing acts they would not be able to do otherwise and that they could not even remember, let alone explain with their senses. They behaved as if they were under a certain pressure, as if they were following impulses, or being under the influence of alcohol or other spirits: thus, in senselessness. Le Bon also noted that individuals often emerged who managed to take advantage of such situations and who could influence, in this moment of general confusion, the behaviour of others by acting as the 'crowd leaders'. We can easily see how the ideas about unconscious impulses were attractive to Freud, as well as why the concern with the emergence of leaders from the masses fascinated elite theorists like Pareto. Even the interest of Durkheim in the phenomenon of 'collective effervescence' can be traced to the ideas of Le Bon.

If Le Bon's ideas were never fully accepted and acknowledged academically, they had an enormous influence. Like a self-fulfilling prophecy, his ideas served as a background for the development of both modern political propaganda machines and commercial advertising. Adolf Hitler personally recorded his admiration for the ideas of Le Bon in *Mein Kampf,* arguing that his book was the single most important source of his ideas about how to gain a mass following. Though this was not put into words in the same way by Lenin or Stalin, the affinities, even the indirect chains of influence, can be reconstructed for this kind of totalitarianism as well.[51]

The first point to notice here is that Marx also reflected upon the events of the Commune. He, however, admired the events, and considered the Paris Commune as a most important and forward-looking political development, a confirmation of his ideas and proof of the suitability of the proletariat for leading the world into a better future. According to him, 'If the Commune was thus the true representative of all the healthy elements of French society, and therefore the truly national Government, it was, at the same time, as a working men's Government, the bold champion on the emancipation of labour, emphatically international' (Marx 1977: 547). It should not be taken lightly that these same events led other, 'bourgeois' observers to reflect upon the sources of mindless violence and the dark side of human existence. Second, there is a very direct link between Le Bon and Lenin. Lenin studied extensively the ideas of Pareto when an exile in Zurich, especially concerning the circulation of elites, and this work contains references to the work of Le Bon. The conjecture that Lenin was aware of the works of Le Bon has also been made. Third, Le Bon's book *Psychology of Socialism* was the follow-up study to the *Psychology of Crowds*, one of the first works that treated socialism as a 'secular religion'. *Psychology of Socialism* was very enthusiastically reviewed by the famous theoretician of violence and the general strike, Georges Sorel,[52] who became closely associated with Pareto and was an important source for the writings of Lenin.

Still, the recognition of mass power needs another element, which is guidance. This came into political science through elite theory, which began as a criticism of mass democracy. It argued that a political class must maintain some degree of exclusiveness and superiority under the conditions of mechanisation and massification. Members of this class are those who possess valued characteristics of pre-eminence such as intellectual ability, moral authority, high prestige or widespread influence. They have social significance, and are assigned responsibilities for and influence over society. 'Ruling classes do not justify their power exclusively by a de facto possession of it, but try to find a moral and legal basis for it, representing it as the logical and necessary consequence of doctrines and beliefs that are generally recognized and accepted' (Mosca 1939: 70). These political tools are not 'mere quackery aptly invented to trick the masses into obedience'; quite the contrary, 'they answer a real need in man's social nature', the need, common to both rulers and ruled, to feel the established order is based not on force but on 'moral principles' (ibid.: 71). This elite was not exclusive, as access to it remained open, and recruitment of new personnel from non-elite strata was considered central in order to renew its ranks continuously.

Much of this critique of mass democracy consists of rather simple truisms, such as the idea that no matter how democratic mechanisms are used, a minority will always monopolise and direct them (ibid.: 50). More interesting are Mosca's perceptions about the apathetic, inward-looking majority, without a public spirit – the exact opposite of democracy's self-image – because there is no authentic desire for the good and beauty, no urge 'to feel any loyalty or sincere devotion to any principle or to any person' (ibid.: 319). Sadly, Mosca is not a fashionable read nowadays. He is often considered a pseudo-scientific subversive, though this judgement reveals as much of his strength as his shortcomings. Mosca starts from the assumption that scholars usually fail to appreciate the value of everyday perception and the morality of common sense (Femia 1993). His down-to-earth statements contain many tautologies, such as the idea that the ruling class is composed of the people who rule, and an elastic and variable terminology, as well as trivial observations.

However, Mosca's ideas were critical of both the bourgeoisie and socialism; and although they had strange affinities both with radicals and conservatives, he remained hostile towards both. Despite his inconsistency and impressionism, he could take a penetrating look at issues that often proved valid. His criticism of democracy was followed by Schumpeter (1943); his critique of socialism was taken up years later by Hayek (2005 [1943]); and what he predicted about Marxist utopianism and collectivism became a sour reality in the course of time. For Mosca, just as later for Voegelin, communism came to be a mortal threat to civilisation, and he considered Marxism the most evil of all contemporary ideologies because it was inspired by hatred and destructiveness

(Mosca 1939: 479). The central point made by Mosca, which is less frequently cited than his slightly exaggerated domination/ submission dualism, although important to his understanding, is that no political unit can thrive in the long run without being animated by a moral force. People must be faithful to personal merit, which is always embodied in elite; otherwise any community is doomed, their fate being moral death. Mosca passionately argues that a forgetfulness of virtues undermines and corrodes the inner spirit of any community. Therefore the ruling class has the duty of remembering the higher values. The function of the elite is to maintain and preserve the value of concentration and discipline, and direct it towards the collective interest or the public spirit. By keeping alive such principles, they protect the fundamental and characteristic ideas of community, which provide the sole defence against the disintegration of the society. The elite are the potential pool of leaders; they are the pledge preventing society immersing itself into the liminal abyss. Mosca followed his words with acts: he was the only person in the Italian parliament to stand up against Mussolini's investment with power.

Mosca, the economist Pareto and the German–Italian sociologist Robert(o) Michels did not simply try to justify the ruling class and its privileges. Their argument had rather two levels. First, ruling minorities are simply facts of life. Modern democratic politics, just any other political system, implies the permanent existence of organised minorities who impose their will on the disorganised majority. Furthermore, they legitimise their own power by using the set of values and beliefs held in common in society – values that are not exclusively political but social, cultural and so educative – and where the legitimate role of the political is at best to defend these from the exclusive domination of one or other of the subsystems, like the logic of the economy. Appearing at first in the writings of Ostrogorski, this conviction became a sociological axiom that Mosca revisited, Pareto extended on an international scale and Michels – Weber's main collaborator and disciple in the years 1906–11 – applied to the case of the socialist or working-class parties as the most typical example where the spirit of mistrust and irritation determined every single action. This is because the demagogic claim to do away with all elites through a radical call for equality not only ignores the hard facts of reality, meaning the inevitability of inequalities of power and influence, but at the same time inflicts lasting and often lethal damage on its more sensitive and vulnerable meaning structures. This type of politics, misnamed as 'radical', pursues mirages. So its achievements will always be illusionary and ephemeral, but its negative effects can easily become permanent.

Elite theorists were also close to theories of totalitarianism, a concept first applied in a comparative sense by Franz Borkenau in 1934. The Communists used the term 'vanguard' for their movement, the fascists had a similar self-consciousness, and both had the same idea of prosperity and happiness as the main principle, helping to identify themselves with the masses. They both considered the life of their people as their own, sharing a deep, never-ending interest to transform their subjects towards their goals by continuously provoking more and more efficient sensations. Both believed in moral purification, the radical cleansing of the objective world, and both endlessly longed for redemption through apocalyptic transformation, the violent disruption of normal everyday life, rejecting any compromise. Fraternity, equality, justice and solidarity were the guiding principles in their holy transformations, and the resemblance of their ideals to a renewal of medieval ascetic values was more than astonishing. Even more, their surrealism applied a mode of mobilisation that could be called spiritual: their movement had a religious character, and their leaders were considered charismatic. Everything seemed to have come together in posing an ideal contrast to the faded, tired and cynical liberal democracy, or so it was argued.

Reality, however, proved to be quite different. Good will and noble intentions do not matter if the entire undertaking is intellectually untenable, seriously flawed. If the leadership of liberal democratic systems was often characterised by ignorance, totalitarian leaders were outright barbarous in their undertaking, having no capacity for understanding the work of government. Thus their accession to power posed a great danger even for their own existence. They never-endingly slotted minor facts and observations into the masses, proclaiming them as deep insights, hunting down and cornering all those who opposed, and even those who did not agree quickly enough, and then nursing all of them. In their case the extraordinary qualities, fascinating power and magnetic attractiveness, the unique and irreplaceable personality that describes a charismatic leader according to Weber (Lindholm

1990), are completely misguiding. It soon became apparent that totalitarian leaders manifest fallibility, signs of incorrectness, stubborn dullness, failings in their professional and social life, and perversion and disaster in their private life. Beyond personal idiosyncrasies and contingent circumstances, strict processes of counter-selection assured that infallibly the worst rose to the top at every level of social life.

This stunning dilemma was not restricted to East–Central European Communist regimes, but had a much more general validity. In the concluding page of his series of lectures on Hitler, Eric Voegelin used the cases and works of Karl Kraus and Heimito von Doderer to characterise the puzzle. Karl Kraus was the most outspoken political satirist of Austria for four decades, writing and publishing alone an entire journal. However, he never even touched Hitler. He considered that Hitler simply *was* a farce, so he could not be *made into* the object of a satire, adding, 'I can't think of a thing to say about Hitler' (Voegelin 1999b: 256). Doderer's epic novel *The Demons*, with a title consciously echoing Dostoevsky, is a panoramic vision of the world in which totalitarianism could become possible. It contained a crucial analytic description of the figure of the revolutionary, who is an atavistic idiot, unable 'to endure himself' (ibid.).

However, most scholarly approaches to totalitarianism not only take it as self-evident that totalitarian leaders are charismatic, but specifically argue that the general features of oppressed persons, their lack of attachments, clear instincts and an acute sense of their interests, help them to obtain charisma; or even prove that they possess genuine charisma. However, the spiritual effervescence that surrounds the men at the front (Patocka 1996) is essentially a feature of liminality, which can only come into being when the previously stable structures of social order are temporarily dissolved. The 'state of war' by definition is not normal; it is a liminal condition that provides unprecedented opportunities for weak personalities. Weakness is properly at home in the liminal, often helps to generate it but is also entrapped there, as its existence lacks those authentic personal characteristics that must be cultivated and developed. How else can one reconcile the fundamental impersonality of these leaders, their dull conformism and disharmonic soul with power, if not through deceit? The following quote from Linz shows how discourses on totalitarian regimes attempted to find a way around the paradox of the actual pettiness of such leaders and their mass appeal and effect: 'Undoubtedly charisma has played an important role for masses and staff under Hitler and Lenin: totalitarian regimes have also made demands on their civil service, based on legal authority; and democratic prime ministers have enjoyed charisma. Authoritarian regimes may also have a charismatic element, since they often come into being in serious crisis situations, and control of mass media facilities the creation of an 'image' of the unique leader. Genuine belief in charisma is likely to be limited, since the man assuming leadership was often unknown before, and to his fellow officers is often a primus inter pares, who owes his position often simply to rank' (Linz 1970). Instead of using the word charisma (a 'gift of grace'), the term 'decisive power' would be more appropriate. However, it is the merit of Linz to talk about the paradox posed by the spiritual attachment and appeal exerted by these regimes, and their very empty appearance.

Charisma and beyond

Under the notion of charisma as a type of legitimate authority, Max Weber introduced spiritual power into political science (Weber 1978). Though Weber detached the notion from its theological usage and relied on examples from anthropology and mythology, it has never lost its original transcendent meaning as a divinely inspired gift of grace for action. The powers of acting, power for creation, the will to power are Nietzschean categories, and we should not to forget that Weber was profoundly inspired by Nietzsche. For both of them the existence of extraordinary power is a fact that finds extraordinary characters as its subject carriers: 'charisma is a gift that inheres in an object or person simply by virtue of natural endowment. Such primary charisma cannot be acquired by any means [...] [though] charisma of the other type may be produced artificially in an object or person through some extraordinary means [...] charismatic powers can be developed only in people or objects in which the germ already existed but would have remained dormant unless evoked by some ascetic or other regimen' (Weber 1978: 400).

Although Weber was neither anti-rationalist nor pro-religious, rather a conservative–nationalist with an allegiance to bourgeois values and political institutions, he considered charisma a central category for his interpretive or *Verstehen* sociology. This was because he realised that the process of mechanical 'rationalisation' had already overrun its limits and become specifically irrational and meaningless (see Lowith 1982). In important parts of the *Protestant Ethic* or *Economy and Society*, Weber talks about the consequences of a radical disenchantment of the world and the way in which the mechanisation of existence had come to be a shocking result. He recognised in the mystical qualities of existence in grace the answer to his painful, tormented questions about the way out of this machinery, and in the person of the charismata he recognised a source of legitimate authority.

Although charisma as an ideal type plays a pivotal role in Weber's sociology, it is a concept that somehow fits uneasily into the standard interpretation of Weber. According to this, Max Weber is the sociologist of power and bureaucracy, of the modern state and capitalism, of the Protestant ethic and the comparative study of the economic ethic of the world religions. Ever since the publication of *Economy and Society*, the professional understanding of Weber's work has tried to pack his work into the Procrustean bed of the 'rationalisation' and 'bureaucratisation'. It is only in relatively recent times, mainly through the works of Tenbruck (1980) and Hennis (1988), that interpreters have shifted attention from the quasi-positivistic pursuit of identifying the sources of the rational culture of the West, thus investigating the driving forces behind modernisation, towards a view that is more nuanced, profound and closer to the spirit of Weber. However, by then the misreading inaugurated by Parsons had become impossible to dislodge.

For sociologists following Parsons, rationalisation meant that capitalism was based on the economic ethic of Calvinism as the concluding stage in a continuous and evolutionary process of rationalisation, in opposition to the emphasis on the forces of production by Marx. This was at best a one-sided selection out of the many question marks that could be found in Weber's work, giving special emphasis to the ascetic conduct of life as the source of a practical social ethic. Unfortunately, this was the first stage in a series of reductions of Weber's complex problematisation of the religious processes that started with Judaism and terminated in the innerworldly asceticism of Puritanism. These approaches regarded the conceptual part of *Economy and Society* as a final and conclusive presentation of Weber's views. In the past decade, however, a more elaborated approach to Weber's insight on modernity has appeared, which has salvaged his sociology of religion from the shortcomings of conventional sociology.

In the notion of charisma/grace, Weber found a spiritually sensitive concept for a particular state of attuning through which certain individuals manage to overcome the limitations of a particular situation in which they find themselves, and succeed in solving the crisis. Charismatic persons or charismatas are mediators between the realm of the divine and human beings; hence they become immortal through their works and with their actions, bringing salvation for the community. Although this notion is heavily based on Plato, it somehow lacks the individual effort that Plato emphasised in the 'care of the self/ soul' (Foucault 1986; Patocka 2002); that the greatest good of man is examining considerateness (understanding, *sophrosyne*) and truth in one's soul. Otherwise, life is not 'worth living', as that would be a life without grace. The noble origins of the aristocracy, so important for Nietzsche's *Genealogy of Morals*, is to be understood in this context, as genuine aristocrats are direct descendants of the mediators of grace. In Weber's work, however, this component is not present.

Weber was especially interested in those moments in history when belief in the regular order of things and its institutional basis was suspended. This state of fermentation is also central for the purposes of this book, as charisma is an authority that is derived not from office, but from the capacity of particular persons to maintain faith in themselves as bearers of legitimate power and to capture the imagination and enthusiasm of people, thus becoming sources of revitalisation in face of both chaos and ossification. The touch of the metaphysical, the possession of spiritual power, is a specifically innovative, exceptional force, an exclusive source of authority, connected to persons who assert their own sense of mission against the demands of tradition, law and order; irritating innovators who burn in their own flames. The effect of such persons on their social and political environment under out-of-order or out-of-the-ordinary conditions is enormous, as in this way they can fulfil their task of reordering the social and political framework of the community. Therefore Weber gave a rebellious reading to grace that it never contained before, a notion of the agitator type, which was alien from the framework of grace, which

emphasised the easy chains of love and obedience to the meaningful order that emanated from the Divine.

The irrational influence therefore remains a delicate point
in Weber's work. Although non-rational irritability due to the
endangered state of stability indeed mobilises the unconscious
by stimulating energies, generating enthusiasm and renewing
vitality, the outcome may turn out to be quite different from
grace, the positive quality of charisma. Weber put great stress on
the unintended consequences of social action. Spirituality stirs
up feelings, beliefs, and faith in reforms and in nation building or in the restoration of *Volk*, in the resuscitation of order or
the serving of the community, or in other kinds salvation from
crisis, without giving any charismatic guarantee. This latter is
an extraordinarily effective power emanating from supernatural
forces, but the mere relaxation of social control simply turns
attention away from the strengthening of common bonds, and
can lead towards obscure ends. The mobilisation of the irrationality of the unconscious – the power of feelings, enthusiasms, zeal
and faith – is geared towards the creation of the authority that
was suspended. Whatever the case may be, the enchanter stands
in the middle of a storm, whether accepting Weber's concept of
charisma or using similar ideas belonging to political psychology.
The only fixed meaning in his concept is the personal spell of
the extraordinary, the distinctive ability to enchant followers by
means of suggestivity.

It might be useful at this point to provide some more details
about this personality through whom the spiritual content is
passing. Socrates had a definite spell on the people around him:
he transfixed them, forcing them to hear him, whether they
approved or disapproved of his ideas, or the entire situation.
Alcibiades, one of his earliest companions, even complains about
the charms he had over the souls by his powers of breathing; that
he was a possessor of the souls: 'so soon as we hear you, or your
discourses in the mouth of another, – though such person be
ever so poor a speaker, and whether the hearer be a woman or a
man or a youngster – we are all astounded and entranced' (Plato,
Symposium 215d). Socrates affected people so much that they
felt themselves drunk in his presence; they would have liked to
transform themselves according to his principles, sitting forever at
his feet. Others just wanted to touch him as they thought that it

caused benefit for them: 'Here, Socrates, come sit by me, so that by contact with you I may have some benefit from that piece of wisdom that occurred to you' (Plato, *Symposium* 175c–d).

The magnificent flowering of pictures, just like a series of video-clips, comes from the authentic strength of the guide who possesses sensuality that is able to captivate the mind. The mobilising power comes from the person who is giving form to the new volition, determining the different combinations of images that appear on the screen of events. In *Ion*, Plato tries to give a compact description of the unique functioning of spirituality, which is a sort of magnetic divine inspiration, curling into suspended rings. Each ring derives its power from the same single magnetic stone and they have a similar power; thus, 'by means of those inspired persons the inspiration spreads to others, and holds them in a connected chain' (Plato, *Ion* 533e). Returning to Weber, charisma is not the product of collective needs, values, crises or negotiated actions. In other words, it is not contextual. It is indissolubly bound to the particular person possessing this unique power, bearing the weight of spiritual influence; to the interpreters of God, by whom they are possessed (see also Willner 1983).

But greatness is a mystery. It is based more on ardent feelings than on sober judgements. Thus the understanding of charisma in reality still remains an enigma. There is a long line of interpreters of divine power: from the first, who is the master (the lawgiver, like Solon; the poet, like Homer); to the second-hand interpreters (actors, like Ion himself); up to the last one, the audience, which is crying or laughing, owing to pity or firmness gained by the experience of divine. Neither fame nor success, neither faith nor power, exhausts the manifestation of grace in a particular person; it keeps waking up the soul forever: 'your soul dances' (Plato, *Ion* 536b–c).

Inspiration or possession by 'spirits' is a loose idea. Consequently the Weberian concept of charisma became one of the most elusive categories in political science. It did not help the understanding of charismatic leadership that the personality trait enabling an individual to induce others to accomplish a given task was called hypnotic suggestion. In fact, several approaches trying to explain the political sense of charisma followed this direction. These fall into two categories. One focuses on the individual characteristics of certain persons, presumed to have charisma, and proposes psychological explanations for these (see Lindholm 1990). The other puts the emphasis on certain political regimes that are supposed to give rise to charismatic leaders (see Linz 1970). However, neither psychological theories nor the literature on totalitarianism and authoritarianism could give a proper, comprehensive description of the spiritual type of legitimate authority; and in the meantime the most important characteristic of grace was lost. This concept implies wholeness, purity, the sun-like qualities of warmth and radiance, which is nourishing and procreative, gay and joyful, able to conjure happiness. The poems of the fourteenth century humanist poet Petrarch perfectly capture this meaning of alleviating, assuaging existence: 'Vergine bella, che di Sol vestita,/ Coronata di stelle, al sommo Sole/ Piacesti si che 'n te sua luce ascose;/ Amor mi spinge a dir di te parole,/ Ma non so 'ncominciar senza tu' aita/ E di Colui ch'amando in te si pose./ Invoco lei che ben sempre rispose,/ Chi la chiamo con fede./ Vergine, s'a mercede/ Miseria extrema de l'umana cose/ Gia mai ti volse, al mio prego t'inchina;/ Soccorri a la mia guerra,/ Bench'i' sia terra, e tu del ciel regina'.[53] These words contribute some very useful features to rounding up the picture of *grazia*/grace, emphasising its uplifting, elevating aspects, evoking its kind and forgiving nature, but always with a sense of non-disturbance or sternness, a kind of inconsolability that the word 'virgin' could express more or less. Yet the Hungarian word *tiszta*, connected to Russian *chist'*, emphasises better the cleanness, the unaffected, uncalculated oneness with nature, which has a connotation with dignity, respect and age as well: *tiszlet* ('respect'), *tisztesség* ('honour'), *tiszt* ('officer'). Petrarch read Plato, made a first attempt to have him translated into Italian and probably had an influence on the naming of the 'Nostra Donna', which was called the 'Regina Republicana' until Cosimo I. Plato treats Athens the city itself with compassion, just as Athena had a special disposition for her people, gifting and maintaining the rule of law and order that gave everybody a lenient forbearing, always on the side of orphans, concerned with the welfare of everybody, disseminating benevolence and generosity. In a similar vein in Florence, the Madonna could start to assert authority in the civil sphere as well; this legitimate authority was accepted for centuries (Paolucci 2004).

The word charisma can be traced back to Greek *charis*. This same word appears in the graces, the *charites*: Thalia the plentiful,

Euphrosyne the delightful and Aglaia the brilliant one are the Greek goddesses of attraction, alleviation and lightness. However, grace is at the same time a community value as the Hungarian/ Russian word for 'clean' shows. It instigates the guardian of grace to the total service of the social in the Republic, to a complete cooperation with the goddess for the benefit of the community. Grace is a gift of spiritual talent granted by powers to the recipients for the benefit of others. In doing so the graces are infiltrated in their entire being: the guardians become attractive, alleviating, radiant, sun-like people. Using their qualities of love, charity and beauty, the graces fasten the wheel of souls towards their bent. This is their famous circular movement, or dancing, which was so masterly drawn by Botticelli and Raphael in their *Three Graces*. During their dance the graces exchange the divine gifts and increase the divine knot that binds men and divine together into a mutual relationship of gift-giving (Wind 1958). There is a no question of a personal characteristic that enables somebody to impress and influence others, nor of a power-game of attraction and subordination. It is much more a moment of birth-giving, with toil and effort on both parts, revealed by the intense concentration on the faces of the Renaissance graces, and mutual release and alleviation, the generation of a solution in a nature-like oneness in pleasing and rejoicing without self-interest. The Weberian concept is too heavily focused on a special intervention by God on man's faculties and operation, and could not avoid the reference to accidents or transitory categories. Therefore his examples are often clumsy, as is often recognised.

The concept of a special, unsolicited divine eruption into human affairs is rooted in classical prophecy and the idea of a chosen people. However, a different perspective is gained if instead we turn our attention to the Platonic idea of the immortality of souls. According to this, the human soul is immortal, it can never be destroyed; if it is dying one time, another time it is born again, thus it can experience all things that ever existed. Therefore at any time one can evoke everything that one owns about virtue, holiness and perfection. In the Weberian perspective the everlasting pursuit of virtue turns into an idle undertaking or ruthless interference into nature. For Plato, the constant efforts made in the search or inquiry (*zetema*) after grace mobilises remembrance or recollection (*anamnesis*), through which man makes his own contribution to reaching nature's aboriginal qualities (Voegelin 1978). The human part cannot be reduced to a passive role of merely accepting fate; grace is not allowed to thrive in anyone, before one cultivates and develops oneself. An inactive person has a futile life from the perspective of divine: 'it is no wonder that [the soul] should be able to recollect all that she knew before about virtue and other things. For as all nature is akin, and the soul has learned all things, there is no reason why we should not, by remembering but one single thing – an act which men call learning – discover everything else, if we have courage and faint not in the search; since, it would seem, research and learning are wholly recollection' (Plato, *Meno* 81c–d).

What Weber is indicating with charisma is much closer to a magic power, a kind of captivating bewitchment, than grace. As grace continuously and eternally exists in everything, the question always rather concerns its conception. Plato calls prudence or wisdom (*phronesis*) the ability to recognise the dividing line between the divine and folly. The former turns every effort of the mind into participation, whereas the second in an opposite way brings division: 'the guidance of wisdom makes profitable the properties of the soul, while that of folly makes them harmful' (Plato, *Meno* 88d–e). Therefore Weber's spiritual power is like the void coming and going away. It can be given to shamans and then again taken away; though it has a constancy, it also has a strong schismatic power, so it is not so surprising that its description could fit communism as well: 'At the outset, "spirit" is neither soul, demon, nor god, but something indeterminate, material yet invisible, non-personal and yet somehow endowed with volition. By entering into concrete objects, spirit endows the latter with its distinctive power. The spirit may depart from its host and vessel, leaving the latter inoperative and causing the magician's charisma to fail' (Weber 1978: 401).

As always, Weber himself is extraordinary. His genius found something that nobody before him captured in the modern social and political sciences: the potential presence of void, also called Metis (khóra/poros/trickster/Sophist), in every created thing; the supple, indeterminate being that continuously operates between two opposite poles; a swift, ambiguous entity which – to dupe its victims – always assumes a mask. There is a danger inherent in its creative potency, as unproductiveness, passivity and paralysis remain after its possession. Its impact reduces the human space where it appeared into a state of confusion, resembling the primordial chaos. This chaotic power also has a lot to do with grace. But in his analysis of power, Weber tried to extend by generalisation the Christian concept of grace, which with this operation has lost its association with beauty, present in Plato. Without a power of oneness, it is impossible to consolidate with void. Spiritual power in liminality is turned into nude witchcraft, a brutal and barren surrealism exerting hypnotic influence over man with all kinds of spell, if it does not find its counterpart in man. 'But man is god, as soon as he is a man', emphasising the necessary similarities in between the two, the freedom from wants (Hölderlin 1994: 110).

The forged imitations that drive the schismatic and multiplicative aspects of void cannot be understood without the figure of underprivileged weakness: the trickster that simply submits itself to the flux of liminality, encapsulating in its very body the energy beyond and forging the process of transformation captured in rites of passage through the stages of separation, submission and re-aggregation into a plastic technicality. There is another point as well, though rarely emphasised: the parasitic side of technology, the fact that no machine that can function without an attentive person beyond it.

This has two consequences. First, that the machine is dependent on the human mind; and second, that the quality of this mind is quite indifferent from the point of the view of the machine. Therefore technicalisation softens and debilitates the energy of its masters by absorbing their attention and care. In this way it deteriorates their life, which becomes worse in condition and in quality, but more efficient from the perspective of the automatic purpose. This softened and subjugated being, caught in a web of mechanical networks, is quite weak, radically losing its dexterity and skilfulness.

5
Charisma in Eroticised Political Formations

Emptying oneself of one's self, thought or opinion, even at the price of pain, offering one's own body to suffering, these features marked the extraordinary senselessness and inner determination of the liminal, as Turner says about the *communitas*, giving liminal authorities the capacity to transmogrify initiands outside the boundaries of reality and meaningful conduct, a capacity that comes only from breaking the association of reality with ratio. In liminality, the essential fabric of social life is eradicated, being swapped for surrealistic desires and wills. Effervescence always occurs, the outburst of emotions, but meaning often fails to materialise in rites, as basic and sensuous passionate interests only widen the distance from the social, and so the rite produces an ever more absurd level of devotion to a cause without any comprehensible principle. The reason for the initiands' dedication becomes blurred, only mad beliefs and ill desires keep proliferating, calling always for more passionate interests and for the giving up of the sanity of one's mind, where for every trick there is always a new ritual pretext gaining legitimacy and then legalisation. In such cases the completion of the liminal stage, instead of re-aggregation, simply means that the initiands become themselves stalkers, scum and cheating figures, by now completely assimilated into a bullying system. Bateson notices that 'When pain is inflicted in other part of the initiation, it is done by men who enjoy doing it and who carry out this business a cynical, in a practical joking spirit' (Bateson 1958). An alienated, self-impoverished *wild man*, with a sharp perception and an even keener sense of mimicry, as Darwin noted about the aboriginals of *Island of Tierra del Fuego* (see Darwin 2010: 17), they are in a complete subservience to a 'denominator machine', where an original fractioning continues to produce further and further schisms automatically, in line with the mechanism of infinite series, as discovered by Archimedes. Just as cave painters lived and worked in the thrall of *imago dei*, stalkers want to transform the world into their own image: whoever took a leap into the void, giving up himself, being resigned to a broken, schismatic existence, wants to break others, entrap them in the same vicious circle of excruciating boredom and pain, justifying his own foolishness by theirs, and have a mocking laughter on this all.

A similar 'wild man' transformation was offered by the totalitarian regimes, though in a less straightforward manner. According to Lenin's well-known theory, a communist takeover is possible only at a single, precise moment. This is the instance in which the capitalist system is already established, but still weak. It cannot happen earlier, as the very basis of communist power, the working class, is a product of capitalism and without capitalism, there is no working class. However, it cannot happen after the consolidation of capitalism either, and for similarly obvious reasons. Thus, if there is too much delay in provoking the revolution of the proletariat, then capitalism takes too strong roots and becomes impossible to defeat. Although on the one hand this implies that the Western European working class movement has in fact missed the opportunity, thus containing a strong implicit criticism of Marx and Engels, on the other it provides a key for understanding the instauration of communist regimes as an alchemical 'opus' that holds fast onto the elements, no matter how much they may try to flee, until they are transformed under the tight grasp of the alchemist to the prescribed type. The alchemist usually concentrates his gaze on particular marks of weakness, looking for base, unsound elements in order to eject them, as a *pharmakos*.

Such a single precise instance in history can be defined as a 'liminal' moment, understood by anthropologists as the middle part of a rite of passage that transforms the status of the performers and their relationship to the world. The establishment of a communist regime everywhere closely conformed to the words of the Albertus Magnus (1193/1206–80), medieval theologian but also alchemist, according to whom things could be forced to change their character by the pressure of extremely harsh circumstances that weaken them: 'I wish to make myself clear because we know whereof we speak and have seen what we are asserting: we see different species receive different forms at different times: then it is evident that by decoction and persistent contact what is red in *arsenicum* will became black and then will become white by sublimation, this is always the case.'[1] In Lenin's theoretical framework this manipulation and deprivation of others appear in the sense that the takeover could become stimulated by provoking resistance and fight through further weakening the already weak. Gaining such a superior perspective about the possible experiential basis of establishing communist rule, however, does not have much to do with the economic realities of capitalism, or the actual evolution of the Western European working class movement. It is, rather, connected to an artificially generated descent into weakness, by aggravating the situation of those already weakened by the realities of capitalism, and of war. Griffin in his *Fascist Century* gives a similar account of the sporadic and capricious emergence of fascist regimes, which continuously relied as resources on magic, sensuality and ecstasy, all part of a palingenetic agitation of the weak, in order to take root in the public, fusing the public and the rebellious revolutionary self (Griffin 2007). He coined the term 'liminoidality' for situations that generate a continuous crisis, with endless purifications, sacrifice, re-sacralisation; a ritualised politics, without re-aggregation.

It is only under such conditions of utmost uncertainty and disorientation that liminal entities like a communist or fascist party can gain access to power, for two reasons. First, because the normal mechanisms of social and political order have become so weak that even the minuscule forces that a liminal party manages to mobilise are enough to grasp power. This, however, in itself would not discriminate a liminal takeover from a coup by any adventurers and bandits. In fact, the Bolshevik party made use of such figures in 1917 (Mauss 1992), and the post-communist conditions in many countries demonstrate a close affinity. However, the communist takeover proper had another crucial element, thus constituting an eminent 'ideal-type' of quasi-politics. Stalin was a double agent of the Okhrana, the Tsarist secret police, during the early period of his life: kidnapping, robbery, jail; always in prison, but always escaping, and with suspicious ease (Smith 1967); comparable to the allegations about the suspicious links Hitler had with the financial world. It was out of these experiences that a new type was created; the *schismatic occasionist*,[2] who conflates the genuine risks taken by a criminal double agent with the transmogrification of his own pangs of conscience into metaphysical sufferings, heroic escapades and the image of always coming out at the top. The resulting utmost deprivations that the Russian communists radiated in Western Europe were incomprehensible for representatives of the Western working class movement. They, however, rang a bell to an already weak population pushed to the brink of total collapse by the fourth year of a world war; thus it was possible to capitalise on their weakness. With communism a catastrophic escalation of violence and persecution occurred, causing their victims to lose grip on themselves and thus literally erupt the Bolshevik presence and force inside their minds and veins.

This kind of systematic alienation from existing bonds and the subsequent making of a subnormal personality are not novel: they are the regular interim results of every kind of initiation ceremony studied by anthropologists. In the communist case, however, the liminal stage became as if incarnate in the coat of a modern political system, strangely enough without any ethos or programme itself: their efficiency to deteriorate was repeated in the fascist case when similar esoteric organisations canalised a utopian fantasy of political revolution, inaugurating in a radically new age, a *palingenetic*[3] rebirth as Griffin used it. Bolsheviks achieved influence in Russia and later in Spain during the civil war not, as Borkenau wrote, because a few thousand workers had been convinced by the Bolshevik propaganda, diffusing the idea, rather because of a breakdown of the entire nation (Borkenau 1937: 282). Scholars like Merle Fainsod, who used the word 'totalitarianism', noted that this was an 'inefficient totalitarianism', as its efficiency was beyond any rational comprehension (Fainsod 1958). The demolishing forces of collectivisation (Conquest 1986), which meant killing and deportation, and the abolition of private property,[4] were all directed towards vague goals. Others like Koestler (1980) or Getty and Manning (1993) suggested that the communists were effectively using a particular technique for unearthing energy and directing it towards the undefined end: the technique of sacrifice. According to them this technique was not a merely secularised version of religious sacrifice, nor could it be conceived of as being channelled towards state building, as in these cases it would be just another attempt at the formation of a religion or a class, a national or a party identity. Rather, it was a sacrifice per se: a technicalised desire making, subjugating oneself to transform another entity into an automatic mode of existence; this was the totalitarian ethos that nourished itself by human desires, wishes and feelings. Gilles Deleuze says that *desire produces*, as a technological device: desire is automatically producing another desire mechanism, which he calls desiring machines (Deleuze 2004b: 232–4, 243).

Strangely enough, this totalitarian ethos is just a repetition of the broader ethos of modernity, sublimating every subject into and under state governance. For Claude Lefort (1986), the power of democracy is structured around an empty place. Taking this idea a step further, the entire history of modernism can be characterised by a Hermetic oscillation between reality and unreality; or rather two sides of the same unreal. On the one hand, modernism is a pure utopian fantasy world, with no connection to reality; even more, it is based on a deliberate escape from and rejection of reality that, nevertheless, is projected as being 'more real' than reality itself. This, in itself, would only render the entire development a proper subject for a case study in 'popular delusions' (Schaefer 1998).[5] However, on the other hand, alternating with utopian delusions, modernism always manifested a very subtle receptivity, a keen apprehension of strategic thinking, an attention to minute psychological detail. The apparent contradiction can be resolved by pointing out that these were both rooted in the same modernist experience of *irreality*.[6] For modernism, reality implied suffering (in the passive sense of 'experiencing'; see Greek *pathos*, also directly linked to 'pathology' and 'pathetic'), an imaginary escalation and exaggeration of reality, it necessarily led to a world of delusions, *nonknowledge* (Bataille 2001: 176);[7] but any experience of suffering, whether genuine or not, is strong enough to alter reality itself. All this produced a special, harrowing lifeworld, transforming those living this experience into extremely receptive and sensitive *occasionists*.

The corollary of this thesis can be now advanced: totalitarians need the feeling, whether of suffering or of happiness; they cannot exist without them. Thus, they need to produce it even when they are at the heart of reality, being in power: in leadership, possessing authority and state power. This is the moment when ignorance is forever lost; and in fact both communism and fascism sat quite uncomfortably in authority. Suffering is both a very genuine and a very strong experience, closely linked to sexual passion, often expressed in identical words (see Latin *passio*, Hungarian *szenvedély/szenvedés*): it has the power to transform the real into irreal, and vice versa, so it is a suitable stage for a successful alchemical opus. The exaggeration of suffering calls out for sacred substance, and the production of the sacred. Etymologically 'to sacrifice' means 'fare sacro',[8] or to make the sacred: it offers the possibility of becoming present in the world for those who otherwise have no presence, having no personality, just robotic obedience, and who cannot give gifts or presents. Sacrifice is thus forcing presence, a magical effort to 'produce' sacred, thus the reversal of creation, which is a divine gift. Sacrifice, a corollary to the cult of suffering, is the constructivist religion. But suffering and sacrifice will never create unity. The same is found with happiness or catharsis, in which we cannot recognise the neurotic, isolated Hitler, Mussolini, Stalin or Rákosi, with their photographs revealing an accelerated ageing process, demonstrating a growing gulf between their ten years younger self, reflecting their bankrupt regime and its emotions. Their highly chaotic irrationalism developed into a mechanised society and political system, living parasitically on the back of former cultures and civilisations. They created a technically equipped anarchical machine driven by regressed desires.

Totalitarianism can be understood as the proliferation of a scattered, fragmented divine realm, where a whole gamut of sacred elements like sacrifice, repentance, conversion, punishment, the cunning trickster, the sacred clown and the wild man gained shape through disintegration. The population had already suffered immensely in economic crises and World Wars. But now, with the establishment of a surrealistic power, its entire past, its history, identity and memory were demolished, until a new and total imprint was stamped by cunning thinking and trickery as the form of a new type of 'objective' existence. The idea 'the more it tortures the better, as the easier it allows to be saved' as a political technique was already used by the Inquisition and by Machiavelli. However, through totalitarian politics it became the exclusive manifestation of a 'sacred power', becoming factual as a result of the objectivation of another essential element of

liminality, the 'sacred clown' (Handelman 1990). The clown sacrifices in order *not to be* sacrificed, using the trickster saying 'today
for you, tomorrow for me', as the trickster knows only too well
that he can easily become the first scapegoat in the act of sacrifice,
as he is the eternal loser.

Still, the totalitarian devotion not just to violence but to self-
destruction until the last breath simply defies understanding. One
may object that, in the case of communist or fascist politics, understanding is irrelevant from the perspective of the social sciences. It
may be relevant for historians, as they attempt to understand the
motives and actions of persons of obscure and forgotten historical
periods. This book, however, is interested in understanding from a
different perspective. The problem is the following. Communism
and fascism were by no means unique cases, only examples of a
general modern phenomenon: that of being attracted by weakness. This was already characteristic of at least certain versions of
Christianity, and its various secularised versions only transposed
suffering into history. The question therefore is the extent to
which a similar phenomenon of devotion to suffering and the
broad overall process of (self-)punishment has impaired, and with
lasting effects, the sane mental powers of the political psyche by
subverting the means of political action into means of disintegration. I argued that all these elements contributing to the weakening of self-support are necessary and inevitable components of
the liminal stage in rites of passage, as without this the torturous
and deceitful artificial process could not have been imposed with
success. Void is the receptacle, which lives on desires, feelings and
emotions, and recreates them endlessly.

Here the impersonation of insanity and a freedom from social
bonds ruthlessly aimed at maintaining a never-ending readiness
for accepting the models proposed by the social illuminator.
The peculiarity of totalitarianism is not that the impostor was
accepted as a hero. This is again not special in itself: Ulysses was
a quite similar case; it is a standard attribute of the trickster that
it is also a culture hero (Hyde 1998). The strange thing was the
schismogenic nature of the solution. This was quite close to the
way communism identified itself with the phrase 'permanent revolution', except that it meant a never-ending frustration through
victimisation and self-victimisation, and the corresponding happiness for giving up oneself. This victimisation was also a peculiar

case, as it was based on the principle of surrogacy (the totalitarians on power and their ever more eager victims), and trying to find out just how far they (the totalitarians) could push their own style, because this style provoked fascination all around the world. At the beginning of the opus the trickster–initiator did not hurt anyone, the unending provocation of disorder was in itself not outrageous under real conditions; only by the passing of time did the model become truly wicked, as it fed and exasperated conflict into dizzying depths, and thus left the community no chance for recovery from sinking into the unreal.

Permanent revolution was not just a Trotskyist utopia, but the living everyday reality of totalitarian countries, though in a form different from the classic model: it involved the forced witnessing of extreme kinds of human behaviour, especially in the form of suffering; and then getting punished for such a guilty pleasure. All that is harmful and that did not yet exist at the precise moment of the totalitarians' take-over was about to become real by the acceptance of their cruel and vulgar style, where atrocities were presented with a sense of comedy and a smug satisfaction of being clever and successful, so radiating suffering all around, combined with a cunning ability to survive. Had they been real, nobody would have noticed them, as one can only negotiate with, debate, attack, persuade a real person and not a phantom; but they were not real, only representations of the liminal phase. This is how the survivors of the first purification, clear-up, *razzia*, finally understood the message: you have to copy their model; there is no other way for surviving than subordinating oneself to the bizarre new image, which exists though being repressed, is frustrated yet communal, is enlightened and secure, and still promises release from the drudgery of making decisions, by taking pains on oneself.

Sacrifice as subjugation technique

The technique of sacrifice explains the possibility of exchanging roles, both in victimisation and in the sharing of enthusiastic glory. Sacrifice channels and celebrates annihilation. It takes away life in order to promote life. However, the life that is offered for sacrifice is again the very same that rendered the committing of sacrifice possible in the first place, both being joined by a belief in the necessity of the sacrificial act, as if a serpent was biting its own tail.[9] This explains the increased importance attributed to the common understanding of the final aim: unity, or wholeness. Both sides of the statement are equally emphatic, as agreement with the sacrificial reasoning is just as crucial as agreement with the gigantic aim of the sacrifice. During totalitarianism all kinds of sacrificial acts were committed, directed towards the most different of objects. Social, political and economic life were reduced to an unending series of sacrifices that aimed at honour and glory, constituting a unification of eroticised individual bodies into a similarly eroticised political body. 'The party's blood is the blood of the workers'; 'The party must be not only respected but loved', these were typical words of the communist leaders,[10] where 'being loved' appeared as the main, erotic reinforcement between the communists and the nation, the path towards unity and wholeness. The passion for possessing each other, where all guilt is assumed (Fitzpatrick 1994: 31), and all knowledge is withheld, is the fascination between the party and the whole nation, while they are interchangeable with each other through their mutual subjugation.

Already at the start there were two problems with this ambiguously aggressive idea of sacrifice. Here we must go beyond the standard approaches, based on the early work of Mauss, like the works of Durkheim and even Girard. In particular, the interpretation offered by Girard, sacrifice being the foundation of culture, can be itself considered as merely a symptom of social or political disorder, much as the thinking of Newton merely reflected the liminal chaos of his times. It is rather necessary to address the political anthropological aspects of sacrifice in the context of *Eros*: both its multiplicative and regressive character, its divisive and fracturing qualities, but also its infinitude and circular completeness. The manner in which *Eros* might contribute to the steady, almost irreversible though unintended decomposition of form, eroding its meaning and substance, destroying its wholeness and shape, while being capable of creating, building up and elevating as well, is captured by Socrates in his speech: 'Love (*Eros*) was a great god, and was of beautiful things', though Diotima showed, using Socrates's own words, 'that god was neither beautiful nor good' (Plato, *Symposium* 201E). *Eros* stands 'halfway between skill and ignorance' (202A), where trickery and double thinking occur; *Eros* stands at every in-between or liminal level of the society, and might receive a special and dangerous significance through sacrifice as denominator, which releases a feeling of happiness with every division and break of limits.

The first problem is that because of its possessiveness, *Eros* objects to possessions that are other than its own, whether we are talking about the individual or the social level: 'desiring thing desires that in which it is deficient' (Plato, *Lysis* 221E). What *Eros* is deficient in, what Desire suffers from, is the deprivation from existence. Existence, the state of unity with itself, is a delightful condition that brings wholeness, wisdom, thought, kindled freedom and independence, while the 'standing reserve' is not a mode of being at all, but deprivation. Consequently, once *Eros* reaches its aim, it empties its target of all possessions, and thus of all independent being. The second problem is that this targeting is blind: 'the unjust will be as much a friend of the unjust and the bad of the bad, as the good of the good' (Plato, *Lysis* 222D). Cupid (*Eros*) is often pictured with bandaged eyes; the union of Penia and Poros (Cupid's parents) was the sexual union of a drunken man with a beggar women who possessed very little to attract a sober person; the drunkenness of Poros allowed him to be easily deceived by erotic substitution. In fact, substitution is still one of the main techniques of sacrifice and scapegoating, where one existence takes away the erotic pressure over the community (see also Robertson Smith 1969 [1894]). During sacrifice a dislocation of existence occurs, the unsettling of ordinary conditions, a breaking or fractioning.[11] During this destruction a transformation takes place, which transports the subjects of sacrifice – all those touched by the sacrifice and not just the victim – out of the existence into the 'standing reserve' (Heidegger 1977). In this drama the sacrificer and the sacrificed stand in seemingly sharp opposition: the former designs the act, whereas the latter is subjected to its violence.

It is important to notice that the sacrificer is the guiding person, the master of ceremonies, who is standing apart from danger, possessing knowledge of the sacrificial technique; just as in metallurgy it is the smith who makes the ore suffer to transform it into iron, whereas his subject is vulnerable, its integrity, the hardness of the stone, being softened up. But in fact they are both victims. The opposition between the sacrificer and the sacrificed is not absolute, as they both become involved in a technological vicious circle, based on self-defeat, because each initiation of the cycle reinforces this very first impulse. The self-contradictory first impulse of giving up oneself to prevent unavoidable pressure leads to the communication paradox that Bateson called double bind, as each act reinforces the desire for more subjugation, with no tendency anymore for harmony. As Euripides said with the Chorus in *Medea*: '*May moderation attend me, fairest gift* of the *gods. May* Aphrodite never cast contentious wrath and insatiate quar-relling upon *me* and madden my heart' (Euripides, *Medea* 640). Indeed, it is hardly possible to explain the incredible speed of the build-up of economic and military potential under commu-nism in any other way than a maddened heart with contentious wrath and insatiate quarrelling inflicted upon people, unearthing energy through sacrifice. Communism never moved away from its original co-ordinates, and during its whole history went around in cycles, obstinately searching for the impossible. Both its begin-ning and end were about sacrifice, where the circle started and finished, without any mental progress, confirming Girard's theory about the connection between situations of crisis and the mobili-sation of the sacrificial mechanism.

The combination of *Eros* with sacrifice is inevitable, as they are two sides of the same coin. One empties oneself out to give way to possession by *Eros*. In this manner it loses the meaning and substance of his mind, becoming idle and more foolish, deserving more slavery, because existence is not our concern anymore, 'in all those for which we have failed to acquire intelligence, so far will anyone be from permitting us to deal with them as we think fit, that everybody will do his utmost to obstruct us [...] we on our part shall be subject to others in such matters, which will be no concern of ours' (Plato, *Lysis* 210B). In particular, this act of self-evacuation is hostile to life, leading to a loss of the notion of the self, which is cultivated through the care of the self (the core of Plato's thought, according to Foucault and Patocka): 'Nor can you have a great notion of yourself, if you are still notionless' (Plato, *Lysis* 210D). To avoid this state implies a fight for things to belong to us, a striving for understanding until it may be entrusted with existence (Heidegger 1977); or as the essence of play, the struggle for excellence (Huizinga 1970).

Void has a hypnotising effect on things around it, as it tries to get in contact with them, to capture them, to infiltrate them, while with a good reason units try to avoid this contact, as it divides, breaks and annihilates everything that is contacted. The new palingenetic entities – new man, new order, new state, or new society – propagated by totalitarian movements generated hopeless desires through impossible demands, to be traced back to the first appearance of alchemy.[12] Their anthropological revolution incorporated rival and conflicting entities, feelings, emotions and desires into one big automatic machinery, which holds and nurses them into a perpetuated cycle of death and re-birth, into eternity. There is no proportion, measure, ratio or will in this mechanism, no word for man, as it became a constructed existence without meaning or goal. Its new cosmology means technicalised perfection, a hygienic hyper-being of sensations, without being disturbed by units that require maintenance, control and care. Consequently real, objective things, bodies, units are all hated, external disturbances that must be destroyed (annihilated, liquidated, liquefied), in order to transform them in a 'healthier', manipulable state'; a 'standing reserve' (Heidegger 1977). The totalitarians' ravenous hunger for technology and for efficiency becomes intelligible from the point of view of nemesis and harm, aiming for an accelerated way to reach the void. Their state sanctified violence and drove for a fully designed constructed world through social engineering (Verdery 2000); their massification, bureaucratisation, 'rationalisation', was the pursuit for a hygienised, clear and pure transformation into machine. They shared industrial concerns, the will to destroy and to rebuild, the purification of human existence, not only metaphorically but in a pragmatic manner, like the Katyn massacre. These were all part of one iron will to transform the weak matter, as embodied in concrete beings, into a strong eternal one, equivalent of the void. The megalopolises and hyper-countries all followed this logic of annihilation, damaging all things and units.

Getting hold of things is a way to express the formation and growth of any being. Obtaining something means you are learning and adopting, you are developing, you are struggling for your improvement, in the hope of becoming concerned with it.[13] Passionate interests subvert hierarchies; it is outside and against institutional structures, and can easily pay a costly price for the ambivalence introduced through undermining existence. Under liminal conditions, however, the terms of the game are inverted.

In the absence of a stable order, everything is ambivalent, no values are sacred, and perpetuating this state of affairs by tricky inventions like sacrifice is the easiest of things. Far from being brave path breakers, the communists tricked through the easy road, capitalising on the unsettled, riotous aspects of post-war conditions, turning the orgiastic excitement produced by pain and suffering into an autopoietic system, injecting the toxin of destruction *ad infinitum*, and in an ever-growing manner. The communist ideology, according to which not a single problem was ever solved in history except through class struggle, successfully transformed society, promoting destruction as a driving principle, having a perfect equivalent in racism, as Foucault realised so well (Foucault 2003). According to such a subversive way of thinking, only traitors and spies were conspiring against the regime, using insidious, dishonest or violent methods, thus conjuring up enemies to their own image. When *Eros* is joined to subversive thinking, it produces base and greedy monstrosities. Thus seditions and illicit rebellions occupied the scenery, with never-ending attacks on institutions, searching for the blame for the surreptitious erosion in the regime, setting people against each other.

'You can lose nothing but your chains' was the much-revered slogan of Marx. But it was never really understood to mean an alchemical process; that communism urged giving up existence, stepping outside everything that one has, losing violently one's possessions (Verdery 2000) for the sake of 'unreasoning sensation, since it becomes and perishes and is never really existent' (Plato, *Timaeus* 28A). In contrast to it, existence is a definite bonding; it is visible and tangible, it ties together the world with the distribution of milliards of bodies, each with well-defined form and identity; whereas the aim of sacrifice is their destruction. The opposite of reason and knowledge is the subjection to *Eros*, which launched fear, alienation, schism into the world through liminality, leading to the loss of the central object of life, producing an explosive relation to the self: 'reason and knowledge of necessity result. But should anyone assert that the substance in which these two states arise is something other than soul, his assertion will be anything rather than the truth' (Plato, *Timaeus* 37C).

There are two twists contained in the destruction of the soul: the first is destruction in sacrifice, the giving up of the self; the second is its mockery, to be punished and ridiculed because of a trust in and desire for the dismal. In this sense, communism was a perfectly coherent system: 'it ends up by forcing people to use evil ways even to escape it',[14] it overstepped the conditions of remaining safe and sound within existence, so it produced all kinds of corrupt alterations.

Subjugation to passionate interests cannot exist in the midst of warfare, as there the task of survival takes up all physical strength and mental energies; the same is true of the meaningful order of a state of law. Once a war is over, life soon returns to normal, and the mundane tasks of reconstruction replace the joint feelings of bewilderment and *ressentiment* for the guilty, as normality implies weariness of the excesses of paranoia. Therefore the communists enacted an elaborate series of manoeuvres to preserve and maintain confusion, into which during the first years after the war the population was hermetically locked, as entire countries were transformed into closed institutions with the closing of borders, facilitating the alchemical opus. The central trick, as already discussed, was played by the newly devised rituals of sacrifice, connected to pervasive trials as scapegoating rituals. However, I have not yet mentioned how people were tricked into the position of being outcasts, becoming just as ill-balanced and unsteady as their communist leaders (Horvath 1998).

An existence driven by fatigue, insomnia and solitude, the communist feeling of the tyranny of the universal, and a leap into the void complemented the hermetic isolation of communist Eastern Europe. Here the communists easily dressed up themselves in the role of the painful sufferer, who takes away the pain of mankind by way of their own suffering, imposing an ice-cold sacred terror of pressure on the population and on their own self for the sake of salvation. So communism never trusted its own people. It considered them as foolish victims of deception and self-deception, whom it had to teach how to seek out class interests behind all moral, religious, political and social ideas, declarations and promises. They never entered into a true relation with either good or bad. Instead they entertained their own separate peculiarity, being 'set apart' as the leading vanguard, a reverse of Mary Douglas's ideas about dirt, which protects the masses from the deteriorations produced by a desperate war, until it becomes transformed into a soft tissue of common sensation. Everything that happened afterwards was a direct outcome of this starting point. Communism became a unified system, where sacrifice was designed, ritualised, tested and tried in various modes; a 'lucid consciousness of horror' (Andrle 1992), which mechanised sacrifice into a state institution, with complete infiltration of the social body, in the name of equality between all ranks, thus between the people and the Party, resulting in their easy substitution with each other. The victim *as* victim thus was cast into the role of the protagonist, the one who took the place of the sacrificer, the one who got involved with and substituted in the sacrifice, who could preserve the order of things by implicating himself into pain, and whose acts continuously had to be re-enacted, as the system could not survive without victims: whether as enemies to be destroyed, or as sufferers to be saved. The victim thus redeems the whole: and *you*, each one of you, must play this role. Until its very end, communism never ceased to emphasise the attributes of victimhood and use it in the same breath. For its entire duration, communism relied upon the gradual infiltration of a weak and subjected being into the heart of the social body: *the loser*, the suffering servant with its eternal connotations of unreliability and vengefulness.

Emptying oneself to passionate interests

Totalitarianism flew in the face of anthropological certainties by amputating the social from the moral, emotional and aesthetic dimensions, where 'there is no symmetry or want of symmetry greater than that which exists between the soul itself and the body itself' (Plato, *Timaeus* 87D). Such an opposition to anthropological fundamentals is not unique in itself historically, but it always brings as a result idleness and eroded values. Whenever symmetry is decomposed between these substances they became reversed and corrupted. Passionate interests have no enjoyment of themselves, they need opposition, the perpetual exchanging of places: 'What I state is this, – that in children the first childish sensations are pleasure and pain, and that it is in these first that goodness and badness come to the soul, but as to wisdom and settled true opinions, a man is lucky if they come to him even in old age, and he that is possessed of these blessings, and all that they comprise, is indeed a perfect man' (Plato, *Laws* 653A). Passionate interests need rightful training: 'this consent, viewed as a whole, is goodness, while the part of it that is rightly trained in respect of pleasures and pains, so as to hate what ought to be hatred, right from the beginning up to the very end, and to love what ought to be loved' (ibid., 653B). But the continuous and spontaneous agreement between different egoisms, central for various modernisms, whether called social contract or consensus, liberty, democracy or reason, were never more than a mimed copy of the authentic, which mixed different types of pleasure, blending utilitarian constraints with overall harmony. Such egalitarian public concerns eventually occupied the social, in a genuine sense of possession, as the social became increasingly filled with proselytising zeal. Technical discoveries, in particular in the field of mass communications, helped the quick spread of the distorted vision about what is right and just. A thirst for power/knowledge (Foucault 1980b) enframed the social, transforming its content into a standing reserve that could be mechanically reproduced and substituted.

The first infinite series in mathematics, discovered by Archimedes, illustrates but does not explain this point. The infinite geometric progression by the ratio of ¼ starts with a first fraction and continually adds further sequences to this first one until exhaustion breaks down all resistance in the unit, as the denominator annihilates it, possessing it; thus a harmonious *ratio*, established between equally self-contained natural numbers, is turned into fraction, with its numerator and denominator: the denominator 'breaks', just creating the 'fraction', and the numerator only counts the number of fragments. This is well captured in the etymology and conceptual history of 'proportionality', which in modern times came to replace *ratio*, as that word lost its meaning through 'rationalism': Latin *portio* 'portion' developed out of *pro ratio*, implying a distribution of segments, as if dividing up the spoils derived from the break-up of a unit; and so 'proportionality' only implies a certain imposed principle of distribution on these fragments, no longer the original *ratio*, the animating harmony. This sequence, which diminishes properties until they are cancelled out of existence, dissolving one unit at a time, continually adding further sequences until full exhaustion is reached by the appearance and triumph of any system (as it is captured in the 'salami tactics' of Mao), is equal to the undermining of borders, and is exemplified by humans' giving up of reasoning. This liquefies the mind and leads to the loss of care, which implies a resistance to giving up stable, meaningful bonds, until the same desires cover the space opened up and then left behind; that is to say, it leads to totalitarian thinking, where everything is driven by fatigue, insomnia and solitude; a leap into the void of a subjugating system unified by passionate interests. The injecting of the toxin of self-destruction *ad infinitum*, for always more conquest, puts the worst in positions of leadership. This leads to more humiliation, as they gain position over you, and even more possession, as they start to dominate every angle of your mind: if you fight against them, even more so than when you are for them.[15] Here cruelty and injustice become highly functional, as they take away the sanity of your mind to promote bland mechanism, improperly called as 'rationality': but the mind that is offered for idleness is again the very same that rendered schematic thinking possible in the first place. To function, this set-up needs a joint belief in the necessity of such acts, thinking, logic and epistemological frame. We have been reduced to use a faulty 'rationality' in trying to understand and engage with these liminal authorities; we have become infected by this mechanical frame of mind while becoming fascinated by a dreadful unreality that we cannot understand. It is difficult to resist the suggestion that resistance is futile, and that choosing to following Socrates is the only human option.

Communism was a splinter movement before 1917 and receded into practical insignificance after 1989, or at least after 1991. Yet in between it became a dominant force over one-third of the planet, threatening the rest. And it still presents several enigmas that include the following. First, the question of its democratic or totalitarian character: how could it always claim that it was more and not less democratic than Western 'merely liberal' democracies? Second, its striking appeal: how could it exert such a fascination over such a large part of the Western cultural and intellectual avant-garde for so much of the past century? Third, what is the exact reason for its sudden and almost bloodless collapse? Finally, why and how does its dissolution not simply mean its complete end, rather only its 'liquification', which gives it an even more wide-spread and in-depth latent effect, and not only in the areas that were formerly under its control?

Robotic obedience

I gave an account of the effect of the 'passionate interests', using Tarde's expression, or *Eros*, as Plato called it, that invests totalitarianism with a possessive and conquering zeal, allowing it to captivate, or literally capture, the mind. This book was interested in the technique used to achieve this goal, and how deeply this mechanism was rooted in modernity. This can be illustrated by the everyday routine of pat-downs in today's airports, where one might see the case how people lost their rights for integrity, an undisturbed mind, social bonds, friendship and solidarity, by purchasing a ticket, which sets up a direct contractual position between themselves and liminal authorities, in airport authorities.[16] We all know that complaints about such degrading, obscene invasions of the self do not arrive either at the Brussels Commission on Human Rights or at the American Congress. However, thousands of people are mistreated daily, exposed to humiliation and traumatised by the activity of the incommensurable liminality. The liminal practices effected on the social go against every tenet of the social; they are performed by employees systematically rendered dumb and shut off from all norms of human decency as a matter of professional obligation, continuously doing something that not even a law enforcement officer is allowed to do, at least without clear suspicion of unlawful behaviour. But such employees are cut off from reality, unable to read or interpret differentials, often power-mad agents in the midst of a peaceful environment of thousands of holiday tourists, businessmen or conference travellers. The silence is contractual, people allow themselves to be molested, they subjugate themselves to indecent groping, they tolerate hideous sexual abuse because they lost their reason to stand up. First, because they signed a contract by buying their ticket, they are in equal rights with the authority. With this contractual basis they come to share the logic of searching for possible gaps in security; also, they have a common interest of reaching the targeted flight. Their interest intervenes no doubt, but the attention is less tight in understanding that this also means the agreement viewing the world as a net of terror, cyber security, crimes and disasters where they are mere subject and object of the terror, subjugated and violated, much before the terror effectuates. What is more, the terror is conditional on their subjugation. If they rebel against the rough, fumbling incompetence, the unwanted touching that crosses the line of the obscene in every sense of the word, in front of the eyes of their children and hundreds of unknowns, they become themselves the violators of law. They are forced to throw out health and beauty aids before entering, removing shoes before arriving at the security gates. They become treated as war objects, the idle and mindless ones. Suddenly they are shut off from reality, family bonds, friends and colleagues, job and hierarchy, respect and dignity. They are reduced to a sweating, fearful body exposed to search.

Although they all know, both parts are conscious that the whole procedure is useless and inefficient, as there is no way to find exposits stuffed into body cavities; they know that a flight attack has the lowest risk in human accidents. But still about 20% of passengers go through body handlings deliberately on the threshold of the self, against the property of the mind, the most secret parts of our history, memory being in love, having children. The constitutional right for oneself, house, papers and effects against searches and seizers is broken, because the new judgement and determination is made that it must be destroyed. Even one's disagreement or showing disapproval brings a fine of many thousands in penalty.

Everything happens smoothly; people become docile, idle and mindless; they act as if they suddenly become shut off from reality, family bonds, friends and colleagues, job and hierarchy, respect and dignity. They are reduced to state bodies, exposed to the searching law in order to become a new generation of technological body, with sharpened sensations, indestructible health and eternal life.

All this does not happen entirely outside knowledge and awareness. Both sides are conscious of the fact that the whole liminal procedure is producing automatic multiplications, but still both sides are running after the satisfaction of desires, which are eager to occupy any place that is left unguarded, rendering possible further growth and development, as illustrated by Archimedes' discovery of infinite series. This is how Hitler grew into the Noble Dark Knight of the Germans, or Stalin into the Saviour of the Russians. Both became almost exactly as their people, massified through liminality, imagined them, because they happened to be at the place where they were not supposed to be. This is a typical interloper characteristic, conveying all those inhibitions, anxieties, fears and worries to the masses that need salvation even at the price of subservience. Subservience can be considered an anthropomorphic nonsense; at least the Greeks considered it so. But it has had a meaning since alchemy. Artificial creation is simply not possible without it, being connected to the world of indifference and senselessness that has no movement, as it is frozen, barren and uncreative. It is the stage of the liminal *nigredo* in alchemy, the destructive, liminal stage. Yet it is indestructible, reproductive, multiplicative and sensual, both for pain and pleasure: 'nonsense enacts a donation of sense', says Deleuze (Deleuze 2004b: 81).[17] Given the particular obsession of modernity for the capitulation of the self, rooted in the idea of self-sacrifice, the achievement of subservience is not peculiar anymore. Self-sacrifice suffered a particular inflexion and became widely used all around Europe as an exclusive and increasing slogan in modernism, becoming a schismogenic double of egoism, animated by the sense of guilt felt because of the pursuit of passionate interests, promoted in the public sphere by various kinds of extremist political ideologies and movements in the twentieth century. This ended up being, with the 'serving the people' idea (Horvath forthcoming), a major justification of totalitarian forms of government, influencing both left- and right-wing politics, and eventually shaping social and economic policy all over the world, in a manner whose depth is still not fully recognised.

This represented a major remodelling of the classical concept of politics, which was based on the concern with friendship (von Heyking 2008). The new concept implies that the common good can be realised not only through friendship and the promotion of a harmonious relationship between citizens, but through a particular concern of the state with 'caring' for the happiness – even the 'soul' – of its citizens (Gordon 1987). The classical concept was replaced with a drive to offer oneself up for the sake of others, whether as somebody who cares or as somebody who is cared for: the positions can be reversed, just as in the case of sacrifice. The cultivation of the relationship between the state and the community was transferred to the field of political communication, image building, propaganda or political marketing, all deployed to 'care' for satisfying the citizens' pleasures through increasingly institutionalised personal instruction and guidance. It was considered a logical outcome of the 'serving the people' idea that the driving forces of social life should be 'collective values', the only way to overcome the conflict of private interests, because only these values allow for the efficient construction of an organic nation, well reflected in Durkheim's idea that 'organic solidarity' can be reached through the division of labour. The reversal that took place with communism was the mirror image of modern politics, which turned the sublime into its foolish torsion by interpreting it verbatim. Judging the depth of every heart and ruling over desires remained core interests of the communist regimes as well: when we interviewed political instructors, members of the district-level Communist Party apparatus, in Budapest in 1987–8, this was one of the most astonishing results (Horvath and Szakolczai 1992).

Considerations related to the economic prosperity of nations were re-formulated accordingly to this desire for subservience. Such considerations were important especially as means for attaining the crucial goal: strengthening and promoting the ideal unity of the state (or the public – the two can easily metamorphose into each other) over the citizens. But as time elapsed, the substance of this 'unity' became less and less elevated, if ever it was, as the quality of existence diminished, together with the quality of the ruling elite. Eventually, it arrived at the lowest common denominator, following the principle of corruption as 'joint fractioning', the political foundation characteristic of our times: pain and suffering, as propagated originally by the communists. Since the beginning, from their early appearances in the nineteenth century, the communists were a peculiar kind of people with a particular faith that differed, though only slightly, from the general fascination with 'serving the people'. The difference lay in their mystical longing for giving themselves up, exposing themselves to suffering and dislocating their integrity by offering up their own body for the sake of a 'big structure'. This elevates a state of disorder onto the pedestal of order; fragments that lack a delightful proportion both in relation to themselves and in relation to each other result in a vacuity, but a vacuity that actively brings decay and more pain through infinite schisms. But as an ethos, the desire for subservience has stalked around for a very long time, as this book has tried to show.

However, there was dissent from the fold, like the nineteenth century French anthropological sociologist Gabriel Tarde. He belonged to the classical type of scholar, warning against the attribution of an integrative role to 'structure'. Accordingly, the social structure is quasi-empty, implying only narrow, standardised connections that are of no value compared with the concrete and the local, with the sympathy animating the social tissue, and with day-to-day relations and proven friendships; everything that is not concrete represents useless totalisation. Nevertheless, Tarde's work remained a lonely voice in the wilderness, as 'integration', the 'co-ordination' of social functions and social institutions, and every type of call for the transmission of the personal into 'big' structures and 'social movements' sadly swallowed up his ideas. Tarde was sidelined for many decades. His quarrels with Durkheim and his school remained unnoticed and an entire science, structuralist–functionalist sociology, was built up on examining fictional, empty relations, which no longer preserved the delight of their natural composition, having no enjoyment of themselves anymore, the regular political constitution becoming dissolved. Consequently, when finally the communists, with Lenin, set themselves the ultimate aim of abolishing the state, they used organised and systematic violence against political authority; they aimed at an absence, but aimed it infinitely, so all this violence was used against concrete people, without any end, but with ever-growing and debilitating pressure.

How much this technique is rooted in modernity

During the Enlightenment the commercial harshness and hysteria of capitalism hijacked, through 'passionate interests', the central and difficult values associated with European culture. This eventually resulted in the complete dissolution of the classical ideas of reason and knowledge, leaning back to antiquity, and their connections with the care of the self, replacing them with an obsession with self-abandonment in the service of ideological considerations for the sake of the 'public' (Koselleck 1988). The Enlightenment, this strange, artificial machinery that freed people from pre-existing moral commitments, generating a wholesale disengagement from the social, was paradoxically hinged through its every effort on the principle of 'rationality'. This was used to justify the crudest egoism and self-interest, investing every living being with a possessive and conquering zeal, very far away from rational temperance or harmonious *ratio*. Capitalism was born without protest, although also without approval, once everything had been processed at the end of the eighteenth century: that is to say forged and turned around. And once European societies were persuaded about the rightness of this change, justifying the unjustifiable, they were enveloped in an emotional storm of unsatisfiable interests. Mechanical rationalisation on the one hand, and the mere stimulation of the senses on the other, guided the exclusively utilitarian vision of society, as was masterly analysed in his *Protestant Ethic* book by Max Weber (Weber 2002). The accumulation of absent content only further animated a continuous process of destruction, progressing from one mobilising campaign to another. The Age of Revolutions periodically dragged populations into the fearful passions of terror, moaning and suffering, continuously at war with the stable.

The nineteenth century was already ripe for the establishment of totalitarianism, repeating *ad nauseam* the old saying that life itself is an illness from which one should be cured by offering oneself as a sacrifice for salvation by 'serving the people', a converted version of the Enlightenment.[18] As for the weakest link, Eastern Europe, where everything is considered intellectual, and thus where all things become over-intellectualised, thus abstract, impressing this non-quality on everything,[19] this converted suggestion had a deadly appeal, especially when spatial liminality came to be combined with temporal liminality. Being endowed with a faith and a desire actively to subscribe to and promote the intellectuals' own version of the world, advocating a giving up of one's personal integrity and entrusting everything in the hands of the collective, is very much a way to undermine one's existence. This geographical area, also called 'the lands in-between' (Kumar 2001: 1),[20] was easy prey to 'passionate interests', becoming a realm of emotions and passions, where reason is easily suspended; a territory of alienation and rootless fatalism (Dostoyevsky). All these features now became enlisted in the service the creation of a standing reserve, with an impossible existence of suffering rendering real and thus true the vision of intellectuals.

When the occasion finally came, after the World Wars, to put into practice the ideas dreamed up by the philosophers of the Enlightenment and their followers, giving power to those liminal agents who could ascertain their truth, there resulted only a softly open receptiveness to a new unexpected impetus characterised by the fascination with the weak: an ugly uninvited quest for the feast of pure intellectual idealism (Kundera 1984). Passionate interests are invasive, targeting the soft and the defenceless with a dissolving, annihilating power; a power that at a fundamental anthropological level, in antiquity as much as in modernity, is rooted in memories, images and dreams. The basic difference between the original and the copy can thus easily evaporate, leading to the conflation of genuine and fake emotions, dragging down the incautious into abject slavery and ugliness, as 'pleasure was itself infinite, and belonged to the class which, in and by itself, has not and never will have either beginning or middle or end' (Plato, *Philebus* 31A). Passionate interests are not functional, not even necessary; their power is in copying and proliferating opportunities that spread with infinite, contagious speed. All the possible states of the void, all passions that are both fearful and unavoidable, like pain and pleasure, fear, anger and lust, become vehicles for seduction, resulting in subservience.

We can appreciate passionate interests better if we consider *Eros*. Homer said about Ananke, as cited in Plato's *Symposium*, about the power of *Eros*: 'She spreads not, only on the heads of men' (*Iliad*, XIX, 92–3). *Eros'* sensitivity, which searches out for genuine properties that are inside a soft tissue and thus can be attacked, ready for possession or take-over through infiltration, is a very delicate poison, which can paralyse. Its training is different from restraint, thus it cannot be restricted to morals or the law. Rather, it poses more fundamental questions of goodness in one's entire being, as *Eros* possesses the power of identity deprivation or integrity dissolution, causing idleness.[21] *Eros* easily captures the outsider who 'just does not like the way things are down here' (see Alberti, *Momus*) in a double bind (Bateson), as *Eros* sets up faculties and takes possession of the self with the strong poison of alienation from the social; it empties the mind, but also troubles it with depravities, urging the infiltrated mind to repeat similar conquests itself, thus increasing the distance from wisdom and prudence.

There is an ample literature on paralysed societies, starting with Gibbon's classic analysis of Byzantium. This was written in the much renowned eighteenth century, which started just after a revolution, the 'Glorious' English one, and finished just about 100 years later with another revolution, the French one, while in between it was ruled by 'enlightened' monarchs, famed for their passions, greed and ignorance. But contemporary societies do not often get this label, probably because it does not fit into

Enlightenment optimism and the belief in progress. This is why the phenomenon of communism held such a fascination for so many people; it seemed to exist as if behind a glass, at a mysteriously undefined level of busy events, where no sounds or noises could trace the interactions among groups and parties, the contours being blurred, only passions burning on their own, without giving any heat. Behind the unforgettable awkwardness of communism, which shocked both its adherents and opponents, it was not easy to recognise its most distinguishing feature: terrifying emptiness. One of the few was Borkenau, who recognised already in 1939 that communism was unable to escape from idleness. During its entire existence communism was out of the touch with the world, breeding in it a spirit of lawlessness, yet continuously passing judgements on it. Neither the communist vanguard nor the population under its control ever managed to systematise the direction in which their joint deeds were carrying them. Where were the final ends? What was the limit of their co-operation, apart from a contempt for any existence: honour, pride, rank, fraternity, virtue, solidarity, right opinion, true reasoning, wisdom and thought, its only determination being derived from presumptions of being attacked?

Already after the first years of the deadening communist rule, through nationalisation, the trials, deportations, detentions, the tectonic shocks of the disaster, the communist presence was profoundly stamped on the nations under its control. After the Second World War, the passing away of the immediate danger did not lead to a clarification of a common direction, but only intensified the disappearance of distinctive forms, leading to a general disorientation characteristic of liminality. In this vagueness, pressures, both emotional and physical trauma, ensnared people, whatever could intensify the unifying malleability inside society. Motley and depraved habits inflicted fear upon people in order to unite them in weakness. In this way, everyone under communism lived on the edge, constantly beyond themselves, so danger became a part of daily life, ending up being routinised and endured with a fatal taken-for-granted factuality, with no knowledge of the reasons why all this commonly shared pain and suffering was necessary, apart from the imperative to accept robotic obedience.

The year 1989 was a turning point in modern history, not because it implied an epistemological break, but because it showed that such a change might happen without a revolution or a radical split, or any other action that took place to upset the previous regime. Communism collapsed without guidance or a master plan; it perished simply because it never really existed, it had no idea how it might oppose its own exhaustion; nothing remained to be destroyed or undermined by 1989, things having become levelled to a uniformly dull and boring state. It lacked wisdom, knowledge and proportion (*ratio*), which makes every living thing real, and which prevents things from dying from exhaustion, as it submitted itself to the void. Arguably, post-communist political discourses continued the same formulae of their precursors, repeating the same discourses of democracy, collective, state, nation, security, equity, rights, changing only the intensity of their combination (Urban 2010). But paradoxically, as a final undeserved triumph, Eastern Europe has learned to devalue the values that make up the modern world as well.

These days it seems to be considered as self-evident all around the world that the main spiritual cohesive force of any political community is the amount of common suffering. Electoral campaigns increasingly hinge upon slogans that delight in evoking images of deprivation – whether in the form of taxes, various crises or simply the pains associated with living – thus giving up living spaces for occupation by passionate interests. Contemporary societies are undergoing a kind of sensual self-transformation in which the very foundations of the community are shifted from noble to base symbols and feelings, transforming the political body into a community of senselessness: submitted, enslaved (to passions) and weak, who desperately need guidance, help and protection, which the political parties and their 'charismatic' leaders are more than happy to provide, thus bringing to the fore the underground, with which everybody has become utterly fascinated. It is a fact that all those who base their power on weakness will lose it once their subjects regain their force. Therefore, they are very keen to maintain the electorate's subjection and submission: *by their own weaknesses*, especially their feelings of suffering and victimhood, throwing sensuality into the affairs of the state. Without any doubt this installs a schismatic logic at the very foundation of social life, a genuine double bind situation: a search for weaknesses, but only to reinforce and proliferate them, using the denominator force of erotic sensuality, which takes over any space that is left uncared for and unguarded.

This results in a very particular kind of play, in which there will be no clear winners or losers anymore, as the more you suffer from various deprivations, the more you win. This leaves open the possibility that, in the absence of reality, obscene tyranny could come to rule the scene, as was evidently already part of the game in the cases of communism and fascism. They both manifested a very subtle receptivity, a keen apprehension of strategic thinking, and attention to minute psychological details, through which they could extract people out of themselves and forge them into passionate obedience to fabricated interests. The apparent contradiction between fascism and communism can be resolved by pointing out that both were rooted in the same total experience of *irreality*, just as happened with the obscene Shaft scene, with metallurgy and alchemy, and then with Renaissance humanism and the Enlightenment. As totalitarian reality implies suffering (in the passive sense of 'experiencing', see Greek *pathos*, also directly linked to 'pathology' used by Koselleck as pathogenesis for the modern world and 'pathetic' as sensation), an imaginary escalation and exaggeration of reality, it necessarily leads to the world of delusive emptiness; but any experience of suffering, whether genuine or not, is strong enough to alter reality itself. All this produced a very special, harrowing surrealism, transforming this liminal experience into the infinite fractioning of the natural and the rational.

Notes

Editorial Preface to Modernism and Charisma

1. Letter from Vincent van Gogh to his brother Theo, written in Arles and sent 24 September 1888. Source: *Vincent van Gogh: The Letters, Van Gogh Museum*, Amsterdam, http://vangoghletters.org/vg/letters/let686/letter.html

Introduction

1. See several papers devoted to these concepts in *International Political Anthropology*, including the special issue on liminality May 2009 (www.politicalanthropology.org), and Horvath (2010); Horvath and Thomassen (2008); Szakolczai and Thomassen (2011); Wydra (2008, 2011a).
2. For similar approaches, see in particular Giesen (2010); Sakwa (2006, 2009); Urban (2008, 2010).
3. See in particular Griffin (2007, 2008).
4. See also Szakolczai (2009).
5. See Derrida on void (1995), or Baudrillard's application of the void to modernity: 'in reality we are accelerating in a void, because all the goals of liberation are already behind us' (1993: 3).
6. Tocqueville saw equality as a depraved taste of modernity, which impels the weak to bring the strong down to their level, and which makes men prefer equality in servitude. See 'Political Consequences of the Social State of the Anglo-Americans', in Tocqueville (2011).
7. Max Weber, in his *The Protestant Ethic and the Spirit of Capitalism* (2002) derives the main principles of modern economic and political conduct from religious ascetic ideas and its maxims.
8. Weber on Charisma (1978: 216–9; 241–8).
9. See also Deleuze's exemplary definition of schizophrenia, whose 'pure lived experience' is outside the logic of sensible qualities', as 'lived experience does not correspond with their feeling. They feel intensity and the passing of intensities, but their body is crossing a threshold of intensity. […] A schizophrenic is still crossing it [experience], going above it, beyond it' Deleuze (2004a: 238).
10. See Parmenides, for whom only a form could be known and recognised as an object of knowledge: 'It is necessary to assert and conceive that this is Being. For it is for Being, but Nothing is not. These things I command you to heel' (Parmenides, Fragment 5 in Coxon 1986: 54).

11. About the way marginality and liminality can mutate into each other, see Szakolczai (2009).

12. The political anthropologist Pierre Clastres formulates in a similar way the love of the subjects for their masters, writing about Etienne de la Boetie's *Discours*, which is the secret of domination, their own love for their own subjugation (Clastres, 2010: 171–89).

13. '[So] long as the two things are different, neither can ever come to be in the other in such a way that the two should become at once one and the same thing and two' (Plato, *Timaeus* 52C-D, as in Cornford 1937: 193).

14. For details about schismogenesis, see Horvath and Thomassen (2008).

15. In his book, Koselleck developed the term 'pathogenesis' to explain how the Enlightenment sowed the seeds of political tensions that led to the French Revolution. He pictures the Enlightenment intellectuals as uprooted groups of onlookers who fostered the divorce from reality characteristic of their age.

16. About this, see Voegelin (1978).

17. About Tarde, see a recent issue of *International Political Anthropology* (2011, No. 1).

18. For more details about this, see Horvath (forthcoming).

19. The term is from Szakolczai (2009: 221–6).

20. The link between metallurgy, religion and the rise of new kind of political authorities in the Bronze Age has been recognised: 'Myths and religious texts indicate the strong associations that people in the past drew between metal and divinity, temporal authority and moral imperatives, in which the significance of metal and metalwork extended well beyond their sheer economic importance' (Peterson 2009: 191).

21. Famously, Clastres refused the separation between the social and the political, considering the two as one. Societies remained under the sign of their own law, autonomy and political independence, excluding social change in this sense, so remaining an undivided unit. This is why submission is unknown between members in a pre-historical a society (Clastres 2010).

22. This logic concerns not only the denial of individuality, the oneness of being, but also that such violation generates *Eros*, 'towards the furthest bounds of possibility' (Bataille 1998: 24).

23. See Griffin (2007).

24. In a recent book, Zizek made the following claim about totalitarianism: 'the notion of "totalitarianism", far from being an effective theoretical concept, is a kind of *stopgap*: instead of enabling us to think, forcing us to acquire a new insight into the historical reality it describes, it relieves us of the duty to think, or even actively *prevents* us from thinking' (Zizek 2011: 3). The case, however, is the exact opposite, as Zizek alleges: it is he who wants to prevent us from seeing clearly, ignoring the fact that 'total' is the best word to describe the power characteristic of these states, who exactly wanted to control everything, every thought, every element of everyday existence. Zizek therefore attempts to prevent us identifying the *nulla* who wanted to acquire control, the non-entities who were the

communist agitators and leaders, and who could only be taken seriously by their – absurd, irreal – pretence for *everything*. Fascism and communism were both unreal, *thus* they produced a total and totalising feeling. But as far as there is no better expression for these *new ovens*, which work for the *greater than one*, heating and cooking entities into transformation, signs of *chaos*, the brotherhood of *salami tactics* and *kill-out squad*, we use the word 'totalitarian'. The term 'totalitarianism', coined by Borkenau in 1934, as a stunning analytical feat, perceiving *then* the common features of Italian fascism and Soviet Bolshevism, captures this perfectly. Thus it remains a necessary tool for social and political analysis.

1 Squaring the Liminal or Reproducing it: Charisma and Trickster

1. The connection of order with beauty as the basic characteristic of Forms defines an undertaking related to the origin of philosophy, a discipline that was concerned with due measure as the ruling principle of the world. For the Presocratics, the rule of forms represents the immortal element in nature: beauty is imprinted on every living being. Plato furthermore emphasised that any deviation from this rule leads to disorder, resulting in an erratically ordained life that is governed by fraud, counterfeit and trickery (Plato, *Laws*). Repositioning (C. Schmitt) is the defining feature of the Trickster (Radin), who breaks all existing bonds, natural or cultural, and recreates a multiplicative *techné* (Heidegger) out of nothingness, or the *nulla*.

2. The cave paintings, these particular projections of the prehistoric mind, can be considered as mental imprints, similar to Tarde's 'photographic plate' (Tarde 1993: viii, 75, 80–1), which – instead of simply indicating light and shade – stamp low or high sensuality onto the surface, transmitting an experience of happiness, in harmony with the understanding of beauty. Intimacy with lawful order brings that gracefulness to the shapes and movements, which generate weight in things and sharpen the quality of the worthy objects, forming memories and traditions that overcome mere flux. For a particularly captivating introduction to the world of cave art, see the Lascaux home page at http://www.lascaux.culture.fr/#/fr/00.xml, which guides through the entire cave.

3. The delightful experience of visiting the Chauvet cave is captured in a 2009 film by Werner Herzog, 'The Cave of Forgotten Dreams'. The cave cannot be visited.

4. Altamira is fully Magdalenian, whereas Lascaux has been partly dated back to the Solutrean. In the discussion of archaeological material offered in this chapter, the following texts were also consulted: Beltrán, Antonio (1999); Chauvet, Jean-Marie, Eliette Brunel Deschamps and Christian Hillaire (1996); Clottes, Jean (2003, 2006); Clottes, Jean and Jean Courtin (1996); Davenport, Demorest and Michael A. Jochim (1988); Vialou, Denis (1998); Whitley, David S. (2008).

5. About this, see Huizinga (1970).
6. Note the similarity here with Minoan Crete, where the overwhelming majority of seal impressions and frescoes also depict animals.
7. In fact Plato's debating practice, the *diairesis*, begins in the same way: both participants, A and B, believe in the same thing, in the same principle. Until A has found an indifferent statement that B could not accept, the debate cannot start.
8. See, for example, the video of a Bear fight at http://www.metacafe. com/watch/1147549/great_grizzly_bear_fight. The scene is originally from *Grizzly Man* (2005), a film composed by Werner Herzog.
9. This is captured in the idiosyncratic figure of the 'stalker' in Andrey Tarkovsky's 1980 film *Stalker*; a *memento mori* of communism.
10. Wrestling, a genuine arch-sport, still preserves these characteristics. The central aspects and techniques of wrestling fights, like 'joint lock', 'takedown' and 'throws', are modes of liberation from a magic bondage, spelt by a sorcerer. Note that in Italian the word for wrestling, *lotta*, following Latin, is also the word for fight.
11. A break is the same thing as a schism; and in Hungarian 'history' *történelem* is connected to 'broken' *tört*, a further support for a Batesonian reading of historical processes as being often schismogenic (Bateson 1972).
12. For more details, see Horvath (2010).
13. The Greeks also called the Trickster by the name *mechaniota*. It is the opposite of creation out of nothing, says Carl Schmitt (2008: 128–9), as creation out of nothingness is the condition for the possibility of self-creation in an ever new worldliness, where 'Freedom replaces Reason, and Novelty replaces Freedom' (Schmitt 2008: 130). *Poeisis* diverts from the right formal principles, therefore does not know good from evil, being ignorant of truth. It is born in thrownness, being a product of *ek-stasis*, where all objects are 'opening up' (Heidegger), or – in another terminology – is born out of liminality. This is the reason for the basic idleness of the Trickster as world-creating poet (Hyde 1998); it is never at home, remaining always an outsider, a stranger: alienated, passive or subjectivated, inoperative, worthless and futile; the fool, incubator of the liminal. Strangely enough, a whole episteme is linked to the fool, a *techné* that opens up in liminality, dislocating the circle of the beautiful into an awkward automatism. This is why technological knowledge is an idle knowledge that has no purpose or motive, it just happens, coming into existence owing to an accident, as in this way an opportunity – a *foolish* occasion – has arisen (we do not have metals because we needed them; how could we have known that we would need a metal before it was discovered?). It is also a mystical, unreal and illusory kind of knowledge: we will illustrate this point later, when discussing the *aletheia* (opening) and labyrinth motives. Its unreality is shown by its ending, just as by its emergence out of liminality. It never reaches an end-point as a conclusion, it simply runs out of steam: 'But the revealing never simply comes to an end' (Heidegger 1977: 298).

14. See Plato on the two components of the beauty, *cosmetikos* and *andreios*, as discussed at the end of the *Statesman*.

2   The Rise of Liminal Authorities: Trickster's Gaining a Craft, or the Techniques of Incommensurability

1. Indeed, archaeologists would date the first major moments in the emergence of metallurgy with the crises of the Neolithic (*ca.*7000 BC) and of the Bronze Age (fourth millennium BC).
2. The Greek term *met'allurgy*, according to one etymological interpretation, means 'one after one', alluding to a sequence of 'rites of passage' to which stones are subjected to transform them into metals; the technique of purifying metal, altering the character of the original ores, first by weakening, then by moulding them, imposing on them a new property.
3. See Husken (2012) on incommensurable rites in Buddhism, Hinduism and in various areas in Africa; and App (2010) for a scholarly view of the fundamental connection between Asian rites, and their difference from the European.
4. On the other side, Hephaestus is also the brother of Athena. Together, they founded Athens.
5. Graceful being (Greek).
6. About the first alchemical text from China, see Hong Ge (1981: 63). In the discussion of alchemy and metallurgy offered in this chapter, the following texts were also consulted: Abbaschian, Reza, Lara Abbaschian and Robert E. Reed-Hill (2010); Campbell, John (2011); Clagett, Marshall (1969); Dave, Patrick (2011); Giardino, Claudio (2010); Grimwade, Mark (2009); Hellebust, Rolf (2003); Kienlin, Tobias L. and Roberts Ben W. (2009); Lembert, Alexandra and Schenkel, Elmar (2002); Linden, Stanton J. (2003); Morrisson, Mark S. (2009); Newman, William R. and Anthony Grafton (2001); Nummedal, Tara E. (2007); Olsen, Berg, Evan Selinger and Søren Riis (2009); Peng Yoke, Ho (2007); Plamper, Jan (2012); Pregadio, Fabrizio (2006); Principe, Lawrence M. (2007); Shumaker, Wayne (1989); Szulakowska, Urszula (2006); Williams, Kim (2010); Yates, Frances (1964).
7. For a detailed definition, see John Scarborough (1988), alluding to the similarity with the unreal in Mozart's *Magic Flute*: the mixture of the fantastic, the intellectual and the evil sombreness, which adds to the exotic dreaminess and power of the opera.
8. See Hermes the craftsman in Brown (1989).
9. See von Franz (1980) on how close alchemical symbolism is to liminality.
10. See the Argentine tale about Juan Pobreza, a barefooted man with a hunchback (Brusca and Wilson 1992); but similar tales are told in many countries inside and outside Europe. See also a particularly intriguing Yakut legend about the blacksmith, the shaman and the potter (Popov 1933).

11. For an exception, see Bateson (1958) about the humiliating and violent Naven ritual.
12. See also the milking sow motif in Çatal Höyük.
13. See Kerényi (1987), also about the significance that Circe's names means circle.
14. See also the 1952 Don Siegel film, *Invasion of the Body Snatchers*, made at the height of the Cold War.
15. 'Immortal mortals, mortal immortals, living their death and dying their life' (Heraclitus, Fr. 62, as in Kirk and Raven 1957: 210).
16. On the shaman's trance, see Eliade (1964).
17. The same holds for active and passive, or any other proper principles, like the Moon and the Sun.
18. On Albertus Magnus, see Crisciani (2002), in particular concerning Papal interest in alchemy.
19. See Plato, the *Statesman*; or see Victor Turner about the rituals of twins (Turner 1969: Chapter 2).
20. 'Goethe used alchemy in his drama *Faust*. Carl Gustav Jung pointed out that *Faust* is an alchemical drama form beginning to end, but he did not elaborate his statement. The main theme in the first part is the desire to preserve one's virility and youth [...] We find evidence of Paracelsus in Goethe's elixir for preserving youth and the elemental spirits. In the second part of the drama, the idea of creating a homunculus comes from Goethe's readings of Paracelsus. Paracelsus had written that this is a secret God had given to human beings, but it must be kept a secret until the end of all time' (Gebelein 2002).
21. At the end of this attempt stands the 'synthetic human'; see the subtitle of the 'Introduction' to Newman (2004), 'From Alchemical Gold to Synthetic Humans'.
22. For this semantic complexity, see further Détienne and Vernant (1978), with liminality or the limitless being the *apeiron* (path), *peras* (bond) or the end of the passage (*tekmor*).
23. The following Rig-Veda passages illustrate this point: 'The non-existent was not; the existent was not/ Darkness was hidden by darkness/ That which became was employed by The Void' as in Close (2007: 156).
24. On 'axial age', see Szakolczai (2003); and Thomassen (2010, 2012).
25. For a recent discussion close to the ideas exposed here, see Derrida (1995).
26. See also 241D: 'In defending myself I shall have to test the theory of my father Parmenides, and contend forcibly that after a fashion not-being is and on the other hand in a sense being is not'.
27. I prefer this neologism to the usual 'opportunist', as the latter implies a positive opportunity that just emerges, and which therefore can be captured or let pass; whereas an occasionist just turns a neutral – or even negative – occasion into a positive opportunity to gain something.
28. This is why envy and vanity are the par excellence property of empty, mimetised individuals (see Girard 1991). Emptiness (so nullity) and

vanity are etymologically connected, in the Indo-European languages as well as in Hungarian.

3 Liminal Mimes, Masks, and Schismogenic Technology: The Trickster Motives in the Renaissance

1. About this pope, see especially Giotto's fresco in Assisi, 'The Dream of Innocent III', where in his dream St Francis was supporting the crumbling Lateran Basilica.
2. Momus is the ancient god of pleasantry, an attractive yet repulsive figure according to Hesiod; but being divorced from any cult, maybe it is more correct to call him a personified literal figure of wantonness, usually represented as keeping a mask in front his face, and holding a small figure in this hands (Hammond and Scullard 1970).
3. The trickster, as it was Alberti who first recognised it, is a figure dominated by a fundamental deficiency, a profound sense of insecurity, rendering him unable to give gifts and thus to take part in normal everyday social life. To compensate for his deficiency, however, he is obliged to present his own deprived being as the norm, trying to lure others into his own status.
4. The Greek word *arkhé* meant both origins (in the sense of initial, original, as in archaic or archaeology) and power (as in *archon* or in *monarchy*).
5. The etymological root of Greek term for grace, *charis*, or *gher, meant pleasure, referring to the social pleasure that was generated by the practice of gift giving.
6. This can be observed in the close etymological ties between the main characteristic of the magnanimous, gift-giving person, 'generosity' and the verb expressing creative power, to 'generate'.
7. See Mauss (2002).
8. 'To neglect to return a favour is to ensure that you will be cut off from social interchange, left alone and without a return gift' (MacLachlan 1993: 6).
9. 'The bitter, anti-heroic elements in the play, Thersites's juxtaposition of war and obscenity, valour and stupidity, look more responsible than ignoble since the slaughter of 1914–18' (Martin 1976: 22).
10. In the words of Shakespeare, 'a crooked figure may/ Attest in little place a million' (*Henry V*, Prologue, 15–16). The nose actually appears on his mask, and will be analysed in more detail.
11. From Girolamo and Giannantonio Tagliente's *Libro de Abaco*, originally published in Venice, 1515; as quoted in Jaffe (1999: 41).
12. See Marinoni's classic paper on Leonardo's discussion of the *nulla* (Marinoni 1960).
13. For details on medieval and Renaissance mathematics, see Bovelles (1994); Clagett (1979); Flegg, Hay and Moss (1995); Field (1997); Franci and Rigatelli (1982); Jaffe (1999); Menninger (1969); Molland (1995); Netz (2004); Sigler (2003); Swetz (1997); Vendrix (2008).

14. About the Trickster, see Horvath (2008); concerning the problem of place and non-place, see also Plato on *khóra* in the *Timaeus*.
15. The main characters of the *Commedia dell'Arte* were not called as 'personalities' or 'characters', but as 'masks' (Nicoll 1963b: 40–1).
16. For details on such characters, see Nicoll (1963a, 1963b) and Niklaus (1956).
17. See Schechter (1994), especially chapters 5 and 6, concerning Hitler and Stalin each having their mime doubles.
18. Here we need to recall the enormous importance attributed by Plato to the role of memory in preserving and transmitting knowledge.
19. A recent book on the Renaissance mathematician Nicholas Chuquet called attention to the early opposition to the new algorithmic method of the zero, as it was considered that forged alterations of the numerals could be made too easily, for example changing 0 to 6 or 9. As a safeguard the practice continued in the writing of cheques with written names of the numbers (Flegg, Hay and Moss 1985).
20. An expression of Robert Musil, author of *Man without Qualities*, a key novel of the twentieth century, brought into social and political analysis by Eric Voegelin.
21. See the *Treviso Arithmetic* (1478), as quoted in Swetz (1997).

4   Attraction and Crowd Passions: Isaac Newton and Jacques Callot

1. The puzzle of infinite divisibility was posed by Zeno, suggested even by Parmenides and other Presocratics, so has a long pedigree in philosophy.
2. See, among others, Cardano, Galileo, Kepler, Copernicus, Descartes, Leibnitz or Hobbes, as analysed by Cesare Maffioli, Simon Schaffer and Quentin Skinner. The idea of releasing the void from the prison of forms could also be traced back to Sophist thinking (e.g. Protagoras), or to Gnostic and Kabalistic monism (see Shoham 1994). About Newton's liminal world view, see the following: 'What the real substance of anything is we know not. In bodies we see only their figures and colours, we hear only the sounds [...] but their inward substances are not to be known either by our senses [...] much less, then have we any idea of the substance of God' (from his *God and Natural Philosophy*, as in Thayer 1974: 44).
3. Liminal phenomena as 'go-betweens' have been studied most recently by Simon Schaffer and his associates (see Schaffer et al. 2009), in the sense of messengers or agents who draw boundaries and cross them. See also Szakolczai (2009) for the term 'permanent liminality'.
4. Concerning contemporaries about Newton, see Shank (2008), Durkan (2008) and Fara (2002).
5. 'Nature may be lasting, the Changes of corporeal Things are to be placed only in the various Separations and new Associations and Motions of these permanent Particles, compound Bodies being apt to break, not in the midst of this Particles, but where those Particles are laid together, and only touch in a few Points' (Newton, *Queries* 1–7 and 31, as in Cohen and Westfall 1995: 53).

6. As Newton says in the *Questiones*, 'atoms were [...] divided by means of vacuum,' *Questiones*, 5 90', in McGuire and Tamny (1983: 345).

7. In 1713 Newton states the following about contagious attraction for this kind of suction impulse automatism that moves into infinity: 'If body attracts body contagious to it and is not mutually attracted by the other, the attracted body will drive the other before it and both will go away together with an accelerated motion in infinitum' (from Newton's letter to Cotes, as in Cohen and Westfall 1995: 119).

8. 'Perhaps', concludes Newton in his letter to Oldenburg, 'the whole frame of nature may be nothing but various contextures of some certain ethereal spirits or vapours'; as in Thayer (1974: 84).

9. 'If by spirit, how comes the spirit to be so easily united to the body, and not slip through it, and when united to it how comes the spirit to be so cease so soon and the spirit to leave it. Hence, every little atom must have souls in store to cast away upon everybody they meet with. If a quality, then *qualitas transmigrate de subject in subjectum* [...] In a word how can that give a power of moving which itself has not.' *Questiones* 52 113'; in McGuire and Tamny (1983: 407).

10. See *Questiones* 63 119'. Nakedness, in English, and even more in Italian (see Agamben, *nuda vita*), represents vulnerability.

11. For Hesiod, it was self-evident that giving is good, while taking away is bad.

12. About Boyle, whose mechanical philosophy had the goal of eliminating forms form the 'explanatory armory of natural science', see Newman (2006: 157–90).

13. 'The shock of every single ray may generate many thousand vibrations and, by sending them all over the body, move all the parts, and that perhaps with more motion than it could move one single part by an immediate stroke; for the vibrations, by shaking each particle backward and forward, may every time increase its motion,' in Thayer (1974: 95).

14. About the Trickster, see Horvath (2008), Hyde (1998) and Radin (1972).

15. Newton, as cited by Voegelin (1990: 165).

16. Newton's Proposition 57 in the *Principia* is an example of this: two bodies attracted to each other mutually describe similar figures about their common centre of gravity, and about each other mutually.

17. In numbering the images I follow Posner (1977).

18. See also Harvie Ferguson's analysis of the war experience (Ferguson 2004).

19. About Italian satiric-political popular dances, see Bragaglia (1952: 36); as for the many types, see Piedigrotta, La Zingara, La Capricciosa, il Diavolo in Camicia, la Spagnoletta from Naples, a real bacchanalia, a sort of mystery play at the cave where Venus was celebrated.

20. See De Giorgi (2004), on the Tarantella being a marriage dance.

21. See Baudelaire, 'Mon Coeur mis à nu', about the desire to torture being a form of sexual repression.

22. These are the exact spots where moresca dancers wore bells, with the explicit apotropaic purpose of chasing away demons; see Brainard (1981: 727).

23. See Tessari (1981), with its particularly telling subtitle *The Mask and the Shadow*; and Horvath (2010).

24. About grotesque, ugly and aberrations as the unreal see Acidini Luchinat (1999), Baltrusaitis (1973), Bora et al. (1998), Castelli (1952), Pellegrini (2003) and Scaramuzza (1995).

25. In a letter dated 25 January 1675 to Oldenburg, Newton formulated his idea on light, saying that it is something very thinly and subtly diffused in every matter; as in Thayer (1974: 87).

26. 'Anybody can be transformed into another body of any kind whatsoever, and can assume successively all intermediate degrees of quality' (Newton, *Principia I*, Book III, Proposition 6, Hypothesis 3).

27. See the excellent book of Patricia Fara (2002) about how the accomplishment of Newton was understood.

28. On the relation between trance, dance and marriage, and about the sexual nature of the trance dance, see Meier (1967).

29. Similar doubled feminine and masculine sexual meanings can be seen on a Moche jug, in which the vessel is feminine, and the neck masculine, forming a phallus, in Johnson (1992: 121).

30. On the box signifying the receiving female body, see Arasse (2005).

31. About the Tarantella dance as a *hieros gamos* rite, see De Giorgi (2004: 103–34).

32. See also the open mouth of the box as something that can cause harm or bite; see the tarantella literature about Taranta, the spider, which is always female (Danforth 1989) to fill it with quite evident sexual activity signed by the semen button and the between-legs stick of the box holder, seminating and to be seminated: 'O Lucia, ah Lucia/ cocozza da vino bonora mi sa/ vide, canella, ca tutto me scolo,/ tiente, ca corro, ca roto, ca volo/ Cucuricu / Rota me su/' (song from the Tarantella, 'Dance of the Cock', in Bragaglia 1952: 179).

33. About buffoonish Heracles, the wandering demon and half god, see Kerényi (1959) and Welsford (1966).

34. Newton used the word *attraction* in his *Principia* in this peculiar way for something centre oriented, promiscuous and indifferent. See his letter *An Account of Commercium Epistolicum*, in Cohen and Westfall (1995: 162).

35. See the Introduction to del Giudice and Deusen (2004); see also Caillois (1981).

36. Here probably we should refer to Newton's Arianism.

37. 'Newton accepts the view that parts are distinct just in case they are separable and, if in fact divided, are divided by the presence of voids between them' (McGuire and Tamny 1983: 41).

38. Strangely enough, there are other works of art that express exactly this same, reproductive quality of the void, which bring us back not simply to the mime but outright to pre-history. One of the most striking aspects of the *mask* is his long, crooked nose, widely recognised as a phallic symbol. But similar figures or masks exist in several parts of the world, beyond Greco-Roman Antiquity, including American

Indians, Africans or Melanesians. In some cases the length of the nose is exaggerated out of all proportion, so much so that it reaches, and becomes at one with, the penis. Such statues, of course, leave much room for interpretation; but they clearly allude to the reproductive 'auto-fertilisation' of the void.

39. See Szabo (1978). It is loathing a desolate existence, obscure and abhorrent: to break the ability and dynamics of form.

40. On Ptolemy (100–178 AD), Alexandrian alchemist, see Hutchins (1963).

41. About how, under the idea of prosperity and happiness, which identifies the state with its subject, life becomes an object of police, enslaving their own people, see Foucault (1982).

42. See again Szakolczai (2009, 2013) about permanent liminality.

43. About seduction, see John Forrester's genealogy about the spread of psychoanalysis in the twentieth century (Forrester 1990). Forrester is wondering what the prime mover of its success is, if not that it is able to map out for a subject one's actions.

44. *Spagyric* (Greek, meaning to separate and to join together again)

45. No matter how strange it may seem, this is what Nietzsche is saying, following Hölderlin, for example in his ideas about 'free spirits'.

46. See Elias about the doubt of Descartes being the 'worm in the apple of modernity' (Elias 1991: 15); a particularly striking metaphor.

47. On John Dee, see Yates (1979).

48. In Hungarian, 'despair' (*kétségbeesés*) literally means 'fall into doubt'.

49. See Szakolczai (2013).

50. According to Serge Moscovici, in spite of general knowledge about the name and work of Le Bon, his case is a mystery, as 'for the last fifty years, works in French have made no mention of his extraordinary influence on the social sciences, preferring to devote inordinate space to minor scholars and amorphously general schools of thought'. Still, '[t]o be quite honest, no French thinker apart from Sorel and probably de Tocqueville has had an influence as great as Le Bon's' (Moscovici 1985: 49).

51. In fact, crowd psychology and commercial or political propaganda represent one of the most obvious direct contacts not only between the two major totalitarian powers, justifying in itself the legitimacy of the concept 'totalitarianism', but also between totalitarian propaganda and such forms of influencing accepted in democratic polities like commercials or political campaigns. In this context, it is of considerable importance that the arguably single most important characteristic of modern market economies, the omnipresence of advertising, is simply absent from economic theory. This is because it challenges the given unity of the tastes of the rational subject that underlies economic choice.

52. About this, see the author's Preface to the 1902 third edition of the book.

53. 'Beautiful Virgin who, clothed with the sun and crowned with stars, so pleased the highest Sun that in you He hid His light. Love drives me

to speak words of you, but I do not know how to begin without your help and His who loving placed Himself in you. I invoke her who has always replied to whoever called on her with faith. Virgin, if extreme misery of human things ever turned you to mercy, bend to my prayer; give help to my war, though I am earth and you are queen of Heaven'. Note how much even in this beautiful poem the inspiration motivating Segni's work, the 'extreme misery of mankind', is present, though in a spiritually transformed, pacified, translucent manner.

5 Charisma in Eroticised Political Formations

1. See Albertus Magnus (1958: 102).
2. I prefer this neologism to the usual 'opportunist', as the latter implies a positive opportunity that just emerges, and which therefore can be captured or let pass; while an occasionist just turns a neutral – or even negative – occasion into a positive opportunity to gain something.
3. Palingenetic for *palin* (Greek, again) and *genesis* (Greek, birth); see Griffin (2007).
4. On property being linked to identity, see in particular Verdery (2000).
5. This appears in particular force in Etienne La Boétie's *Discourse of Voluntary Servitude* (1548) (see Schaefer 1998), where La Boétie argues that people lose their freedom through their own blindness. The desire to serve the tyrant is something that they themselves want.
6. Following Augé on *surmodernité*, or 'supermodernity', one needs a neologism to capture this at once absurd and 'hyper-real' experience of communism.
7. Bataille has attempted several times to describe *nonknowledge*, the 'horror of ceasing to be personally, the distances from the world' (Bataille 2001: 177).
8. See especially Burkert (1984).
9. See the story of the serpent sacrifice of Janamejaya in the Mahabharata.
10. From the speeches of Mátyás Rákosi; see Horvath (2000: 119, 122).
11. See also Hubert and Mauss (1981), Milbank (1995).
12. Alchemical operations following this logic persisted in modernity: 'Thus the Board of Mines of the first half of the eighteenth century still had room for two different types of knowledge about the world. The first type was mechanical science. Here interesting connections lead towards further redefinitions of the mining crafts into mining sciences. These redefinitions would eventually lead to the transformation of the entire business of mining into scientific enterprise. Further down this road waited the scientific mining engineers of the nineteenth century. The second type of knowledge concerned knowledge about spirits and the paranormal' (Fors 2007: 252).

13. This idea was emphasised by Pierre Hadot and Michel Foucault, two of the most important French philosophers of the past decades. Interestingly, both recognised a crucial East–Central European dimension with this concern, Foucault through the ideas of Jan Patocka, whereas Hadot through the book of Juliusz Domanski.

14. See Solzhenitsyn's Preface to his 1978 Harvard address.

15. Jumping to the present, this is clearly illustrated in our days by the case of Berlusconi.

16. Airports are par excellence liminal places, being thresholds between two countries, also considered as illustrations of 'non-places' in Augé's analysis of 'surmodernity'.

17. Deleuze's book *The Logic of Sense* offers a comprehensive analysis of this theme. The strongest indications about the meaning Deleuze intended to explore are contained in the chapter 'Eleventh Series of Nonsense'. The central idea is that the senses become enacted by nonsense, as their specific names, designating classes and properties will be lost. Thus their distribution happens in a way independent from the precise relation of signification in which their originally emerged, thus becoming senseless.

18. The last words of Socrates were also interpreted in this way; even by Nietzsche (*The Gay Science*: 340).

19. What Koselleck (1988) showed about the Enlightenment in the West – a secret conspiracy of disgruntled intellectuals, far both from political and social life – stands true even more for the case of Eastern Europe, as was repeatedly argued (see Konrád and Szelényi 1979). See also Boland (2008).

20. The original Hungarian title of the book co-authored with Arpad Szakolczai was *Senkiföldjén* 'On the No Man's Land'.

21. It was by seeing this danger and the need for proper training that Plato said: 'Interpreting and transporting human things to the gods and divine things to men' (*Symposium* 202 E).

Bibliography

Abbaschian, Reza, Lara Abbaschian and Robert E. Reed-Hill (ed.) (2010) *Physical Metallurgy Principles*, Stamford, CT: Cengage Learning.

Acidini Luchinat, Cristina (1999) *Grottesche: Le volte dipinte nella Galleria degli Uffici*, Florence: Giunti.

Agricola, Georgius (1950) *De Re Metallica*, ed. Herbert C. Hoover and Lou H. Hoover, New York: Dover.

Albertus Magnus (1958) *Libellus de Alchimia*, ed. Stanton J. Linden, Cambridge: Cambridge University Press.

Andrle, Vladimir (1992) 'Demons and Devil's Advocates: Problems in Historical Writing on the Stalin Era', in Nick Lampert and Gábor T. Rittersporn (ed.) *Stalinism: Its Nature and Aftermath*, London: Macmillan.

App, Urs (2010) *The Birth of Orientalism*, Philadelphia: University of Pennsylvania Press.

Arasse, Daniel (2005) *Non si vede niente*, Rome: Artemide.

Ariès, Philippe (1985) *L'uomo e la morte dal Medievo a oggi*, Rome: Laterza.

Assmann, Jan (2002) *La morte come tema culturale*, Torino: Einaudi.

Augé, Marc (1992) *The Anthropological Circle: Symbol, Function, History*, Cambridge: Cambridge University Press.

—— (2008) *Non-Places: Introduction to an Anthropology of Supermodernity*, London: Verso.

Aujoulat, Norbert (2005) *The Splendour of Lascaux*, London: Thames and Hudson.

Baltrusaitis, Jurgis (1973) *Il Medioevo fantastico: Antichità ed esotismi nell'arte gotica*, Milano: Adelphi.

Barry, Ann Marie (1997) *Visual Intelligence: Perception, Image, and Manipulation in Visual Communication*, Albany: State University of New York.

Bataille, Georges (1998) *Eroticism*, London: Penguin.

—— (2001) *The Unfinished System of Nonknowledge*, ed. Stuart Kendall, London: University of Minnesota Press.

—— (2005) *The Cradle of Humanity: Prehistoric Art and Culture,* Cambridge: MIT Press.

Bateson, Gregory (1958) *Naven*, Stanford: Stanford University Press.

—— (1972) *Steps to an Ecology of Mind*, New York: Ballantine.

Baudrillard, Jean (1993) *The Transparency of Evil: Essays on Extreme Phenomena*, London: Verso.

—— (2009) *Why Hasn't Everything Already Disappeared*, London: Seagull.

—— (2010) *The Agony of Power*, Los Angeles: Semiotext(e).

Beltrán, Antonio (ed.) (1999) *The Cave of Altamira*, New York: Harry Abrams.

Bernheimer, R. (1952) *Wild Men in the Middle Ages*, Cambridge, MA: Harvard University Press.

Boland, Tom (2008) 'Critique as Imitative Rivalry: George Orwell as Political Anthropologist', *International Political Anthropology* 1, 1: 77–91.

Bora, Giulio, Manuela Kahn-Rossi, Francesco Porzio, Giacomo Berra, Museo cantonale d'arte (Lugano, Switzerland) and Christian Beaufort-Sponton (1998) *Rabisch: Il grottesco nell'arte del Cinquecento*, Milan: Skira.

Borkenau, Franz (1937) *The Spanish Cockpit: An Eye-Witness Account of the Political and Social Conflicts of the Spanish Civil War*, London: Faber.

—— (1939) *World Communism: A History of the Communist International*, Ann Arbor: University of Michigan Press.

Borsi, Stefano (1999) *Momus, o Del principe: Leon Battista Alberti, i papi, il giubileo*, Florence: Polistampa.

Bovelles, C. de (1994) *Il piccolo libro del nulla*, ed. Piercarlo Necchi, Genoa: Il Melangolo.

Bragaglia, Anton Giulio (1930) *Evoluzione del mimo*, Milan: Ceschina.

—— (1952) *Danze popolari italiane*, Rome: Enal.

Brainard, Ingrid (1981) 'An Exotic Court Dance and Dance Spectacle of the Renaissance: "La Moresca"', in Daniel Heartz and Bonnie Wade (eds) *Report of the Twelfth Congress, Berkeley, 1977, International Musicological Society*, Philadelphia: American Musicological Society.

Brown, Norman O. (1989) *Hermes the Thief*, New York: Vintage Books.

Brusca, María Cristina and Tona Wilson (eds) (1992) *The Blacksmith and the Devils*, New York: Holt.

Burke, Peter (2005) 'Performing History: The Importance of Occasions', *Rethinking History* 9, 1: 35–52.

Burkert, Walter (1984) 'Sacrificio-sacrilegio: Il Trickster fondatore', *Studi Storici* 25: 835–45.

Caillois, Roger (1981) *I giochi e gli uomini: La maschera e la vertigine*, Milan: Bompiani.

Cajori, Florian (1919) *A History of the Conceptions of Limits and Fluxions in Great Britain from Newton to Woodhouse*, London: The Open Court.

Calasso, Roberto (2006) *Il rosa Tiepolo*, Milan: Adelphi.

Callot, Jacques (1971) *Incisioni*, Florence: La nuova Italia.

—— (1992) *Le incisioni di Jacques Callot nelle collezioni italiane*, Milan: Mazzotta.

Camesasca, Ettore and Marco Bona Castellotti (1996) *Alessandro Magnasco 1667–1749*, Milan: Electa.

Campbell, John (2011) *Complete Casting Handbook: Metal Casting Processes, Metallurgy, Techniques and Design*, Oxford: Butterworth-Heinemann.

Castagno, Paul C. (1994) *The Early Commedia Dell'Arte (1550–1621): The Mannerist Context*, New York: P. Lang.

Castelli, Enrico (1952) *Il demonico nell'arte*, Milano: Electa.

Chauvet, Jean-Marie, Eliette Brunel Deschamps and Christian Hillaire (1996) *Chauvet Cave: The Discovery of the World's Oldest Paintings*, London: Thames and Hudson.

Chikashige, Masumi (1936) *Alchemy and Other Chemical Achievements of the Ancient Orient: The Civilization of Japan and China in Early Times as Seen from the Chemical Point of View*, Tokyo: Rokakuho Uchida.

Clagett, Marshall (1969) 'The Scholar and the Craftsman in the Scientific Revolution', in Marshall Clagett (ed.) *Critical Problems in the History of Science*, Madison, WI: University of Wisconsin Press.

—— (1979) *Studies in Medieval Physics and Mathematics*, London: Variorum.

Clastres, Pierre (2010) *Archeology of Violence*, Los Angeles: Semiotext(e).

Close, Frank (2007) *The Void*, Oxford: Oxford University Press.

Clottes, Jean (2003) *Return to Chauvet Cave: Excavating the Birthplace of Art*, London: Thames and Hudson.

—— (2006) 'Spirituality and Religion in Paleolithic Times', in F. LeRon Shults (ed.) *The Evolution of Rationality: Interdisciplinary Essays in Honor of J. Wentzel van Huyssteen*, Grand Rapids, MI: Eerdmans Publishing.

Clottes, Jean and Jean Courtin (1996) *The Cave Beneath the Sea: Palaeolithic Images at Cosquer*, New York: Harry Abrams.

Cohen, I. Bernard and George E. Smith (eds) (2002) *The Cambridge Companion to Newton*, Cambridge: Cambridge University Press.

Cohen, I. Bernard and Richard S. Westfall (eds) (1995) *Newton: Texts, Backgrounds, Commentaries*, London: W. W. Norton.

Conquest, Robert (1986) *The Harvest of Sorrow: Soviet Collectivization and the Terror-Famine*, Oxford: Oxford University Press.

Cornford, Francis M. (ed.) (1937) *Plato's Cosmology: The Timaeus of Plato*, London: Routledge.

Couliano, Ioan P. (1981) 'Magia spirituale e magia demonica nel rinascimento', *Rivista di storia e letteratura religiosa* 27, 3: 360–408.

Coxon, Allan H. (1986) *The Fragments of Parmenides*, Maastricht: van Gorcum.

Crisciani, Chiara (2002) *Il Papa e l'alchimia: Felice V, Guglielmo Fabri e l'elixir*, Rome: Viella.

Danforth, Loring M. (1989) *Firewalking and Religious Healing*, Princeton: Princeton University Press.

Darwin, Charles (2010) *Evolutionary Writings*, ed. James Secord, Oxford: Oxford University Press.

Dave, Patrick (2011) *The View Beyond: Sir Francis Bacon: Alchemy, Science, Mystery*, London: Polair.

Davenport, Demorest and Michael A. Jochim (1988) 'The Scene in the Shaft at Lascaux', *Antiquity* 62: 558–62.

De Giorgi, Pierpaolo (2004) *L'Estetica della tarantella*, Galatina: Congedo.

Deleuze, Gilles (2004a) *Desert Islands and Other Texts*, ed. David Lapoujade, Los Angeles: Semiotext(e).

—— (2004b) *The Logic of Sense*, ed. Constantin V. Boundas, London: Continuum.

Del Giudice, Luisa and Nancy Van Deusen (2004) *Performing Ecstasies: Music, Dance, and Ritual in the Mediterranean*, Ottawa: Institute for Medieval Music.

Détienne, Marcel and Jean-Pierre Vernant (1978) *Cunning Intelligence in Greek Culture and Society*, Brighton, Sussex: The Harvester Press.

Derrida, Jacques (1995) '*Khóra*', in *On the Name*, ed. Thomas Dutoit, Stanford: Stanford University Press.

Douglas, Mary (1966) *Purity and Danger*, London: Routledge.

Dunn, John (2000) *The Cunning of Unreason*, London: HarperCollins.

Durkan, Anthony (2008) *Newton's Boobs: Gravitational Anomalies*, Brighton: Pen.

Durkheim, E. (1995 [1912]) *The Elementary Forms of Religious Life*, New York: Free Press.

Eliade, Mircea (1964) *Shamanism: Archaic Techniques of Ecstasy*, London: Penguin.

Elias, Norbert (1991) *Symbol Theory*, London: Sage.

Eshleman, Clayton (2003) *Juniper Fuse: Upper Palaeolithic Imagination and the Construction of the Underworld*, Middletown: Wesleyan University Press.

Fagan, Brian (2010) *Cro-Magnon: How the Ice Age Gave Birth to the First Modern Humans*, New York: Bloomsbury Press.

Fainsod, Merle (1958) *Smolensk Under Soviet Rule*, London: Macmillan.

Fara, Patricia (2002) *The Making of Genius*, London: Picador.

Femia, Joseph (1993) 'Mosca Revisited', *European Journal of Political Research* 23, 2: 145–61.

Ferguson, Harvie (2004) 'The Sublime and the Subliminal: Modern Identities and the Aesthetics of Combat', *Theory, Culture and Society* 21, 3: 1–33.

Field, Judith V. (1997) *The Invention of Infinity: Mathematics and Art in the Renaissance*, Oxford: Oxford University Press.

Fitzpatrick, Sheila (1994) *Stalin's Peasants*, Oxford: Oxford University Press.

Flegg, Graham, Cinthia Hay and Barbara Moss (1985) *Nicolas Chuquet, Renaissance Mathematician*, Boston, MA: Riedel.

Forrester, John (1990) *The Seductions of Psychoanalysis*, Cambridge: Cambridge University Press.

Forbes, Robert J. (1950) *Metallurgy in Antiquity*, Leiden: Brill.

Fors, Hjalmar (2007) 'Occult Traditions and Enlightened Science: The Swedish Board of Mines as an Intellectual Environment 1680–1760', in Lawrence M. Principe (ed.) *Chymists and Chymistry: Studies in the History of Alchemy and Early Modern Chemistry*, Sagamore Beach, MA: Science History Publications.

Foucault, Michel (1980a) *The History of Sexuality, Vol. 1: An Introduction*, New York: Vintage.

—— (1980b) *Power/Knowledge: Selected Interviews and Other Writings by Michel Foucault, 1972–1977*, ed. Colin Gordon, Sussex: Harvester.

—— (1982) 'The Subject and Power', in Hubert Dreyfus and Paul Rabinow (eds) *Michel Foucault: Beyond Structuralism and Hermeneutics*, Chicago: University of Chicago Press.

—— (1986) *The Care of the Self, The History of Sexuality*, Vol. 3, New York: Vintage.

—— (2001) *Fearless Speech*, Los Angeles: Semiotext(e).

—— (2003) '*Society Must Be Defended*': Lectures at the Collège de France, 1975–76, ed. Mauro Bertani and Alessandro Fontana, London: Allen.

Franci, Raffaella and Laura Rigatelli (1982) *Introduzione all'aritmetica mercantile del Medioevo e del Rinascimento*, Siena: Quattro Venti.

Freud, Sigmund (1949 [1912]) *Group Psychology and the Analysis of the Ego*, London: Hogarth.

Ge, Hong (1981) *Alchemy, Medicine and Religion in the China of A.D. 320*, ed. James R. Ware, New York: Constable.

Gebelein, Helmut (2002) 'Alchemy and Chemistry in the Work of Goethe', in Alexandra Lembert and Elmar Schenkel (eds) *The Golden Egg: Alchemy in Art and Literature*, Berlin: Galda + Wilch Verlag.

Geneste, Jean-Miche, Tristan Horde and Chantal Tanet (2004) *Lascaux, A Work of Memory*, Perigueux: Fanlac.

Getty, John A. and Roberta T. Manning (eds) (1993) *Stalinist Terror: New Perspectives*, Cambridge: Cambridge University Press.

Giardino, Claudio (2010) *I metalli nel mondo antico: Introduzion all'archeometallurgia*, Roma: Laterza.

Giesen, Bernhard (2010) *Zwischenlagen: Das Ausserordentliche als Grund der sozialen Wirklichkeit*, Göttingen: Velbrück.

Girard, René (1991) *A Theatre of Envy: William Shakespeare*, Oxford: Oxford University Press.

Goethe, Johann W. (1995) *Scientific Studies*, ed. Douglas Miller, Princeton: Princeton University Press.

Gordon, Colin (1987) 'The Soul of the Citizen: Max Weber and Michel Foucault on Rationality and Government', in Scott Lash and Sam Whimster (eds) *Max Weber, Rationality and Modernity*, London: Allen & Unwin.

Grafton, Anthony (2003) *Leon Battista Alberti: Un genio universale*, Rome: Laterza.

Grayson, Cecil (1998) *Studi su Leon Battista Alberti*, Florence: Olschki.

Greco, Franco C. (ed.) (1990) *Pulcinella maschera del mondo: Pulcinella e le arti dal Cinquecento al Novecento*, Naples: Electa.

Greenblatt, Stephen (2001) *Hamlet in Purgatory*, Princeton, NJ: Princeton University Press.

—— (2004) *Will in the World*, London: Jonathan Cape.

Griffin, Roger (2007) *Modernism and Fascism: The Sense of a Beginning Under Mussolini and Hitler*, Basingstoke: Palgrave Macmillan.

—— (2008) *A Fascist Century*, ed. Matthew Feldman, Basingstoke: Palgrave Macmillan.

Grimwade, Mark (2009) *Introduction to Precious Metals: Metallurgy for Jewellers & Silversmiths*, London: A&C Black.

Guenther, Mathias (1999) *Tricksters and Trancers: Bushman Religion and Society*, Bloomington: Indiana University Press.

Hammond, Nicholas Geoffrey and Howard Hayes Scullard (1970) *The Oxford Classical Dictionary*, Oxford: Clarendon.

Handelman, Don (1990) *Models and Mirrors*, Cambridge: Cambridge University Press.

Hanks, Bryan and Linduff, Katheryn (eds) (2009) *Social Complexity in Prehistoric Eurasia: Monuments, Metals, and Mobility*, Cambridge: Cambridge University Press.

Hayek, Friedrich A. von (2005 [1943]) *The Road to Serfdom*, London: Institute of Economic Affairs.

Hennis, Wilhelm (1988) *Max Weber: Essays in Reconstruction*, London: Allen & Unwin.

Heidegger, Martin (1977) *Basic Writings*, New York: Harper & Row.

Hesiod (1978) *Works and Days*, Bristol: Bristol Classical Press.

Hellebust, Rolf (2003) *Flesh to Metal: Soviet Literature & The Alchemy of Revolution*, Ithaca, NY: Cornell University Press.

Hirschman, Albert (1977) *The Passions and the Interests*, Princeton: Princeton University Press.

Hölderlin, Friedrich (1994) *Hyperion and Selected Poems*, ed. Eric L. Santner, NY: Continuum.

Horvath, Agnes (1998) 'Tricking into the Position of the Outcast', *Political Psychology* 19, 3: 331–47.

—— (2000) The Nature of the Trickster's Game, Ph.D. thesis, European University Institute, Florence, Italy.

—— (2008) 'Mythology and the Trickster: Interpreting Communism', in Alexander Wöll and Harald Wydra (eds) *Democracy and Myth in Russia and Eastern Europe*, London: Routledge.

—— (2009) 'Liminality and the Unreal Class of the Image-Making Craft', *International Political Anthropology* 2, 1: 53–72.

—— (2010) 'Pulcinella, or the Metaphysics of the *Nulla*: In Between Politics and Theatre', *History of the Human Sciences* 23, 2: 47–67.

—— (forthcoming) 'A Népszolgálat a Szolgálat és a Nép között' (The Problem of Serving the People), in Nándor Bárdi (ed.) *Minority Studies*, Cluj-Napoca: Institutul Pentru Studierea Problemeror Minoritatilor Nationale (Minority Studies Institute).

Horvath, Agnes and Arpad Szakolczai (1992) *The Dissolution of Communist Power: The Case of Hungary*, London: Routledge.

Horvath, Agnes and Bjørn Thomassen (2008) 'Mimetic Errors in Liminal Schismogenesis: On the Political Anthropology of the Trickster', *International Political Anthropology* 1, 1: 3–24.

Hubert, Henri and Marcel Mauss (1981) *Sacrifice: Its Nature and Function*, Chicago: University of Chicago Press.

Huizinga, Johan (1970) *Homo Ludens*, Boston: Beacon Press.

—— (1990) *The Waning of the Middle Ages*, Harmondsworth: Penguin.

Husken, Ute (2012) *Negotiation Rites*, Oxford: Oxford University Press.

Hutchins, Robert M. (1963) *Great Books of the Western World*, London: Benton.

Hyde, Lewis (1998) *Trickster Makes this World*, New York: North Point Press.

Idil, Vedat (2001) *Ankara: The Ancient Sites and Museums*, Ankara: Net Turistik Yayinlar.

Jaffe, Michele Sharon (1999) *The Story of O: Prostitutes and Other Good-for-Nothings in the Renaissance*, Cambridge, MA: Harvard University Press.

Johnson, Harmer (1992) *Arte primitiva americana*, Milan: Bompiani.

Johnson, Paul (2004) *Art: A New History*, New York: HarperCollins.

Jung, Carl G. (1989) *Psychology and Alchemy*, London: Routledge.

Kahan, Gerald (1976) *Jacques Callot: Artist of the Theater*, Athens, GA: University of Georgia Press.

Kerényi, Károly (1959) *The Heroes of the Greeks*, London: Thames and Hudson.

—— (1976) *Dionysos: Archetypal Image of Indestructible Life*, Princeton: Princeton University Press.

—— (1980) 'I misteri dei Kabiri', in *Miti e misteri*, Torino: Boringhieri.

—— (1986) *Hermes, Guide of Souls: The Mythologem of the Masculine Source of Life*, New York: Spring Publications.

—— (1987) *Goddesses of Sun and Moon*, New York: Spring Publications.

Kieckhefer, Richard (1998) *Forbidden Rites: A Necromancer's Manual of the Fifteenth Century*, University Park, PA: Pennsylvania State University Press.

Kirk, Geoffrey Stephen and John Earle Raven (1957) *The Presocratic Philosophers*, Cambridge: Cambridge University Press.

Kienlin, Tobias L. and Ben W. Roberts (eds) (2009) *Metals and Societies: Studies in Honour of Barbara S. Ottaway*, Bonn: Rudolf Habelt.

Kleiner, Fred S. (2010) *Gardner's Art through the Ages: The Western Perspective*, Boston: Wadworth.

Koestler, Arthur (1980) *Darkness at Noon*, London: Folio Society.

Koselleck, Reinhart (1988) *Critique and Crisis: Enlightenment and the Pathogenesis of Modern Society*, Oxford: Berg.

Konrád, George and Iván Szelényi (1979) *The Intellectuals on the Road to Class Power*, Brighton: Harvester.

Kumar, Krishan (2001) *1989: Revolutionary Ideas and Ideals*, Minneapolis: University of Minnesota Press.

Kundera, Milan (1984) *The Unbearable Lightness of Being*, London: Faber & Faber.

Latour, Bruno and Vincent A. Lépinay (2009) *The Science of Passionate Interests: An Introduction to Gabriel Tarde's Economic Anthropology*, Chicago: Prickly Paradigm Press.

Le Bon, G. (1899) *The Psychology of Socialism*, New York: Macmillan.

Lefort, Claude (1986) *The Political Forms of Modern Society: Bureaucracy, Democracy, Totalitarianism*, ed. John B. Thompson, Oxford: Polity.

—— (2007) *Complications: Communism and the Dilemmas of Democracy*, New York: Columbia University.

Lembert, Alexandra and Schenkel, Elmar (eds) (2002) *The Golden Egg: Alchemy in Art and Literature*, Berlin: Galda + Wilch Verlag.

Leroi-Gourhan, André (1982) *The Dawn of European Art: An Introduction to Palaeolithic Cave Painting*, Cambridge: Cambridge University Press.

Lewis-Williams, David (2002) *The Mind in the Cave: Consciousness and the Origins of Art*, London: Thames and Hudson.

Linden, Stanton J. (ed.) (2003) *The Alchemy Reader: From Hermes Trismegistus to Isaac Newton*, Cambridge: Cambridge University Press.

Lindholm, Charles (1990) *Charisma*, Oxford: Basil Blackwell.

Linz, Juan J. (1970) 'An Authoritarian Regime in Spain', in Erik Allardt and Stein Rokkan (eds) *Mass Politics*, New York: The Free Press.

Lock, Andrew and Charles R. Peters (1999) *Handbook of Human Symbolic Evolution*, New York: Wiley-Blackwell.

Lowith, Karl (1982) *Max Weber and Karl Marx*, London: Allen & Unwin.

MacLachlan, Bonnie (1993) *The Age of Grace*, Princeton: Princeton University Press.

Marinoni, Augusto (1960) *L'Essere del nulla: Prima 'Lettura di Leonardo'*, Florence: Giunti.

Martin, Priscilla (ed.) (1976) *Shakespeare: Troilus and Cressida*, London: Macmillan.

Marx, Karl (1977) *Selected Writings*, ed. David McLellan, Oxford: Oxford University Press.

Mauss, Marcel (1992) 'A Sociological Assessment of Bolshevism (1924–5)', in Mike Gane (ed.) *The Radical Sociology of Durkheim and Mauss*, London: Routledge.

—— (2002) *The Gift*, London: Routledge.

McGovern, Patrick E. (2003) *Ancient Wine: The Search for the Origins of Viniculture*, Princeton: Princeton University Press.

McGuire, James E. and Martin Tamny (1983) *Certain Philosophical Questions: Newton's Trinity Notebook*, Cambridge: Cambridge University Press.

Meier, Carl A. (1967) *Ancient Incubation and Modern Psychotherapy*, Evanston, IL: Northwestern University Press.

Menninger, Karl A. (1969) *Number Words and Number Symbols: A Cultural History of Numbers*, Cambridge, MA: MIT Press.

Merezhkovsky, Dmitry S. (1929) *The Life of Napoleon*, London: Dent.

Milbank, John (1995) 'Stories of Sacrifice: From Wellhausen to Girard', *Theory Culture Society* 12, 4: 15–46.

Molland, George (1995) *Mathematics and the Medieval Ancestry of Physics*, Aldershot: Variorum.

Morrisson, Mark S. (2009) *Modern Alchemy: Occultism and the Emergence of Atomic Theory*, Oxford: Oxford University Press.

Mosca, Gaetano (1939) *The Ruling Class*, New York: McGraw-Hill.

Moscovici, Serge (1985) *The Age of the Crowd: A Historical Treatise on Mass Psychology*, Cambridge: Cambridge University Press.

Netz, Reviel (2004) *The Transformation of Mathematics in the Early Mediterranean World: From Problems to Equations*, Cambridge: Cambridge University Press.

Newman, William R. (2004) *Promethean Ambitions: Alchemy and the Quest to Perfect Nature*, Chicago: University of Chicago Press.

—— (2006) *Atoms and Alchemy: Chymistry and the Experimental Origins of the Scientific Revolution*, Chicago: University of Chicago Press.

Newman, William R. and Anthony Grafton (eds) (2001) *Secrets of Nature: Astrology and Alchemy in Early Modern Europe*, Cambridge, MA: MIT Press.

Nicoll, Allardyce (1963a) *Masks, Mimes and Miracles*, New York: Cooper.

—— (1963b) *The World of Harlequin*, Cambridge: Cambridge University Press.

Nietzsche, Friedrich (1974) *The Gay Science*, New York: Vintage.

—— (1976) *The Portable Nietzsche*, ed. Walter Kaufmann, London: Penguin.

Niklaus, Thelma (1956) *Harlequin Phoenix*, London: Bodley Head.

Nummedal, Tara E. (2007) *Alchemy and Authority in the Holy Roman Empire*, Chicago: University of Chicago Press.

Olsen, Berg, Evan Selinger and Søren Riis (eds) (2009) *New Waves in Philosophy of Technology*, Basingstoke: Palgrave Macmillan.

Paërl, Hetty (2002) *Pulcinella: la misteriosa maschera della cultura europea*, Sant'Oreste: Apeiron.

Paolucci, Antonio (ed.) (2004) *Colloqui davanti alla Madre: Immagini mariane in Toscana tra arte, storia e devozione*, Florence: Mandragora.

Pareto, Vilfredo (1954) 'The Menace to Society', in John D. Montgomery (ed.) *The State versus Socrates: A Case Study*, Boston: The Beacon Press.

—— (1966) *Sociological Writings*, Oxford: Basil Blackwell.

—— (1986) *The Rise and Fall of the Elites*, Salem, NH: Ayer Co.

Patocka, Jan (1996) *Heretical Essays in the Philosophy of History*, Chicago: Open Court.

—— (2002) *Plato and Europe*, Stanford: Stanford University Press.

Pellegrini, Franca (ed.) (2003) *Capricci, gobbi, amore, guerra e bellezza*, Padova: Il Poligrafo.

Peng Yoke, Ho (2007) *Explorations in Daoism: Medicine and Alchemy in Literature*, London: Routledge.

Peterson, David L. (2009) 'Production and Social Complexity', in Bryan K. Hanks and Katheryn M. Linduff (eds) *Social Complexity in Prehistoric Eurasia: Monuments, Metals, and Mobility*, Cambridge: Cambridge University Press.

Pizzorno, Alessandro (1991) 'On the Individualistic Theory of Social Order', in Pierre Bourdieu and James S. Coleman (eds) *Social Theory for a Changing Society*, Boulder, CO: Westview Press.

—— (2010) 'The Mask: An Essay', *International Political Anthropology* 3, 1: 5–28.

Plamper, Jan (2012) *The Stalin Cult: A Study in the Alchemy of Power*, New Haven: Yale University Press.

Plato (1914–35) *Plato in Twelve Volumes*, London: Heinemann.

Popov, A. (1933) 'Consecration Ritual for a Blacksmith Novice among the Yakuts', *The Journal of American Folklore* 46, 181: 257–71.

Posner, Donald (1977) 'Jacques Callot and the Dances Called Sfessania', *The Art Bulletin* 59, 2: 203–216.

Pregadio, Fabrizio (2006) *Great Clarity: Daoism and Alchemy in Early Medieval China*, Stanford, CA: Stanford University Press.

Principe, Lawrence M. (ed.) (2007) *Chymists and Chymistry: Studies in the History of Alchemy and Early Modern Chemistry*, Sagamore Beach, MA: Science History Publications.

Radin, Paul (1972) *The Trickster: A Study in American Indian Mythology*, with a Commentary by Karl Kerényi and Carl G. Jung, New York: Schocken.

Robertson Smith, William (1969 [1894]) *Lectures on the Religion of the Semites*, New York: KTAV Publishing House.

Ruspoli, Mario (1987) *The Cave of Lascaux*, New York: Abrams.

Russell, Bertrand (1903) *Principles of Mathematics*, Cambridge: Cambridge University Press.

Rusten, Jeffrey and Ian C. Cunningham (2003) *Theophrastus: Characters; Herodas: Mimes; Sophron and Other Mime Fragments*, Cambridge, MA: Harvard University Press.

Sakwa, Richard (2006) 'From Revolution to Krizis: The Transcending Revolution of 1989–91', *Comparative Politics* 38, 4: 459–78.

—— (2009) 'Liminality and Postcommunism: The Twenty-First Century as the Subject of History', *International Political Anthropology* 2, 1: 110–26.

Scaramuzza, Gabriele (1995) *Il brutto nell'arte*, Naples: Il Tripole.

Scarborough, John (1988) 'Hermetic and Related Text in Classical Antiquity', in Ingrid Merkel and Allen G. Debus (eds) *Hermeticism and the Renaissance: Intellectual History and the Occult in Early Modern Europe*, Cranbury, NJ: Folger Books.

Schaefer, David Lewis (ed.) (1998) *Freedom over Servitude: Montaigne, La Boétie, and On Voluntary Servitude*, Westport, CT: Greenwood Press.

Schaffer, Simon, Lissa Roberts, Kapil Raj and James Delbfurgo (eds) (2009) *The Brokered World: Go-Betweens and Global Intelligence, 1770–1820*, Sagamore Beach, MA: Science History Publications.

Schechter, Joel (1994) *Satiric Impersonations: From Aristophanes to the Guerrilla Girls*, Carbondale: Southern Illinois University Press.

Schmitt, Carl (2008) *Political Theology II: The Myth of the Closure of Any Political Theology*, Cambridge: Polity.

Schumpeter, Joseph A. (1943) *Capitalism, Socialism and Democracy*, London: Allen and Unwin.

Segni, Lotario (2003) *La miseria della condizione umana: De Contemptu Mundi*, Milan: Berlusconi.

Sigler, Laurence E. (2003) *Fibonacci's Liber Abaci*, New York: Springer.

Shank, John B. (2008) *The Newton Wars and the Beginning of the French Enlightenment*, Chicago: University of Chicago Press.

Shapin, Steven and Simon Schaffer (1985) *Leviathan and the Air Pump: Hobbes, Boyle, and the Experimental Life*, Princeton: Princeton University Press.

Shoham, Giora (1994) *The Bridge to Nothingness*, Cranbury: Associated University Presses.

Shumaker, Wayne (ed.) (1989) *Natural Magic and Modern Science: Four Treatises, 1590–1657*, Albany, NY: SUNY Press.

Smith, Edward Ellis (1967) *The Okhrana: The Russian Department of Police*, Stanford: The Hoover Institution Press.

Solzhenitsyn, Alexander (1978) *A World Split Apart*, Cambridge, MA: Harvard University Press.

Swetz, Frank J. (1997) *Capitalism and Arithmetic: The New Math of the Fifteenth Century*, Illinois: Open Court.

Szabo, Arpad (1978) *The Beginnings of the Greek Mathematics*, Budapest: Akadémiai.

Szakolczai, Arpad (2003) *The Genesis of Modernity*, London: Routledge.

—— (2009) *Reflexive Historical Sociology*, London: Routledge.

—— (2013) *Comedy and the Public Sphere: The Re-birth of Theatre as Comedy and the Genealogy of the Modern Public Arena*, London: Routledge.

Szakolczai, Arpad and Bjørn Thomassen (2011) 'Gabriel Tarde as Political Anthropologist: The Role of Imitation for Sociality, Crowds and Publics within a Context of Globalization', *International Political Anthropology* 4, 1: 43–62.

Szulakowska, Urszula (2006) *The Sacrificial Body and the Day of Doom: Alchemy and Apocalyptic Discourse in the Protestant Reformation*, Leiden: Brill.

Tarde, Gabriel (1969) *On Communication and Social Influence*, ed. Terry N. Clark, Chicago: The University of Chicago Press.

—— (1993) *Les lois de l'imitation*, Paris: Éditions Kimé.

Tenbruck, Friedrich H. (1980) 'The Problem of Thematic Unity in the Works of Max Weber', *British Journal of Sociology* 31, 3: 316–51.

Tessari, Roberto (1981) *Commedia dell'Arte: la Maschera e l'Ombra*, Milan: Mursia.

Thayer, Horace Standish (ed.) (1974) *Newton's Philosophy of Nature: Selections from his Writings*, New York: Hafner.

Thomassen, Bjørn (2010) 'Anthropology, Multiple Modernities and the Axial Age Debate', *Anthropological Theory* 10, 4: 321–42.

—— (2012) 'Anthropology and its many Modernities: When Concepts Matter', *Journal of the Royal Anthropological Institute* 18, 1: 160–78.

Thompson, Charles John Samuel (1932) *The Lure and Romance of Alchemy*, London: George G. Harrap & Co.

Thompson, William I. (1996) *The Time Falling Bodies Take to Light: Mythology, Sexuality, and the Origins of Culture*, Basingstoke: Palgrave Macmillan.

Tocqueville, Alexis de (2011) *The Ancien Regime and the French Revolution*, edited with an introduction by Jon Elster, Cambridge: Cambridge University Press.

Turner, Victor (1969) *The Ritual Process*, Chicago: Aldine.

—— (1982) *From Ritual to Theatre: The Human Seriousness of Play*, New York: PAJ Publications.

Urban, Michael (2008) 'Forms of Civil Society: Politics and Social Relations in Russia' *International Political Anthropology* 1, 1: 93–111.

—— (2010) *Cultures of Power in Post-Communist Russia*, Cambridge: Cambridge University Press.

Vendrix, Philippe (ed.) (2008) *Music and Mathematics in Late Medieval and Early Modern Europe*, Turnhout: Brepols.

Verdery, Katherine (2000) 'Privatization as Transforming Persons', in Sorin Antohi and Vladimir Tismaneanu (eds) *Between Past and Future: The Revolutions of 1989 and Their Aftermath*, Budapest: CEU Press.

Vialou, Denis (1998) *Our Prehistoric Past*, London: Thames and Hudson.

Voegelin, Eric (1978) *Anamnesis*, Notre Dame, IN: University of Notre Dame Press.

—— (1990) *Published Essays, 1966–1985*, Vol. 12 of *The Collected Works*, ed. Ellis Sandoz, Missouri: University of Missouri Press.

—— (1999a) *The New Order and Last Orientation*, Vol. 7 of *History of Political Ideas*, in *The Collected Works of Eric Voegelin*, Columbia: University of Missouri Press.

—— (1999b) *Hitler and the Germans*, ed. Detlev Clemens and Brendan Purcell, Columbia: University of Missouri Press.

von Franz, Marie-Luise (1980) *Alchemy: An Introduction to the Symbolism and the Psychology*, Toronto: Inner City Books.

von Heyking, John (2008) '"Sunaisthetic" Friendship and the Foundations of Political Anthropology', *International Political Anthropology* 1, 2: 179–92.

Walker, Daniel P. (1958) *Spiritual and Demonic Magic: From Ficino to Campanella*, London: Warburg Institute.

Weber, Max (1978) *Economy and Society*, Berkeley: University of California Press.

—— (2002) *The Protestant Ethic and the Spirit of Capitalism*, Los Angeles: Roxbury.

Welsford, Enid (1966) *The Fool, His Social and Literary History*, London: Faber.

Westfall, Richard S. (1993) *The Life of Isaac Newton*, Cambridge: Cambridge University Press.

Whitley, David S. (2008) *Cave Paintings and the Human Spirit: The Origin of Creativity and Belief*, New York: Prometheus Books.

White, Randall (2006) 'The Women of Brassempouy: A Century of Research and Interpretation', *Journal of Archeological Method* 13, 4: 251–304.

Williams, Kim (ed.) (2010) *The Mathematical Works of Leon Battista Alberti*, Basel: Birkhäuser.

Willner, Ann R. (1983) *Spellbinders: Charismatic Political Leadership*, New Haven: Yale University Press.

Wind, Edgar (1958) *Pagan Mysteries in the Renaissance*, London: Faber.

Wydra, Harald (2007) *Communism and the Emergence of Democracy*, Cambridge: Cambridge University Press.

—— (2008) 'Towards a New Anthropological Paradigm: The Challenge of Mimetic Theory', *International Political Anthropology* 1, 1: 161–74.

—— (2009) 'The Liminal Origins of Democracy', *International Political Anthropology* 2, 1: 91–109.

—— (2011a) 'Passions and Progress: Gabriel Tarde's Anthropology of Imitative Innovation', *International Political Anthropology* 4, 2: 93–111.

—— (2011b) 'The Power of Symbols – Communism and Beyond', *International Journal of Politics, Culture, and Society* 22, 4: 1–21.

Yates, Frances (1964) *Giordano Bruno and the Hermetic Tradition*, London: Routledge.

—— (1972) *The Rosicrucian Enlightenment*, London: Paladine Books.

—— (1976) *The Art of Memory*, London: Routledge.

—— (1979) *The Occult Philosophy in the Elizabethan Age*, London: Routledge.

Zizek, Slavoj (2011) *Did Somebody Say Totalitarianism?* London: Verso.

Index